P9-CMO-487

Fodor's
LOS CABOS

WELCOME TO LOS CABOS

With coastline that stretches from the Sea of Cortez to the Pacific Ocean, and 350 sunny days a year, Los Cabos is Mexico's ultimate seaside escape. It's endless summer at the tip of the Baja Peninsula, and surfers, golfers, divers, and hikers come here for year-round water sports and outdoor activities. The sister towns of Cabo San Lucas and San José del Cabo offer distinct experiences that range from all-night bar crawls to Thursday-night art walks. Between them the Corridor presents all-inclusive resorts with everything for the perfect honeymoon or family vacation.

TOP REASONS TO GO

★ **Beaches:** More than 80 km (50 miles) of gorgeous strands with towering rock formations.

★ **Golf:** Spectacular views from greens designed by the world's best course architects.

★ **Nightlife:** Cabo's after-dark, into-the-dawn party scene draws a loud, festive crowd.

★ **Sportfishing:** Beginners and pros drop a line in the "Marlin Capital of the World."

★ **Whale-Watching:** The gentle giants that migrate here swim right next to the boats.

★ **Spas:** Desert healing treatments in sumptuous resort wellness centers.

15 ULTIMATE EXPERIENCES

Los Cabos offers terrific experiences that should be on every traveler's list. Here are Fodor's top picks for a memorable trip.

1 El Arco At Land's End

These towering granite formations let you know you've arrived at the tip of the Baja Peninsula. El Arco ("the arch") has become the region's emblem. *(Ch. 3)*

2 Todos Santos

This típico town on the West Cape is a perfect day trip and home to a growing expat community, cozy lodgings, and great eateries. *(Ch. 8)*

3 Whale-Watching

Gray whales migrate to Los Cabos every year from December through April, down Baja's coast and up to the east, making for a memorable viewing. *(Ch. 3)*

4 Shopping

Find hand-painted tiles, pottery, embroidered clothing, silver jewelry, and fire opals, plus the iconic beaded crafts of the Huichol people. *(Ch. 6)*

5 Sailing

Find Windsurfer and Sunfish sailboats docked at the Cabo San Lucas Marina and take a tour along the region's ultra-blue waters. *(Ch. 3)*

6 Marina Golden Zone

Peruse upscale shops and enjoy fine dining at Cabo's downtown marina. You can also visit the Tequila Museum and a traditional Mexican-style cantina. *(Ch. 6)*

7 Nightlife

A major spring break destination, Cabo is known as a party town, but you can also opt for low-key outings in San José del Cabo. *(Ch. 7)*

8 Wirikuta Cactus Garden

Wander through this astounding garden, home to 1,500 species of cacti from all over the world, located just 25 minutes from Cabo San Lucas. *(Ch. 3)*

9 Cabo Pulmo National Marine Park

Stretching five miles from Pulmo Point to Los Frailes, this national park encompasses the only living hard coral reef in North America. *(Ch. 3)*

10 Seafood

Cabo is famous for its seafood, especially dishes like chocolate clams, fish tacos, smoked marlin, lobster, and more. The fish taco originated here. *(Ch. 4)*

11 Sportfishing

Cabo San Lucas is nicknamed the Marlin Mecca, but there are over 800 species of fish here. Sportfishing remains one of the area's most popular pastimes. *(Ch. 3)*

12 Beaches

In Los Cabos, soft, sandy beaches stretch for about 50 miles beside the turquoise and navy waters of the Pacific Ocean and the Sea of Cortez. *(Ch. 2)*

13 Golfing

One of the world's top golf destinations, Los Cabos has courses throughout the area by big-name designers like Jack Nicklaus and Roy Dye. *(Ch. 3)*

14 Spas

Many come to Cabo to relax at one of the many resorts with spas offering scenic outlooks and extensive body and beauty treatments. *(Ch. 6)*

15 Surfing

Los Cabos, with its warm seas, offers both intense and gentle waves, focused in the Pacific Coast, the East Cape, and the Cabo Corridor. *(Ch. 2 and 3)*

Fodor's LOS CABOS

Editorial: Douglas Stallings, *Editorial Director*; Margaret Kelly, *Senior Editor*; Alexis Kelly, Jacinta O'Halloran, and Amanda Sadlowski, *Editors*; Teddy Minford, *Content Editor*; Rachael Roth, *Content Manager*

Design: Tina Malaney, *Design and Production Director;* Jessica Gonzalez, *Production Designer*

Photography: Jennifer Arnow, *Senior Photo Editor*

Maps: Rebecca Baer, *Senior Map Editor*; David Lindroth, Mark Stroud (Moon Street Cartography), *Cartographers*

Production: Jennifer DePrima, *Editorial Production Manager*; Carrie Parker, *Senior Production Editor*; Elyse Rozelle, *Production Editor*; David Satz, *Director of Content Production*

Business & Operations: Chuck Hoover, *Chief Marketing Officer*; Joy Lai, *Vice President and General Manager*; Stephen Horowitz, *Director of Business Development and Revenue Operations;* Tara McCrillis, *Director of Publishing Operations;* Eliza D. Aceves, *Content Operations Manager and Srategist*

Public Relations and Marketing: Joe Ewaskiw, *Manager;* Esther Su, *Marketing Manager*

Writers: Marlise Kast-Myers, Chris Sands

Editors: Rachael Roth (lead editor), Jacinta O'Halloran (editorial contributor)

Production Editor: Elyse Rozelle

Production Design: Liliana Guia

5th Edition

ISBN 978-1-64097-002-1

ISSN 2326–4152

All details in this book are based on information supplied to us at press time. Always confirm information when it matters, especially if you're making a detour to visit a specific place. Fodor's expressly disclaims any liability, loss, or risk, personal or otherwise, that is incurred as a consequence of the use of any of the contents of this book.

PRINTED IN THE UNITED STATES OF AMERICA

10 9 8 7 6 5 4 3 2 1

CONTENTS

Fodor's Features

CONTENTS

MAPS

ABOUT THIS GUIDE

Fodor's Recommendations
Everything in this guide is worth doing—we don't cover what isn't—but exceptional sights, hotels, and restaurants are recognized with additional accolades. Fodor's Choice★ indicates our top recommendations. Care to nominate a new place? Visit Fodors.com/contact-us.

Trip Costs
We list prices wherever possible to help you budget well. Hotel and restaurant price categories from $ to $$$$ are noted alongside each recommendation. For hotels, we include the lowest cost of a standard double room in high season. For restaurants, we cite the average price of a main course at dinner or, if dinner isn't served, at lunch. For attractions, we always list adult admission fees; discounts are usually available for children, students, and senior citizens.

Hotels
Our local writers vet every hotel to recommend the best overnights in each price category, from budget to expensive. Unless otherwise specified, you can expect private bath, phone, and TV in your room. For expanded hotel reviews, visit Fodors.com.

Top Picks	Hotels &
★ Fodor's Choice	Restaurants
Listings	🏨 Hotel
✉ Address	🛏 Number of rooms
✉ Branch address	🍴 Meal plans
☎ Telephone	✗ Restaurant
🖷 Fax	🪑 Reservations
⊕ Website	👔 Dress code
✉ E-mail	▭ No credit cards
🎫 Admission fee	$ Price
⊙ Open/closed times	**Other**
Ⓜ Subway	⇨ See also
✛ Directions or Map coordinates	☞ Take note
	🏌 Golf facilities

Restaurants
Unless we state otherwise, restaurants are open for lunch and dinner daily. We mention dress code only when there's a specific requirement and reservations only when they're essential or not accepted. For expanded restaurant reviews, visit Fodors.com.

Credit Cards
The hotels and restaurants in this guide typically accept credit cards. If not, we'll say so.

EUGENE FODOR

Hungarian-born Eugene Fodor (1905–91) began his travel career as an interpreter on a French cruise ship. The experience inspired him to write *On the Continent* (1936), the first guidebook to receive annual updates and discuss a country's way of life as well as its sights. Fodor later joined the U.S. Army and worked for the OSS in World War II. After the war, he kept up his intelligence work while expanding his guidebook series. During the Cold War, many guides were written by fellow agents who understood the value of insider information. Today's guides continue Fodor's legacy by providing travelers with timely coverage, insider tips, and cultural context.

EXPERIENCE
LOS CABOS

LOS CABOS PLANNER

When to Go

Although Los Cabos hotels are often busiest starting in mid-October for the sportfishing season, the high season doesn't technically begin until mid-December, running through the end of Easter week. It's during this busy period that you'll pay the highest hotel and golf rates. Spring break, which can stagger over several weeks in March and April, is also a particularly crowded and raucous time. Downtown Cabo gets very busy, especially on weekends, throughout the year. Whale-watching season (December–April) coincides with high season, but whale-watchers tend to stay in La Paz, not Los Cabos.

The Pacific hurricane season mirrors that of the Atlantic and Caribbean, so there is always a slight chance of a hurricane from August through late October. In September 2014, Hurricane Odile plundered Los Cabos, making it the strongest hurricane to hit the Baja Peninsula. Hurricanes rarely hit Los Cabos head-on, but the effects can reverberate when a large hurricane hits Mexico's Pacific coast. Still, most summer tropical storms pass through quickly, even during the so-called short "rainy" season, from July through October.

Getting Here and Around

Visitors fly nonstop to Los Cabos from all over the United States, and to La Paz from some U.S. cities. Via nonstop service, Los Cabos is about 2 hours from San Diego, 2½ hours from Los Angeles, 2¾ hours from Houston, 2¾ hours from Dallas/Fort Worth, and 2 hours from Phoenix.

Flying time from New York to Mexico City, where you must switch planes to continue to Los Cabos, is 5 hours. Los Cabos is about a 2-hour flight from Mexico City.

Resources California Baja Rent-A-Car (*CABAJA Rental Cars*). ⊠ *9245 Jamacha Blvd., Spring Valley* ☏ *888/470-7368, 619/470-7368* ⊕ *www.cabaja.com.* **Lewis & Lewis Insurance.** ⊠ *11900 W. Olympic Blvd, Suite 475, Santa Monica* ☏ *310/207-7700, 800/966-6830* ⊕ *www.mexicanautoinsurance.com.*

Safety

Due to criminal activity and violence in 2017, the U.S. State Department warned U.S. citizens about the risk of traveling to Los Cabos and La Paz. Stay up to date with travel warnings on the U.S. State Department website. Standard precautions always apply: distribute your cash, credit cards, and IDs between a deep front pocket and an inside jacket pocket, and don't carry excessive amounts of cash. Leave your passport, along with other valuables, in your in-room safe—and be sure to make copies of your passport and credit cards to leave with someone back home.

Festivals

Festivals include Carnaval (February and March, before Lent); Semana Santa (Holy Week); Día de Nuestra Señora de Guadalupe (Day of Our Lady of Guadalupe; December 12); and Las Posadas (December 16–25). One of Los Cabos' most enjoyable celebrations is Sabor a Cabo (The Flavors of Cabo), which takes place in early December. It's a weeklong celebration of food, drink, and music, and showcases the area's top restaurants. Other popular annual events include the San José Jazz Weekend in February, Los Cabos Open of Surf in June, the Mexican Tennis Open in August, and Los Cabos Film Festival in November.

WHAT'S NEW IN LOS CABOS

Desert Green Thumb

Visitors to the region often ask whether they should stay in San José del Cabo, Cabo San Lucas, or somewhere in between. Those looking for action and nightlife have always opted for the flashier Cabo San Lucas, while San José's hoteliers and restaurateurs have stopped trying to compete on San Lucas's terms, opting instead to market their community for what it is—a cultural, historic, art center with a relaxed vibe.

The city has truly come into its own in the past decade. San José's *zócalo* (central plaza) has been jazzed up as a romantic district where couples stroll after leisurely dining; old haciendas have been transformed into trendy restaurants and charming inns. The city's art scene is thriving with a high-season Thursday Night Art Walk, where those interested in art can visit participating galleries and enjoy free drinks and live music. The latest allure however, are the desert farms on the outskirts of San José, capitalizing on the organic food movement with their farm-to-table restaurants. By adding cooking schools, markets, tours, and lodging, these desert draws provide more of an experience than just an ordinary meal.

Swing into Action

Golf is the name of the game in Los Cabos. There are multiple courses tied to names that read like a who's who of golf legends and course designers: Jack Nicklaus, Greg Norman, Davis Love III, Phil Mickelson, Tom Weiskopf, Robert Trent Jones II, and Tom Fazio. Baja golf is more than just Los Cabos: courses line the entire peninsula, if not in the same density as at its southern extreme.

The Rise of Todos Santos

Once the province of surfers—the breaks are wicked here, making for some amazing waves, but risky swimming—this town overlooking the western cape about an hour north of Cabo San Lucas is home to a growing artists' community. Just don't call Todos Santos Baja's "hot" new destination, because folks here aren't interested in becoming another Los Cabos. The area is refined, and preserves its Mexican culture.

Baja's Boomtown

People often ask, "Is Los Cabos the next Cancún?" which implies potential detriment to the environment and the local culture. Despite the destruction, Los Cabos did benefit from 2014 Hurricane Odile, which battered the peninsula, as visitors canceled plans to vacation there in the storm's aftermath. In the four years that followed, Los Cabos grew immensely, as noted in the Corridor where construction cranes dominate the skyline, multimillion-dollar renovations of existing hotels, and the birth of new ones. Currently Los Cabos has more than 63 hotels with more than 16,000 rooms, with plans to add another 4,000 rooms by 2018. Yet the question remains whether Los Cabos can handle the boom with so little infrastructure in place.

WHAT'S WHERE

1 San José del Cabo.
Thirty-two kilometers (20 miles) east of Cabo San Lucas, San José has remained the smaller, quieter, and more traditional of the two regions. Its 18th-century colonial architecture, artsy vibe, and quality restaurants are all within driving distance. Five minutes from the colonial center is Puerto Los Cabos, home to a flashy marina, golf courses, boutique hotels, and luxury resorts. Drive another five minutes from Puerto Los Cabos to the sand dunes where organic farms are producing extraordinary dining experiences.

2 The Corridor. Along this stretch of road, which connects San José to Cabo, exclusive, guard-gated resort complexes have taken over much of the waterfront with their sprawling villas, golf courses, and upscale shopping centers such as Las Tiendas de Palmilla, and Koral Center.

3 Cabo San Lucas. Cabo San Lucas is at the very end of the Carretera Transpeninsular (Highway 1). Cabo has always been the more gregarious, outspoken of the sisters. The sportfishing fleet is anchored here, and cruise ships anchored off the marina tender passengers into town. Trendy restaurants and bars line the streets and massive hotels have risen all along the beachfront. Here, you'll find Bahía Cabo San Lucas (Cabo Bay), the towering Land's End Rocks, and the famed arched landmark, El Arco.

4 Todos Santos. Only an hour north of Cabo San Lucas, Todos Santos lies close enough to be part of Los Cabos experience—but still be that proverbial world away. This *típico* town on the West Cape is home to a growing expat community, as well as some cozy lodgings and restaurants.

5 La Paz. The capital of southern Baja is a "big little" city, one of the most authentic on the peninsula. La Paz is a laid-back community with excellent scuba diving and sportfishing in the Sea of Cortez. Its lovely oceanfront *malecón* features a number of good restaurants and hotels.

6 Baja California. The beaches and seafood of Rosarito, Ensenada, and Puerto Nuevo draw retirees, RV'ers, and, during spring break, crowds of wild college kids; the Valle de Guadalupe provides respite and fantastic vineyards.

GREAT ITINERARIES

Each of these fills one day in Los Cabos. Together they span the area's most quintessential experiences, from boating to El Arco and visiting the blown-glass factory, to grabbing a beer at a local brewpub and discovering Cabo's Marina Golden Zone.

Learn the Lay of the Land

On Day 1 take it easy, enjoy your hotel, take a swim in the pool, and get to know the beach in your general area. If staying in Cabo, meander around town, mentally noting the many restaurants and shops on the way that you might wish to sample later. Walking the length of the marina boardwalk will introduce you to Cabo's notorious party central: From the boardwalk's western end beginning near the **Marina Fiesta Hotel**, you'll pass through the marina's Golden Zone (along which is the infamous **Nowhere ¿Bar?**). The marina walk ends at the **Tesoro Los Cabos Hotel**. Here you can catch a boat for sunset cruises, whale-watching, and sportfishing.

Traversing the Corridor

To see the Corridor and make it over to San José del Cabo from Cabos San Lucas, it's most convenient and least expensive if you rent a car for a couple of days. (Taxis are frightfully expensive, and buses limit you to their schedule and stops.) Shop around for rentals and you'll be amazed at the range; Alamo and Cactus Car include insurance in their rates. Take your time driving along the Corridor, both to enjoy the sights of the coast, as well as to become accustomed to the unique traits of this quirky highway. On- and off-ramps are challenging, as you'll see. About mid-Corridor you pass **Playa Santa María** and **Chileno Bay,** fun for stops to sun, swim, and snorkel. Bring your own equipment and refreshments.

As you near San José del Cabo, you can't miss the **Koral Center** or **Tiendas de Palmilla** (Palmilla Shopping Center) across from the **One&Only Palmilla Resort.** "Tiendas" comprises upscale shops and some excellent restaurants, including Nick-San. (Walmart, Costco, and Sam's Club have also set up shop along Highway 1 for your more basic shopping needs.) Heading farther east, you'll shortly see a turnout and large parking lot—a great panoramic overlook of the Sea of Cortez. It's a lovely spot to watch the surf at the **Old Man's break,** to your right, in front of the **Cabo Surf Hotel.**

Los Cabos Beaches

All hotels provide beach towels, chairs, and umbrellas. The 7 Seas restaurant at Cabo Surf Hotel will deliver cocktails beachside, meaning you don't even have to leave your sunning spot for a margarita. To get to the most pristine beaches along the Sea of Cortez, head east out of San José del Cabo by car. At the corner of Boulevard Mijares and Calle Benito Juárez in San José, turn east at the sign marked "pueblo la playa." The paved street soon becomes a dirt road that leads to the small fishing villages of **La Playa** (The Beach) and **La Playita** (The Little Beach), about 1½ km (½ mile) from San José. As the gateway between San José del Cabo and the East Cape coastline, this area known as Puerto Los Cabos is marked by a series of round-abouts that branch to the marina, Cacti Mundo (cactus world gardens), organic farms (Flora Farms, Acre, and Los Tamarindos), and luxury resorts like Secrets and JW Marriott.

From La Playita, drive 60 km (37 miles) up the coast to the ecological reserve **Cabo Pulmo,** home of Baja Sur's largest

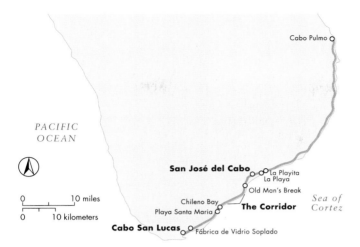

coral reef. Water depths range from 15 to 130 feet, and colorful marine animals live among the reef and shipwrecks. When hunger calls, stroll up the beach from Cabo Pulmo to **Tito's** for a fish taco and an ice-cold cerveza. Try to get back to La Playa by late afternoon to avoid driving the East Cape's dirt road at night. Stop for some fresh seafood and a frozen margarita at **Buzzard's Bar and Grill** right near the beach just north of La Playa. San José is 10 minutes away.

Artsy Los Cabos

Set out from Cabo San Lucas for the **Fábrica de Vidrio Soplado** (Blown-Glass Factory)—a bit hard to find if you're driving yourself. First head toward San José on Avenida Lázaro Cárdenas, which becomes Highway 1. Turn left at the stoplight and signs for the bypass to Todos Santos; then look for signs to the factory. It's in an industrial area two blocks northwest of Highway 1. At the factory, you can watch the talented artisans use a process little changed since it was first developed some 4,000 years ago.

From the factory, head east for the 20-minute drive to San José del Cabo. Park at the south end of Boulevard Mijares near the Tropicana Inn, since

parking is limited from here on in. Grab some lunch at **Baja Brewing Company**, located on Avenida Morelos. The pub has a tasty San José Especial cerveza, and offers international fare to go along with it. Then stroll through the central plaza, or zócalo, directly in front of the **Mision de San José del Cabo Anuiti** (mission church) and peruse the several art galleries north and west of the church.

For dinner, try **Don Sanchez's** in San José proper, where Canadian-born chef Tadd Chapman is elevating the presentation of local ingredients and Mexican wines.

Alternatively, from the glass factory, head north on Highway 19 for the one-hour drive to the laid-back town of Todos Santos. Lunch at **El Gusto!** restaurant in the Posada La Poza hotel promises to be one of the most sumptuous you'll get in Baja. (Reservations are a must.) Spend the afternoon visiting in-town galleries near the **Misión de Nuestra Señora de Pilar** (Mission of Our Lady of Pilar) church.

CRUISING TO LOS CABOS

Cruise lines with itineraries to Los Cabos and Baja California include Carnival, Celebrity, Crystal, Cunard, Holland America, Lindblad Expeditions, Norwegian, Oceania, Princess, Regent Seven Seas, and Royal Caribbean. Most depart from Los Angeles (Long Beach), San Diego, San Francisco, Seattle, Fort Lauderdale, Miami, New York, San Juan, Vancouver, and even Southampton, England, or Bridgetown, Barbados. Most cruises to Baja dock at Cabo San Lucas, with a few calling at Ensenada, La Paz, and Loreto.

Terrific shopping, dining, beaches, and shore excursions and the unforgettable view of Los Arcos upon approach make Cabo San Lucas a crowd-pleaser among cruise ports. Ships need to drop anchor and tender passengers to the marina, about a 10-minute trip. Ensenada is a favorite stop on shorter Baja cruises. Its modern Cruise Port Village terminal berths two full-size ships at a time. La Paz, on the Sea of Cortez, wins rave reviews as being the most "authentically Mexican" of Baja's cruise destinations. A few large ships dock at its port of Pichilingue, about 16 km (10 miles) north of town. Smaller boats can berth at La Paz itself. Tenders transport travelers ashore to the port of Loreto, north of Pichilingue.

Carnival. Carnival is known for its large-volume cruises and template approach to its ships, which both help keep fares accessible. Boats in its Mexican fleet have more than 1,000 staterooms. Seven-night Mexican Riviera trips out of Los Angeles hit Cabo San Lucas and, occasionally, La Paz, among other Pacific ports in Mexico. Carnival wrote the book on Baja-only cruises, with three- or four-day itineraries out of Los Angeles to Ensenada. Las Vegas–style shows and passenger participation is the norm. ☎ 800/764–7419 ⊕ www.carnival.com.

Celebrity. Spacious accommodations and the guest-lectured Enrichment Series are hallmarks of Celebrity cruises. Its *Celebrity Infinity* plies the Panama Canal east- and westbound on 15-day itineraries, hitting Cabo San Lucas along the way, with an extensive choice of departure ports (Fort Lauderdale, Los Angeles, Miami, San Diego, or San Francisco). ☎ 800/647–2251 ⊕ www.celebrity-cruises.com.

Crystal. Crystal is known for combining large ships with grandeur, opulence, and impeccable service. Its *Crystal Symphony* calls at Cabo San Lucas on a variety of itineraries from San Francisco (10 days) and Los Angeles (14 days). ☎ 800/722–0021 ⊕ www.crystalcruises.com.

Holland America. The venerable Holland America line leaves from and returns to San Diego or Fort Lauderdale. Panama Canal cruises spanning 14- to 23-day itineraries include stops in Cabo San Lucas, while a 25-day Hawaii-Mexico calls at Cabo San Lucas and other Mexican ports. ☎ 877/932–4259 ⊕ www.hollandamerica.com.

Lindblad Expeditions. Lindblad's smaller *Sea Lion* and *Sea Bird* take you where the other guys can't go, for an active, nature-themed Baja cruise experience. Eight- to 15-day excursions embark in La Paz and nose around the islands of the Sea of Cortez. Its kayaks and Zodiacs launch from the ship to provide you with unparalleled opportunity to watch whales, dolphins, and seabirds. ☎ 800/397–3348 ⊕ www.expeditions.com.

Norwegian Cruise Lines. Its tagline is "whatever floats your boat," and Norwegian *is* known for its relatively free-wheeling style and variety of activities and excursions. Seven- to nine-day cruises on the *Star* depart from Los Angeles, with full days in Cabo San Lucas, and Panama Canal cruises on the *Jewel, Sun,* and *Pearl* from 14 to 17 days all call on Cabo San Lucas. ☎ *866/234–7350 ⊕ www.ncl.com.*

Oceania. The ships of Oceania are intimate and cozy. Before arrival at Cabo San Lucas or any port, you can attend a lecture about its history, culture, and tradition. The *Sirena* stops here on a 15-day cruise out of Los Angeles to Miami. The *Regatta* stops here on an 18-day cruise from San Francisco to Miami, and on a 15-day cruise from Miami to San Diego. ☎ *855/623–2642 ⊕ www.oceaniacruises.com.*

Princess Cruises. Not so great for small children but good at keeping teens and adults occupied, Princess strives to offer luxury at an affordable price. Its cruises may cost a little more than others, but you also get more for the money: large rooms, varied menus, and personalized service. Seven- to 10-day Mexican Riviera cruises aboard the *Ruby Princess, Grand Princess, Emerald Princess,* or *Star Princess* start in Los Angeles or San Francisco and hit Los Cabos and other Pacific ports. Shorter three- to five-day trips out of Los Angeles call at Ensenada or Los Cabos. ☎ *800/774–6237 ⊕ www. princess.com.*

Regent Seven Seas Cruises. RSSC's luxury liner the *Navigator* offers trips that originate in Vancouver and San Francisco and call at Cabo San Lucas on select Panama Canal and transpacific itineraries. Some stop here for a half day; others stay in port longer, making RSSC a rare cruise company that lets you sample Los Cabos' evening diversions. ☎ *877/505–5370 ⊕ www.rssc.com.*

Royal Caribbean. Royal Caribbean's 16-night Panama Canal cruises on *Vision of the Seas* originate in Miami and Los Angeles, and call at Cabo San Lucas, among other Mexican Pacific ports. Striving to appeal to a broad clientele, the line offers lots of activities and services as well as many shore excursions. ☎ *866/562-7625 ⊕ www. royalcaribbean.com.*

WEDDINGS

Choosing the Perfect Place. Los Cabos is growing in popularity as a Mexican wedding and honeymoon destination. Many couples choose to marry on the beach, often at sunset because it's cooler and more comfortable for everyone; others opt to marry in an air-conditioned resort ballroom.

Consider booking an all-inclusive, which has plenty of meal options and activities to keep your guests busy before and after the main event.

Wedding Attire. Some women choose a traditional full wedding gown with veil, but more popular and comfortable—especially for an outdoor wedding—is a simple sheath or a white cotton or linen dress that will breathe in the tropical heat. Some brides opt for even less formal attire: anything from a sundress to shorts or a bathing suit.

Weddings on the beach are best done barefoot, even when the bride wears a gown. Choose strappy sandals for a wedding or reception that's not on the sand. Whatever type of attire you choose, purchase it and get any alterations done before leaving home. (There's virtually no place here to do either.) Buy a special garment bag and hand-carry your dress on the plane. Don't let this be the one time in your life that your luggage goes missing.

The groom and any groomsmen can take their what-to-wear cue from the female half of the wedding party, but know that Los Cabos has no place to rent formal attire.

Time of Year. Planning according to the weather can be critical for a successful Los Cabos wedding. If you're getting married in your bathing suit, you might not mind some heat and humidity, but will your venue—and your future mother-in-law—hold up under the summer heat? We recommend holding the ceremony between November and February. March through June is usually dry but extremely warm and humid.

By July, the heat can be unbearable for an outdoor afternoon wedding, and summer rains, rarely voluminous in Los Cabos, begin to fall here around the same time. Although hurricanes are rarer along the Pacific than the Caribbean, they can occur August through late October and even early November. For an outdoor wedding, establish a detailed backup plan in case the weather does not comply.

Finding a Wedding Planner. Hiring a wedding planner will minimize stress for all but the simplest of ceremonies. The slogan of one firm here is: "if you have the groom and the dress, we can do the rest." And a planner really can. A year or more in advance, the planner will, among other things, help choose the venue, find a florist, and arrange for a photographer and musicians.

The most obvious place to find a wedding planner is at a resort hotel that becomes wedding central: providing accommodations for you and your guests, the wedding ceremony venue, and the restaurant or ballroom for the reception. You can also hire an independent wedding coordinator, which you can find easily online by searching "Los Cabos wedding," and ask them to provide references.

When interviewing a planner, talk about your budget and ask about costs. Are there hourly fees or one fee for the whole event? How available will the consultant and his or her assistants be? Which vendors are used and why? How long have they been in business? Request a list of the exact services they'll provide, and get a proposal in writing. If you don't feel this is the right person or agency for you, try someone else. Cost permitting, it's helpful to meet the planner in person.

Requirements. A bona fide wedding planner will facilitate completing the required paperwork and negotiating the legal requirements for marrying in Mexico. Blood tests must be done upon your arrival, but not more than 14 days before the ceremony. All documents must be translated by an authorized translator from the destination, and it's important to send these documents certified mail to your wedding coordinator at least a month ahead of the wedding.

You'll also need to submit an application for a marriage license as well as certified birth certificates (bring the original with you to Los Cabos, and send certified copies ahead of time). If either party is divorced or widowed, official death certificate or divorce decree must be supplied, and you must wait one year to remarry after the end of the previous marriage. (There's no way around this archaic requirement, still on the books, designed to ensure that no lingering pregnancy remains from a former marriage.) The bride, groom, and four witnesses will also need to present passports and tourist cards. Wedding planners can round up witnesses if you don't have enough or any.

Since religious weddings aren't officially recognized in Mexico, a civil ceremony (*matrimonio civil*) is required, thus making your marriage valid in your home country as well. (It's the equivalent of being married in front of a justice of the peace.) Cabo San Lucas and San José del Cabo each have one civil judge who performs marriages, a good reason to start planning months in advance. Often for an extra fee, the judge will attend the site of your wedding if you prefer not to go to an office. Civil proceedings take about 10 minutes, and the wording is fixed in Spanish. Most wedding planners will provide an interpreter if you or your guests don't speak the language. For a Catholic ceremony, a priest here will expect evidence that you've attended the church's required pre-wedding sessions back home. If you're planning a Jewish wedding, you'll need to bring your rabbi with you as Los Cabos has no synagogues. Another option is to be married in your own country and then hold the wedding event in Los Cabos without worrying about all the red tape.

Same-sex civil unions are legal in Mexico City, and in the states of Campeche, Chihuahua, Coahuila, Colima, Jalisco, Michoacán, Morelos, Nayarit, and Quintana Roo. Same-sex marriages are also legal in certain municipalities in Guerrero, Puebla, Querétaro, and Tamaulipas. In Los Cabos, unfortunately, they are not. A few Los Cabos wedding planners have organized same-sex commitment ceremonies, but these have no legal standing.

KIDS AND FAMILIES

Los Cabos and Baja don't necessarily leap to mind when planning a vacation with the kids. (This isn't Orlando, after all.) It's not that the region is unfriendly to children, but enjoying time with the kids here does take some advance preparation and research.

Places to Stay

Except those that exclude children entirely, many of Los Cabos' beach hotels and all-inclusive resorts cater to families and have children's programs. A few offer little more than kids' pools, but several of the big hotels and their wealth of activities go way beyond that and make fine options for families with kids. Our top picks:

Dreams Los Cabos has an active Explorers Club for children ages 3–12. (The search for a beach treasure is always a crowd-pleaser.) Older kids will appreciate tennis, badminton, volleyball, and soccer.

Grand Velas houses the best spots for kids and teenagers in Los Cabos. Exclusively for children ages 4–12, the Kids' Club teaches little ones how to make piñatas, jewelry, masks, and kites. The Teens' Club, for ages 13–18, has a dance club, juice bar, pool table, Ping-Pong, karaoke, and private Xbox Kinect cinemas. These supervised services are open all day, and free of charge to hotel guests.

Hilton's Cabo Kids' Club is geared toward kids 4–12, with cookie decorating, arts and crafts, board games, Spanish classes, cinema under the stars, and even spa treatments for kids at Eforea Spa. Baby-sitting service is also available so parents can get some alone time.

Vacation Rentals: Apartments, condos, and villas are an excellent option for families. You can cook your own food (a big money saver), spread out, and set up a home away from home. If you decide to go the apartment- or condo-rental route, be sure to ask about the number and size of the swimming pools and whether outdoor spaces and barbecue areas are available.

Beaches

If you have visions of you and your family frolicking in the surf, revise them a bit. Many Los Cabos–area beaches are notoriously unsafe for swimming, so your day at the beach will be relegated to the sand.

The destination has a handful of beaches you can swim in, the most popular (and crowded) being Medano Beach in Cabo San Lucas. While it may be good for swimming, there are some quick drop-offs, not to mention the waters can get congested with party people. Other swimmable beaches include Playa Solmar on the Pacific side of Land's End, and Santa Maria Beach off the main highway. Chileno Beach is great for families, but part of the cove is now dominated by the recently developed Chileno Bay Resort. Estuary Beach at the north end of hotel row in San José del Cabo is relatively calm, as is Playa Hotelera just east of the San José Estuary. Playa Palmilla, near San José del Cabo, offers tranquil water most days, making it a good spot for stand-up paddleboarding or swimming. Playa Buenos Aires in the Corridor is safest between Hilton and Paradisus Resort, where the man-made Tequila Cove serves as a wave breaker. Playa del Amor (Lover's Beach), at Land's End near Cabo San Lucas, is regarded as OK for swimming on the Sea of Cortez side, but not the Pacific side. (You can't swim in any of the Pacific beaches here.)

After Dark

Nightlife here is mostly geared toward grown-ups, but a few kid-friendly dining spots do exist. El Merkado in the Corridor offers an elevated "food court" concept that explores the best of Mexico's gastronomy. Both Flora Farms and Acre restaurant have "farm-to-table" dining experiences, meaning kids can explore the grounds while mom and dad enjoy live music over a watermelon julep. Most all-inclusives have familiar food that will satisfy the most finicky of eaters, and the U.S. chains are all here, too.

All restaurants in Mexico are nonsmoking (except in outdoor-seating areas). Both San José del Cabo and Cabo San Lucas have modern theaters that show Hollywood movies a few weeks after they premiere back home; note, though, that animated films or G-rated films are often dubbed in Spanish.

Baja Top Five for Kids

Canyon and Beach Action, Cabo San Lucas: For little adventurers, Baja Outback has boogie boarding, surfing, sand-castle building, stand-up paddleboarding, and more at the beach. For teens, Wild Canyon Adventures dishes up desert action with camel rides and zip-lining.

Bucaneer Queen, Cabo San Lucas: Kids of all ages can dress up like pirates and go swashbuckling and hunting for treasure on the *Bucaneer Queen*, one of several pirate cruises that operate out of Los Cabos.

La Bufadora, near Ensenada: Literally "the buffalo snort," this natural tidal-wave phenomenon near Ensenada sprays water 75 feet into the air.

Swim with the Dolphins, San José del Cabo: Kids can swim and play with friendly dolphins at the Marina in Puerto Los Cabos near San José. A second dolphin center is located at the Marina in Cabo San Lucas.

Whale-Watching, Los Cabos, Ensenada, Guerrero Negro, Loreto, Magdalena Bay: You'll find whale-watching venues up and down the peninsula; here, outfitters here take you out to sea in pangas, small boats that let you get an up-close view of the magnificent beasts. No matter what your age, Baja has no greater thrill.

Legalities

All children over the age of two require a Mexican Tourist Card (FMT card) to venture beyond the U.S. border region. Kids 15 and under require only a birth certificate to return to the United States by land from Mexico. If you fly home, everyone, regardless of age, must hold a passport to get back into the United States.

Don't forget Mexico's well-known and stringent laws regarding the entry and exit of children under 18. All minors must be accompanied by both parents or legal guardian. In the absence of that, the parent not present must provide a notarized statement granting permission for the child to travel. Divorce, separation, or remarriage complicate these matters, but do not negate the requirement.

If you are traveling as a full family, multi-ethnic family, or have remarried, adopted, or have different last names, copies of relevant documentation are always benefical for Mexican immigration officials, just in case there are questions.

SNAPSHOT LOS CABOS

Where Desert Meets Sea

A visitor flying into Los Cabos will readily observe the peninsula's stark, brown terrain—indeed, it feels like you're arriving in the middle of nowhere. You'll realize soon after landing that even though the tip of Baja once also resembled the rest of the dry, inhospitable desert, it has been transformed into an inviting desert oasis. The landscape, where once only cacti and a few hardy palms resided, is now punctuated by posh hotels, manicured golf courses, and swimming pools. As shown by the thousands of sun-worshipping, partying people seemingly oblivious to the fact that true desert lies, literally, across Highway 1 from their beachfront hotel, Los Cabos has successfully beaten back the drylands. Pay some respect to the area's roots by taking a hike or tour around the surrounding desert landscape.

A similar phenomenon exists in the northern sector of the peninsula, with the metro area anchored by Tijuana, in reality just a continuation of U.S. Southern California. Irrigation has turned this desert into one of Mexico's prime agricultural regions.

In between far-northern Baja and Los Cabos—the peninsula logs a distance of just over 1,600 km (1,000 miles), which compares to the north–south length of Italy—expect mostly desert scrubland. Two-thirds of the landmass is desert—a continuation of the Sonora Desert in the southwest United States—and receives about 10 inches of rain per year. The remaining third of the peninsula forms a mountainous spine, technically four mountain ranges. The northernmost of these mountains are pine-forested and might make you think you've taken a wrong turn to Oregon. East of San Felipe, Baja's highest peak, the Picacho del Diablo ("Devil's Peak"), measures 10,150 feet and is snowcapped in winter.

The Bajacalifornianos

Geography, history, and economics have conspired to give Baja California a different population mix than the rest of Mexico. The country as a whole is the quintessential *mestizo* (mixed indigenous and white-European descent) culture, but only half of *Bajacalifornianos*—the name is a mouthful—can point to any indigenous ancestry. Historically, the peninsula was a land apart, a Wild West where only the intrepid dared to venture to seek their fortunes—many Mexicans still view Baja through that prism—and has drawn a more international population. The indigenous population that does live here is a recent addition of migrants from the poorer southern states of Oaxaca and Chiapas drawn to jobs in the border cities.

Baja's population is over 3.3 million, but nearly two-thirds of that number lives near the U.S. border. The 1,600-km (1,000-mile) drive from north to south confirms this is a sparsely populated region of Mexico. The state of Baja California Sur, the southern half of the peninsula, is the country's least populous.

U.S. citizens make up around 10% of the population, with retirees, business owners who have set up shop here, or commuters who live in Mexico but work in the San Diego metro area among them.

A Multifaceted Economy

By Mexican standards, the Baja Peninsula is prosperous, but things were not always so. It was only some six decades ago that Mexico even deemed part of the region to be economically viable enough for statehood, creating the state of Baja California north of the 28th parallel in 1953. Baja California Sur became Mexico's newest state in 1974. Prior to that, the region, once considered far-off and neglected, was administered as a territory directly from Mexico City.

This is Mexico, however, and all is relative, even today. Wages here may be double, triple, or quadruple those in the rest of the country, but you pause when you realize that about $5 a day is still the national average. The presence of the *maquiladora* (foreign-run factories in Mexico) economy has brought up the on-paper average level of prosperity to the peninsula. This industry of tariff-free, export-geared manufacturing congregates on the U.S. border with more than 900 factories providing employment for more than 300,000 people, but critics decry the sweatshop conditions. Urban magnet Tijuana—whose population now stands at 1.7 million—attracts people from all over the country looking for jobs.

Agriculture and fishing contribute to Baja's economy, too. Cotton, fruit, flowers, and ornamental plants grow in the irrigated northern region. (Most of the rest of Baja California is too arid and inhospitable to support much agriculture.) Large populations of tuna, sardines, and lobster support the fishing industry.

And it goes without saying that tourism is a huge business in Baja, with an impressive $1 billion flowing into Los Cabos annually. Historically, the border region has tallied those kinds of numbers as well, but fears of drug-cartel violence have greatly eaten into tourism revenues for that area.

Livin' la Vida Buena

Living the good life in Mexico—specifically in and around Los Cabos—seems to get easier year after year. Americans and Canadians are by far the biggest groups of expats, not only at the peninsula's southern tip, but in communities such as Ensenada, Rosarito, Loreto, and La Paz. In addition to those who have relocated to make Mexico their home, many foreigners have part-time retirement or vacation homes here.

Some visitors to Los Cabos and Baja experience "Sunshine Syndrome," and want to extend their stay indefinitely. But many find living in Baja bears little resemblance to vacationing here. Experts suggest doing a trial rental for a few months to see if living the day-to-day life here is for you.

The population of Los Cabos and the larger communities of Baja are a mix of natives and foreigners, so contractors and shopkeepers are used to dealing with gringos and most speak English. Los Cabos has many English-language publications and opportunities for foreigners to meet up for events or volunteer work.

FLAVORS OF LOS CABOS

"Me sube el colesterol, mi amorcita," goes the chorus to cheery popular song here. "My cholesterol's going up, my love," laments the singer about the heavy, fried Mexican food he gets at home. Yet in Baja, innovative chefs are giving a healthy twist to traditional Mexican fare. Not too long ago the dining options in the Cape were limited mainly to (very tasty) *tacos de pescado y cerveza* (fish tacos and beer) or *pollo y cerveza* (chicken and beer). Walking the streets of Cabo and San José, travelers will be pleased to find grand, innovative dining experiences.

Sibling Rivalry

The friendly inter-Cabo rivalry between Cabo San Lucas and San José del Cabo infuses everything—the dining scene included. Historically, it's been a comparison of quantity vs. quality: Cabo San Lucas wins hands down in sheer volume and variety of dining places. What San José del Cabo lacks in numbers, it makes up for with the finesse and intimacy of its dining experience. The Golden Rule of Cabo San Lucas restaurateurs was once: "As long as you keep the margaritas coming, the customer will be happy." (The mass-market eateries still adhere to this rule.) But a growing number of San Lucas dining spots have followed San José's lead and have begun to offer intimate, cozy dining experiences.

Nuevo Mexican

Ask a dozen Los Cabos chefs for a definition of today's Mexican cuisine, and you'll get a dozen different answers. Many prefer the description "Baja chic," to emphasize the peninsula's uncanny ability to find the right mix of fashionable and casual. Major changes have come to Mexican gastronomy in the past decade. Traditionally heavy cuisine is being altered and reinterpreted. The trend is moving toward using quality local, organic ingredients and combining traditional Mexican fare with elements of other cuisines, all the while asserting one's own interpretation. All chefs are quick to point out that they're not abandoning Mexican cooking entirely. "People visit Mexico. They do expect Mexican food," one chef told us. The rise in popularity of north Baja's steadily growing wine region can also be found on many of Los Cabos' menus, so be sure to try some of the quality Mexican varietals that you can't yet obtain in the United States.

Seafood

With 4,025 km (2,500 miles) of coastline and no point more than 110 km (70 miles) from the ocean, seafood figures prominently in Baja's cuisine. Baja's signature dish is the ubiquitous *taco de pescado*, or fish taco: take strips of batter-fried fish (frequently halibut or mahimahi), wrap them, along with shredded cabbage, in a corn tortilla, and top it all off with onions, salsa, lime juice, and a dollop of sour cream or a mayonnaise-based sauce. You'll find as many recipes for Baja-style seafood stew as there are cooks, who refer to the dish as paella or *zarzuela*. Any mix-and-match combination of clams, crab, shrimp, cod, sea bass, red snapper, or mahimahi could find its way into your dish, along with requisite white wine, garlic, and spices. Shellfish is frequently served here as a *coctel*, steamed with sauce and lime juice. While fish tacos might be a travelers "go to" Baja favorite, the peninsula is also famous for chocolate clams, smoked marlin, chicken tamales fajados, and of course lobster.

2

BEACHES

Updated
by Marlise
Kast-Myers

Along the rocky cliffs of the Pacific Ocean and the Sea of Cortez lie many bays, coves, and roughly 80 km (about 50 miles) of sandy beach. The waters range from translucent green to deep navy, and even a stunning turquoise on some days of the year.

The destination has six swimmable beaches including Lover's Beach, Bahía Santa María, Bahía Chileno, Tequila Cove (a small section at Playa Buenos Aires), Punta Palmilla, and Playa Médano—the most popular beach in Cabo San Lucas. Most people come to Médano's active 3-km (2-mile) stretch for the crowds, since there's no better place to people-watch. Gorgeous Playa del Amor (Lover's Beach) near the famous *El Arco* (arch) is five minutes across the bay by water taxi ($10–$15), It's a great spot for swimming, though the waters can be somewhat busy with all the *panga* traffic. Just southwest of San José, the most popular beaches are Costa Azul and Playa Palmilla. Between Cabo San Lucas and San José del Cabo are the Corridor's less congested beaches of Las Viudas, Bahía Santa María, and Bahía Chileno.

No other beaches are within walking distance of either Cabo San Lucas or San José del Cabo; some can be accessed by boat, but most require a car ride (unless you're staying at a Corridor hotel nearby). Since beach service and amenities are limited to hotel guests, it is imperative that you lug extra water, especially if you are adventuring during the searing summer months.

PLANNING

WHEN TO GO

Nearly 360 warm and sunny days per year, few bugs, and fantastic water temperatures (70s in winter and 80s in summer) allow visitors to enjoy this natural wonderland year-round. The winter holiday season is busy, and people often book months in advance. Spring break is another busy time. Late May through September is when it's hottest and least crowded.

SUN AND SAFETY

If swimming in the ocean or sea is at the top of your vacation checklist, opt for a property on a protected cove, where swimming is permitted. Most resorts in the region are on stretches of beach where swimming is dangerous or forbidden due to strong currents. Look for the beach warning flags posted outside resorts: red means conditions are dangerous, yellow signals to use caution, and green signifies conditions are safe. Barely visible rocks and strong undertows make many of the beaches unsuitable for swimming. Use precaution as tides change from serenely calm or dangerously turbulent, depending on the day or even the hour. The Pacific side is notorious for rogue waves and intense undertows. Also, the sun here is fierce: don't underestimate the need for waterproof sunscreen and a wide-brimmed hat.

BEACH ETIQUETTE

As on most beaches in Mexico, nudity is not permitted on Los Cabos beaches. If you head to a beachside bar, it's appropriate to put on a cover-up, although you'd be hard-pressed to find a strict dress code at any of these places unless you're at one of the more posh resorts. As tempting as it is to pick up seashells from the beach, be advised that U.S. Customs commonly seizes these items upon reentry to the United States. Packing a picnic or cooler for a day at the beach is a great idea, as few of the public beaches have restaurants or food vendors. A few beaches have vendors offering umbrella rentals, but if you're really keen on having one for shelter, it's best to take your own.

BEACH FACILITIES

As a general rule, Los Cabos beaches are no-frills, with very few public facilities. There is no established lifeguard program in the entire Los Cabos region. Hotels will often post a red flag on the beach to alert swimmers to strong currents and undertows, but you won't see such warnings on the stretches of public beach along the coasts.

More and more of the public beaches have toilets, but you'll still be hard-pressed to find a shower. The picnic tables, grills or fire pits, playgrounds, and other amenities common at U.S. beaches simply aren't part of the scene in Los Cabos. If you want or need anything for your day at the beach, it's best to pack it yourself. If any of the following facilities are present at a beach, we'll list them: lifeguard, toilets, showers, food concession, picnic tables, grills or fire pits, playground, parking lot, or camping.

Mexican beaches are free and open to the public, though some of the resort developments along the Corridor are doing their best to keep their beaches private for guests. Resort boundaries are usually very well marked; any beach after that is free to all.

SAN JOSÉ DEL CABO

Oh, the madness of it all. Here you are in a beach destination with gorgeous weather and miles of clear blue water, yet you dare not dive into the sea. Most of San José's hotels line Playa Hotelera on Paseo Malecón San José, and brochures and websites gleefully mention beach access. But here's the rub—though the long, level stretch of coarse brown sand

IF YOU LIKE:	IN CABO SAN LUCAS	ALONG THE CORRIDOR	IN SAN JOSÉ DEL CABO OR BEYOND
Crystal-clear water	El Médano, Playa del Amor	Bahía Santa María	San José del Cabo's main beach (aka Playa del Sol)
Snorkeling/ Swimming	Playa del Amor (near the Sand Falls area)	Bahía Santa María, Bahía Chileno	For snorkeling, keep going to the East Cape and Cabo Pulmo area
Surfing	Monuments Beach (at eastern end of El Médano Beach)	Costa Azul stretch, Acapulquito Beach (at the Cabo Surf Hotel)	Shipwreck, 14½ km (9 miles) northeast of San José; Nine Palms, just beyond
Beachside or ocean-view bars	The Office, Mango Deck, Billygan's at El Médano Beach	Zipper's at Costa Azul, or Acapulquito Beach at 7 Seas at Cabo Surf Hotel	Buzzard's Bar & Grill (east of La Playita) or El Ganzo Beach Club
Undiscovered beaches	El Faro Viejo Beach is difficult to access, with dangerous waves, but is a gem for sunbathing	A drive along the highway will reveal many "acceso a playa" signs—be wary of waves	Los Frailes and Cabo Pulmo at Playa Los Arbolitos is distant—a full day's adventure—but pristine for water activities and well worth the time

is beautiful, the currents can be dangerously rough, the drop-offs are steep and close to shore, and the waves can be fierce. While surfers love this type of water and flock here in droves, it's extremely dangerous for the casual swimmer. Warning signs are posted up and down the beach, just in case you happen to forget. Feel free to walk along the beach to the Estero San José, play some beach volleyball, or enjoy a horseback ride along the shore. For swimming, head to protected Playa Palmilla just a few miles southwest, in the Corridor.

Playa Estero (*Estuary Beach*). A sandy beach can be enjoyed at the mouth of the Estero San José, the lush estuary that starts at the north end of Hotel Zone near the Holiday Inn hotel. This oasis is home to more than 350 species of wildlife and vegetation (200-plus species of birds alone), and can be explored on foot, or via kayaks rentable at El Ganzo Beach Club. Horses are available for hire across from Holiday Inn at Bonanza Horseback Riding. Bring bug spray as the wetlands attract lots of mosquitoes. Not recommended for swimming, it is nevertheless a worthwhile trip in an area that is otherwise not known for its lushness. Public parking is available just beyond the Holiday Inn. **Amenities:** parking lot. **Best for:** walking; sunrise. ⊠ *San José del Cabo.*

FAMILY **Playa Hotelera.** The long, wide stretch of beach running in front of the hotels on the coast of San José del Cabo might be stunning, but the riptides and undertows make it deceivingly dangerous for swimmers. There are no public services on the beach, but you can always duck into one of the hotels for a snack, or head across the street to Plaza Del Pescador for a meal at one of the restaurants. This beach often has locals with horses to rent for a beachside ride. Due to the line of resorts, there are only a few access points to reach the sand. **Amenities:** none. **Best for:** walking. ⊠ *San José del Cabo.*

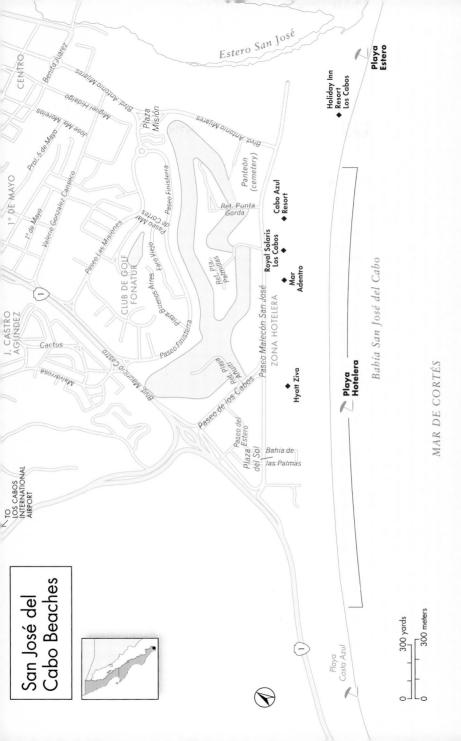

San José del Cabo Beaches

CENTRO

TO LOS CABOS INTERNATIONAL AIRPORT

Benito Juárez

Miguel Hidalgo

Blvd. Antonio Mijares

José Ma. Morelos

Valerio González Canseco

Prol. 5 de Mayo

1° de Mayo

1° DE MAYO

I. CASTRO AGUNDEZ

Cactus

Malvarrosa

CLUB DE GOLF FONATUR

Paseo Las Misiones

Faro Viejo

Buenos Aires

Estafeta

Paseo Finisterra

Plaza Misión

Paseo Finisterra

Paseo Mar de Cortés

Ret. Pta. Palmillas

Ret. Punta Gorda

Panteón (cemetery)

Blvd. Antonio Mijares

Estero San José

Playa Estero

Holiday Inn Resort Los Cabos ◆

Cabo Azul Resort ◆

Royal Solaris Los Cabos ◆

Mar Adentro ◆

Paseo Malecón San José

ZONA HOTELERA

Blvd. Mauricio Castro

Ret. Playa Azul

Paseo de los Cabos

Paseo del Estero

Plaza del Sol

Bahía de las Palmas

Hyatt Ziva ◆

Playa Hotelera

Bahía San José del Cabo

MAR DE CORTÉS

Playa Costa Azul

0   300 yards
0   300 meters

ALONG THE CORRIDOR

The Corridor's coastline edges the Sea of Cortez, with long, secluded stretches of sand, tranquil bays, golf fairways, and huge resorts. Only a few areas are safe for swimming, but several hotels have man-made rocky breakwaters that create semi-safe swimming areas when the sea is calm. Look for blue-and-white signs along Highway 1 with symbols of a snorkel mask or a swimmer and "*acceso a playa*" ("beach access") written on them to alert you to beach turnoffs. It's worth studying a map ahead of time to get an idea of where your turnoff will be. Don't hesitate to ask around for directions, and don't lose hope if you still need to circle back around once or twice. Facilities are extremely limited and lifeguards are nonexistent, though many of the beaches now have portable toilets. ■ TIP→ **The four-lane Highway 1 has more-or-less well-marked turnoffs for hotels. Be alert: signage as a rule appears at the very last minute.** Drivers tend to speed along most of the Corridor highway, which makes for a lot of business for the police officers who patrol the Corridor. Slow buses and trucks seem to appear out of nowhere, and confused tourists switch lanes with abandon. If you're driving, wait until you're safely parked to take in Sea of Cortez views.

Bahía Santa María and **Bahía Chileno** are two beautiful strands in the Corridor. Bahía Santa María is the less busy of the two, and both beaches offer fun snorkeling and safe swimming; the docile fish will actually approach you. For seclusion, drive northeast to the stunning beaches on the dirt road northeast of San José del Cabo. Soon after leaving San José you'll see Playa Las Viudas dotted with shade palapas and surfers looking for the next big break. Don't be put off by all of the private homes or "no trespassing" signs—beaches are plentiful and public access is clearly marked. The dirt road from the highway is well maintained and fine for passenger cars (despite dire-sounding warnings from locals who will tell you that you must have a four-wheel-drive vehicle)—but the dirt roads are best avoided if it's raining.

FAMILY

Fodor's Choice

★

Bahía Chileno (*Chileno Bay*). A calm enclave—with golf courses, residences, and Chileno Bay Resort— is roughly midway between San José and Cabo San Lucas. Consistently ranked one of the cleanest beaches in Mexico, Chileno has been awarded "Blue Flag" certification, meaning 32 criteria for safety, services, water quality, and other standards have been met. The beach skirts a small, crescent-shape cove with aquamarine waters and an outside reef that are perfect for snorkeling and swimming (there are even restrooms, showers, and handicap access). To the east are tide pools great for exploring with the kids. Getting here is easy, thanks to the well-marked access ramps on both sides of the road. Along the western edge of Bahía Chileno, some 200 yards away, are some good-size boulders that you can scramble up. In winter, this part of the Sea of Cortez gets chilly—refreshing for a dip, but most snorkelers don't spend too much time in the water. On weekends, get to the bay early if you want to claim shade under a palapa. **Amenities:** toilets; showers; parking lot. **Best for:** swimming; snorkeling; tide pools. ⊠ *Bahía Chileno, The Corridor* ✛ *The turnoff for the beach is at Km 14.5 on Hwy. 1. Look for the signs whether driving west from San José or at Km 16 when driving east from Cabo San Lucas.*

Continued on page 42

SURFING CABO STYLE

From the gentlest of beginner waves at Old Man's surf spot to the gnarliest winter waves at Los Cerritos, Los Cabos has surf for everyone. The tip of the Baja Peninsula has three key areas: the Pacific coast (often called "the Pacific side"), the East Cape, and the Cabo Corridor between them. This means that there are east-, west- and south-facing beaches taking waves from just about every direction.

There are also warm, crystalline seas and great surf schools. Friendly instructors make lessons fun and are more than willing to tailor them to the needs of anyone—from groms to retirees, aspiring surfers to experts. Schools also offer surf tours so you can benefit from insider knowledge of the local waves and quirky surf spots before heading out on your own.

by Larry Dunmire

LOS CABOS SURF FINDER

Surfer at a right-hand point break

Punta Conejo
Todos Santos
Punta Lobos
Playa San Pedrito
El Pescadero
El Pescadero
Playa Los Cerritos

Pacific Coast

WEST CAPE

Gentle waves during summer time.

19

PACIFIC SIDE

In winter, the Pacific from Cabo San Lucas town north to Todos Santos, often roils with rough, thundering swells. Surf spots here are only for the most accomplished although Los Cerritos, home to the Costa Azul Surf Shop and school, can have gentle waves in summer. Pacific-side beaches face essentially west and slightly north. Hence, winter swells coming from these directions (thanks to Alaskan storms) make landfall head on, creating great waves.

Punta Conejo: a rocky point break north of Todos Santos; unique in that it's surfable on both north and south swells. Has good right and left breaks. *11 km (7 miles) north of Todos Santos; turn off Hwy. 19 near Km 80.*

Punta Lobos: big point breaks with south swells. *South of Todos Santos; turn off Hwy. 19 at Km 54 onto dirt road, and continue for about 2.5 km (1.5 miles).*

Surfer on the nose of his long-board on a clean wave

Perfect waves in Salsipuedes, Baja California

Playa San Pedrito: a beautiful, broad, curved, sandy beach break, surfable on both west and north swells. *About 5 km (3 miles) south of Todos Santos; turn off Hwy. 19 at CAMPO EXPERIMENTA sign, and continue about 2.5 km (1.5 miles).*

El Pescadero: fast, consistent, right reef and beach breaks; watch out for painful sea urchins in shallow water! *Hwy. 19 at Km 59.*

Playa Los Cerritos: highly versatile beach—in summer, good for beginners, with gentle breaks and a safe, sandy bottom; winter waves are gnarly. Best ones are on northwest swells, though south swells aren't bad. Both left and right beach breaks. Home to Costa Azul Surf Shop; can get crowded. *Less than a km (half a mile) south of Todos Santos; Hwy. 19 at Km 66.*

CABO CORRIDOR

The 20-mile stretch of beautiful beaches and bays between the towns of Cabo San Lucas and San José del Cabo has no less than a dozen surf spots, including some that are hard to find and access. Opportunities range from the expert-only Monuments break just outside of Cabo to the beginner-friendly Old Man's spot. For experts, surfing in the Corridor is generally best in the summer and fall, when storms as far away as New Zealand and Antarctica can send south swells all the way up here.

Playa Monumentos: powerful left point break, offering great gut-wrenching waves on south and west swells. Dangerously shallow at low tide; many sea urchins. Great surf and sunset watching from bluff near parking area. *Far south end of Cabo's El Medano Beach, east of Cabo San Lucas on Hwy 1; pull off at Misiones de Cabo, drive to gate, park at right.*

Playa El Tule: long wide beach with great right reef break in El Tule Arroyo, near highway bridge of same name. One of few places you can still camp; need 4WD to get here. *Midway btw. Cabo San Lucas and San José. East on Hwy. 1, look for EL TULE sign, pull off road and drive toward ocean on soft, sandy road.*

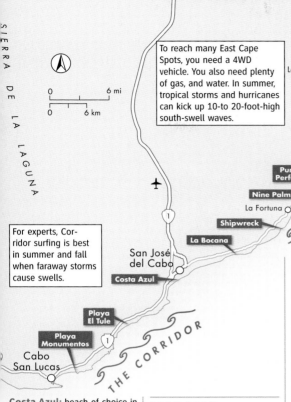

To reach many East Cape Spots, you need a 4WD vehicle. You also need plenty of gas, and water. In summer, tropical storms and hurricanes can kick up 10-to 20-foot-high south-swell waves.

For experts, Corridor surfing is best in summer and fall when faraway storms cause swells.

Costa Azul: beach of choice in summer. World-famous, experts-only Zippers break often tops 12 feet. Has two other popular breaks: Acapulquito (Old Man's) in front of Cabo Surf Hotel—forgiving with a gentle surf break and good for beginners—and The Rock, a more challenging reef break to the east. The rocks are near the surface; quite shallow at low tide. There's a restaurant and a branch of the Costa Azul Surf Shop here. *Hwy. 1.*

La Bocana: freshwater estuary with a river mouth beach break (i.e., giant barrels break upon sand bars created by runoff sand deposited here after powerful summer rains). Both left and right rides. *Hwy. 1, south of Intercontinental hotel.*

EAST CAPE

North and east of San José, up the rough, unpaved East Cape Road, there are many breaks with good waves that are perpetually empty—with good reason. To get here, you need a 4WD vehicle. You also need plenty of gas, sufficient water, an umbrella, and *mucho* sun block. Waves here aren't for beginners, and some of the coast is on private property. Note, too, that locals (both Mexican and gringo) can be protective of their spots. East Cape beaches face south and east, and, in summer, tropical storms and hurricanes can kick up 10-, 15-, and even 20-foot-high south-swell waves—exciting for beginners to watch from the shore.

Shipwreck: fast, right reef break with south swells in summer. Considered the second-best summer surfing spot. Need 4WD to get here. *Off East Cape Rd., about 16 km (10 miles) up a rough, washboard road.*

Nine Palms: right point break with good, long waves and great shape but at least an hour's drive out. *East Cape Rd., near village of Santa Elena and a palm-tree grove.*

Punta Perfecta: right point break; can get big and hollow (i.e., "tubular") during summer's south swells. Out of the way (4WD required) and hard to find; territorial local surfers get testy when asked for directions. *East Cape Rd., near Crossroads Country Club and Vinorama.*

Los Frailes: Waves get big on a south swell. Down a long, dusty, pounding drive (need 4WD). Beautiful white sand beach and tranquil desert surroundings. *East Cape Rd.*

Stand-up paddleboarding (SUP)

LEARNING TO SURF

WHAT TO EXPECT

Expect introductory classes to cover how to lie on the board, paddle properly, pop up into a surf stance, and handle riding white wash (inside waves).

GEARING UP

Both surf shops and schools offer a wide selection of lessons, gear, and boards—sometimes including "skegs," soft, stable beginners's boards with plastic fins. Novices will want to use longboards, which offer the most stability. Rash guards (form-fitting polyester vests) protect you from board chafing and sunburn. Booties, rubberized watershoes, protect your feet from rocks, coral and sea urchins.

GETTING OUT THERE

Most agree that the best place for beginners is San José del Cabo's Acapulquito Beach, home to Old Man's surf spot. It has gently breaking, "feathering" (very forgiving) waves and the region's most understanding surfers. Acapulquito Beach is also home to the Cabo Surf Hotel, with a top school. The **Mike Doyle Surf School** (⊕ *www.mikedoylesurfschool. com*) has five full-time teachers, certified by the NSSIA, the National Surf Schools and Instructor's Association (U.S.) and a great selection of more than 100 boards—short, long, "soft" boards for novices, and even a couple of SUP boards.

Costa Azul Surf Shop (⊕ *www.costa-azul. com.mx*), with branches in San José del Cabo (near Zipper's Restaurant) and south of Todos Santos, near Los Cerritos Beach, is another option for lessons. Staff here can arrange tours to breaks so far off the path that roads to them aren't always marked on maps, let alone paved. The shop's website also has good interactive surfing maps.

Costa Azul's surf excursions—with guides (one guide for every two students), transportation, equipment, and two-hour lessons—cost US$180 a person.

SURF'S DOWN?

If the surf's flat, *no problema!* SUP, or stand-up paddleboarding, is done on flat waters using broad, long, lightweight boards that are comfortable to stand on. You paddle along, alternating sides for balance, using what resembles a single-bladed kayak paddle. SUP is easy to master, great exercise, and highly enjoyable.

Accomplished surfers have pushed the SUP-ing envelope, paddling their boards into the lineup (or surf zone) and right into the waves, be they small or large. The paddle is then used to steer, almost like a boat's rudder. One step at a time, though—this type of SUP is *not* as easy as the masters make it look!

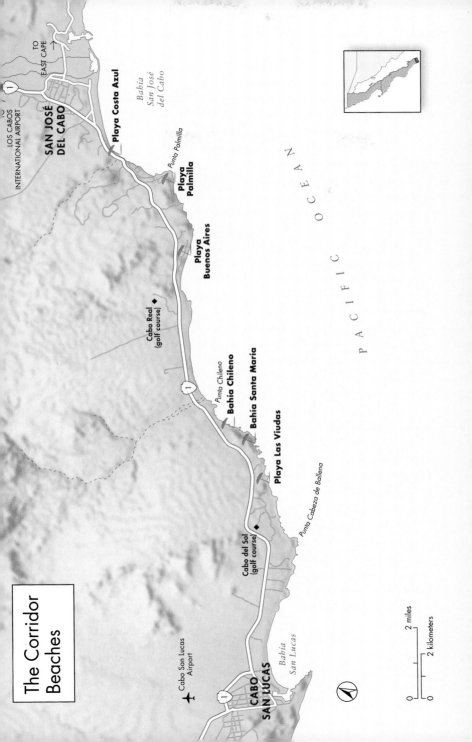

The Corridor Beaches

TO EAST CAPE

LOS CABOS INTERNATIONAL AIRPORT

SAN JOSÉ DEL CABO

Playa Costa Azul

Bahía San José del Cabo

Punta Palmilla

Playa Palmilla

Playa Buenos Aires

Cabo Real (golf course)

Punta Chileno

Bahía Chileno

Bahía Santa María

Playa Las Viudas

Punta Cabeza de Ballena

Cabo del Sol (golf course)

Cabo San Lucas Airport

CABO SAN LUCAS

Bahía San Lucas

PACIFIC OCEAN

0   2 miles
0   2 kilometers

Bahía Santa María (*Santa Maria Beach*). This wide, sloping, horseshoe-shape beach is surrounded by cactus-covered rocky cliffs; the placid waters here are a protected fish sanctuary. The bay is part of an underwater reserve and is a great place to snorkel: brightly colored fish swarm through chunks of white coral and golden sea fans. Unfortunately, this little slice of paradise has limited palapas for shade, so arrive early or bring a beach umbrella. In high season, from November to May, there's usually someone renting snorkeling gear or selling sarongs, straw hats, and soft drinks. It's best to bring your own supplies, though, including lots of drinking water, snacks, and sunscreen. Snorkel and booze-cruise boats from Cabo San Lucas visit the bay in mid-morning through about 1 pm. Arrive mid-afternoon if you want to get that total Robinson Crusoe feel. The parking lot is a quarter mile or so off the highway and is sometimes guarded; be sure to tip the guard. The bay is roughly 19 km (12 miles) west of San José and 13 km (8 miles) east of Cabo San Lucas. Heading east, look for the sign saying "playa santa maría." **Amenities:** toilets; parking lot; showers. **Best for:** snorkeling; swimming. ⊠ *19 km (12 miles) west of San José del Cabo, 13 km (8 miles) east of Cabo San Lucas, The Corridor.*

Playa Buenos Aires. This wide, lengthy, and accessible stretch of beach is one of the longest along the Cabo Corridor, but is rapidly developing with new resorts. Reef breaks for surfers can be good, but the beach is also known for its riptides, making it unswimmable. It's a great beach for long, quiet runs or walks, and it's not uncommon to find locals with horses to rent for a beachside ride. Whales can easily be spotted from the beach from January through March. The small, man-made "Tequila Cove" between Hilton and Paradisus has calm waters, excellent for swimming. Here you'll find a tiny shack renting boogie boards and other water-sports equipment. **Amenities:** toilets; parking lot (exit at Km 22 or 24). **Best for:** surfers; walking. ⊠ *Near the Secrets Marquis Hotel Los Cabos/Hilton and stretching down to Meliá Cabo Real.*

Playa Costa Azul. Cabo's best surfing beach runs 3 km (2 miles) south from San José's hotel zone along Highway 1. The Zipper and La Roca breaks are world famous. Playa Costa Azul connects to neighboring **Playa Acapulquito** in front of Cabo Surf Hotel. Surfers gather at both beaches year-round, but most come in summer, when hurricanes and tropical storms create the year's largest waves, and when the ocean is at its warmest. This condo-lined beach is popular with joggers and walkers, but swimming isn't advised. When getting in and out of the water in front of Cabo Surf Hotel (where surf lessons take place), watch out for the sea urchins that cling to the shallow rocks. Beginner surfers should ask locals to point out the mound of hidden rocks near the break closest to the cliffs; this means it's much safer to take "rights" than "lefts" at this break. Although not overly common, jellyfish can also be a problem here. The turnoff to this beach is sudden and only available to drivers coming from Cabo San Lucas (not from San José del Cabo). It's on the beach side of the highway, at Zipper's restaurant, which is on the sand by the surf breaks. If coming from San José del Cabo, you have to exit at Costa Azul Surf Shop and drive under the highway to the parking area. Food and drinks are available at Zipper's restaurant

Bahía Chileno (Chileno Bay) is a popular swimming and snorkeling spot along the Corridor.

or at 7 Seas restaurant. Surfboards can be rented at Costa Azul Surf Shop or at Cabo Surf Hotel. **Amenities:** toilets; food concession; picnic tables; parking lot. **Best for:** surfing; walking; partiers. ✉ *Just over 1 km (½ mi) southwest of San José del Cabo.*

Playa Las Viudas (*Widow's Beach*). Just west of Santa María Bay, this small public beach is often referred to as Twin Dolphin Beach after the Twin Dolphin Hotel, a longtime landmark that was demolished in mid-2007 to make room for Chileno Bay Club. The reef makes it a great place for snorkeling (bring your own gear), but it is open to the ocean and all the inherent dangers that entails, so swimming is not recommended. Low tides reveal great tidal pools filled with anemone, starfish, and other sea creatures (please leave these creatures in the sea). Rock outcroppings create private areas and natural tabletops in the sand for beach picnics. The waters are also popular for kayaking and paddleboarding. **Amenities:** toilets; parking lot. **Best for:** snorkeling; kayaking ✉ *Hwy. 1, Km 12, Santa Maria Bay* ✛ *Turnoff sign after El Tule bridge.*

Playa Palmilla. Check out the impressive multimillion-dollar villas on the road to Playa Palmilla, the best swimming beach near San José. Turn off the highway as if you're going to the One&OnlyPalmilla and then cross over the highway on an overpass. Continue about half a mile. The entrance is from the side road through the ritzy Palmilla development; take a left before you reach the guardhouse of the One&Only hotel. There are signs, but they're not exactly large. The beach is protected by a rocky point and the water is almost always calm; Punta Palmilla, farther out, is popular with surfers during huge swells (20 feet or more). A few

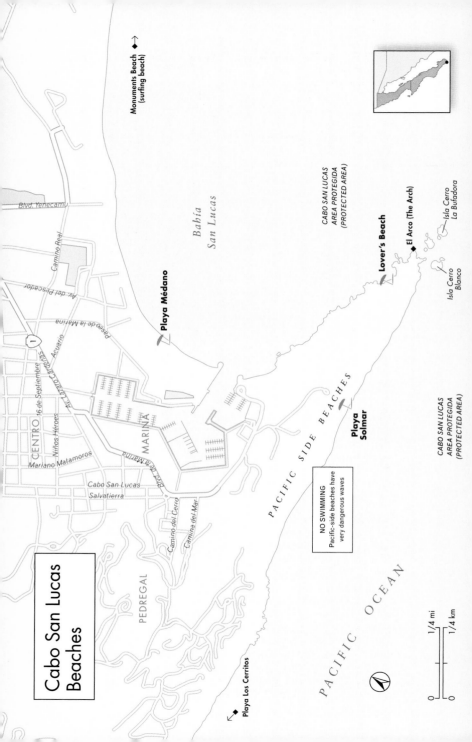

Cabo San Lucas Beaches

Monuments Beach ◆⟶
(surfing beach)

Blvd. Yenecamu

Bahía San Lucas

Camino Real

Av. del Pescador

Paseo de la Marina

Acuario

Playa Médano

*CABO SAN LUCAS
AREA PROTEGIDA
(PROTECTED AREA)*

Lover's Beach

El Arco (The Arch)

Isla Cerro
La Bufadora

Isla Cerro
Blanco

CENTRO

16 de Septiembre

Niños Héroes

Av. Lázaro Cárdenas

MARINA

Mariano Matamoros

Blvd. de la Marina

Cabo San Lucas

Salvatierra

Camino del Cerro

Camino del Mar

PEDREGAL

PACIFIC   SIDE   BEACHES

**Playa
Solmar**

*CABO SAN LUCAS
AREA PROTEGIDA
(PROTECTED AREA)*

NO SWIMMING
Pacific-side beaches have
very dangerous waves

PACIFIC   OCEAN

◆ Playa Los Cerritos

0   1/4 mi
0   1/4 km

thatched-roof palapas on the sand provide shade; there are trash cans but no restrooms. Guards patrol the exclusive section known as Pelican Beach fronting the hotel, discouraging nonguests from entering—although the public legally has access to cross the beach in front of the resort property. Guests of One&Only have access to beachfront cabañas, surf instruction, beach equipment, toilets, and a restaurant. **Amenities:** parking lot. **Best for:** fishing; walking; swimming. ⊠ *Entrance on Hwy. 1, at Km 27, 8 km (5 mi) southwest of San José del Cabo.*

CABO SAN LUCAS

Fodor'sChoice
★
Lover's Beach (*Playa del Amor*). These days, lovers have little chance of finding much romantic solitude here. The azure cove on the Sea of Cortez at the very tip of the Land's End Peninsula may well be the area's most frequently photographed patch of sand. It's a must-see on every first-timer's list. Water taxis, glass-bottom boats, kayaks, and Jet Skis all make the short trip out from Playa Médano to this small beach, which is backed by cliffs. Snorkeling around the base of these rocks is fun when the water is calm; you may spot striped sergeant majors and iridescent green and blue parrot fish. Seals hang out on the rocks a bit farther out, at the base of "El Arco," Cabo's famed arched landmark. Swimming and snorkeling are best on the Sea of Cortez side of Lover's Beach, where the clear, green, almost luminescent water is unquestionably the nicest in Cabo San Lucas. Walk through a gap in the rocks to access Divorce Beach on the Pacific side, which is too turbulent for swimming but ideal for sunbathing. Vendors are usually present, but it's always best to bring your own snacks and plenty of water. The beach is crowded at times, but most people would agree that it's worth seeing, especially if you're a first-timer. To get here, take a five-minute panga water-taxi ride ($10–$15) or the half-hour glass-bottom-boat tour. Opt for the latter if you wish to have some time to photograph the arch from the Pacific-side view. Both boats leave with relative frequency from the Cabo San Lucas marina or Playa Médano. **Amenities:** none. **Best for:** swimming; snorkeling; sunrise; sunset. ⊠ *Just outside Cabo San Lucas, at El Arco, Cabo San Lucas.*

FAMILY
Playa Médano. Foamy plumes of water shoot from wave runners and dozens of water taxis buzz through the calm waters off Médano, a 3-km (2-mile) span of grainy tan sand that's always crowded. When cruise ships are in town, it's mobbed. Bars and restaurants line the sand, waiters deliver ice buckets filled with beer to sunbathers in lounge chairs, and vendors offer everything from silver jewelry to hats, T-shirts, and henna tattoos. You can even get a pedicure. Swimming areas are roped off to prevent accidents, and the water is usually calm enough for small children. Be aware there are quick shoreline drop-offs, so life preservers are a good idea for the little paddlers in your group. Hotels line Médano, which is just north of downtown off Paseo del Pescador. Construction is constant on nearby streets, and parking is virtually impossible. The most popular spot on the beach is around the Mango Deck and The Office, where more than half a dozen bar-restaurants have set up beach chairs and tables. This is a hot spot for people-watching

EN ROUTE TO TODOS SANTOS

Playa Los Cerritos. This long, expansive beach on the Pacific Ocean, about 64 km (40 miles) north of Cabo San Lucas and on the way to the town of Todos Santos, is famous among surfers for its wonderful breaking waves in winter. Great for beginners, the waves here are consistent, accessible, and not overly powerful. Boards and lessons are available at the Costa Azul Surf Shop right on shore. This beach works best on northwest swells. Even if you don't ride the waves, you can watch them crash along the shore. The sandy beach is wide, flat, and ideal for wading and swimming close to shore. Swimming farther out is not recommended because of the strong currents. Most of the surfing crowd camps or stays in RVs near the beach, although there are no organized campsites or RV parks in the area. The developing area covers the basics with a few conveniences—including bustling Los Cerritos Club restaurant and two surf shops. Access to the beach is marked on Highway 19 (which connects Cabo San Lucas and Todos Santos) by a sign for Playa Los Cerritos at Km 64 (13 km [8 miles] south of Todos Santos). The graded dirt road to the beach is 2½ km (1½ miles) from Highway 19. **Amenities:** toilets; showers (for restaurant patrons); food concession; parking lot; camping; surfboards. **Best for:** surfing; swimming; snorkeling; walking. ⊠ *64 km (40 mi) north of Cabo San Lucas, 13 km (8 mi) south of Todos Santos.*

(and for singles). For something a bit more tranquil, grab a bite at Casa Dorada Resort's oceanfront restaurant Maydan, which is open to the public. Be prepared to deal with the many crafts vendors cruising the beach. They're generally not pushy, so a simple head shake and "*no, gracias*" will do. **Amenities:** food concession. **Best for:** partiers; snorkeling; swimming. ⊠ *Paseo del Pescador, Cabo San Lucas.*

Playa Solmar. Huge waves crash onto the sand on the Pacific side of Cabo San Lucas. This wide, beautiful beach stretches from Land's End north to the cliffs of El Pedregal, where mansions perch on steep cliffs. Swimming is impossible here because of the dangerous surf and undertow; stick to sunbathing and strolling. From December to March, you can spot gray whales spouting just offshore; dolphins leap above the waves year-round. The beach is at the end of Avenida Solmar off Boulevard Marina—an easy walk from downtown Cabo San Lucas. Five resorts—Solmar, Grand Solmar, Terrasol, Playa Grande, and Sandos Finisterra—are all on this beach, making it easy to stop for a meal if you get hungry. Crowds are minimal, as guests tend to stick to the hotel pools. **Amenities:** none. **Best for:** walking; solitude. ⊠ *Blvd. Marina to hotel entrances, Cabo San Lucas.*

SPORTS AND
THE OUTDOORS

Updated
by Marlise
Kast-Myers

Long stretches of coastline along the Sea of Cortez and the Pacific Ocean make Los Cabos a beautiful spot for a beach vacation. Be careful about where you take a dip, though—many of the beaches border sea waters that are too dangerous for swimming due to strong undercurrents. Nearly 350 warm and sunny days per year make Los Cabos a natural wonderland, where outdoor activities—both land- and water-based—can be enjoyed year-round.

Los Cabos has something for everyone in a relatively small area. Whether you want a people-packed beach or a secluded cove, high-speed Jet Ski rides or leisurely fishing trips, deep-sea scuba expeditions or casual snorkeling, the waters off Cabo and the surrounding area offer endless possibilities.

Waterskiing, Jet-Skiing, and sailing are found almost exclusively at Cabo San Lucas's Playa Médano, where you can also go kayaking. At least eight good scuba-diving sites are near Playa del Amor. The East Cape, which includes the town of Cabo Pulmo, is a great area for kayaking, fishing, diving, and snorkeling. In fact, Cabo Pulmo has the only coral reef in the Sea of Cortez and there are numerous spots to dive—even just snorkeling right off the beach is an experience. Both the Sea of Cortez and the Pacific provide great waves for year-round surfing whether you're a longboarder or a hotshot on a short board. Still, in the spot known as the "Marlin Capital of the World," sportfishing remains one of the most famous and popular water sports.

If you'd like to mix up your Los Cabos experience with some land-based adventures, the area's desert terrain lends itself to all sorts of possibilities, whether you're a thrill-seeker or a laid-back bird-watcher. You can explore cactus fields, sand dunes, waterfalls, and mountain forests on foot or horseback. Zip-lining is all the rage around Arroyo Azul. Back in town, you can play beach volleyball on Playa Médano, tennis at one of the hotels, or golf at one of the many courses available. If you are fortunate enough to be in Los Cabos during the whale migration (December through April)—when the weather is perfect—a whale-watching trip with one of the many tour-boat operators is a must.

SAN JOSÉ DEL CABO AND THE CORRIDOR

GOLF

3

Greens fees quoted include off- and high-season rates and are subject to frequent change.

Los Cabos has become one of the world's top golf destinations thanks to two factors: the 9-hole course opened by Mexico's tourism development agency Fontaur in San José in 1988, and the area's year-round mild to warm weather—Los Cabos never experiences even the occasional frigid winter possible in the southern United States. Green fairways dot the arid landscape like multiple oases in the desert. You'll encounter many sublime views of the Sea of Cortez, and on a few courses, play alongside it. Otherwise the motif is desert golf. Architects and designers like Jack Nicklaus, Robert Trent Jones II, Tom Weiskopf, Roy Dye, and Greg Norman have all applied their talents to courses in the area.

Cabo Real Golf Course. This visually attractive layout features spectacular views of the mountains and sea, as well as a challenging test. Designed by Robert Trent Jones Jr., Cabo Real has straight and narrow fairways, difficult slopes, and strategically placed bunkers. The first six holes are in mountainous terrain, working their way up to 500 feet above sea level. The course then heads back to the water and eventually descends down to the Sea of Cortez by the 14th hole. Recovering from mistakes here can be quite difficult. Greens fee includes cart (walking is not permitted), water, and towel. Balls are not included. ⊠ *Hwy. 1, Km 19.5, San José del Cabo* ☎ *624/173–9400, 877/795–8727* ⊕ *www.questrogolf.com* ⊟ *$245; $175 after 1:30 pm* ⛳ *18 holes, 6848 yards, par 71.*

Camp Campestre San José Golf Course. Here you are greeted by panoramic views stretching to the Sea of Cortez, canyons, and mountains on a Jack Nicklaus design. This public course also features dramatic elevation changes and undulating tricky multilevel putting surfaces. Attractive bunkering requires well-placed tee shots and very accurate iron play. They have used paspalum grass throughout the course that sets Camp Campestre among the best manicured in the region. The only downfall is that there are no holes on the water. ⊠ *Km 119, Libramiento Aeropuerto, San José del Cabo* ☎ *877/795–8727 in U.S., 624/173–9400* ⊕ *www.questrogolf.com* ⊟ *$135–$190* ⛳ *18 holes, 6966 yards, par 71.*

Fodor's Choice ★ **One&Only Palmilla Golf Course.** At the first course crafted by Jack Nicklaus, you will encounter 27 holes of some of the best resort golf that Mexico has to offer. The Mountain and Arroyo Nines came first, with the Ocean Nine finished later. Generous target-style fairways wind their way through rugged mountainous desert terrain that is beautifully landscaped. The Ocean Nine drops 600 feet in elevation as you visit the edge of the Sea of Cortez, while the Mountain and Arroyo

WIRIKUTA CACTUS GARDEN

Just 25 minutes outside of Cabo San Lucas in an ocean cove is this 12-acre labyrinth, lined with over 1,500 species of succulents and cacti from Africa, South America, and Mexico. "Wirikuta" in the Huichol language means a pilgrimage to the sacred peyote land, and the park honors Mexico's indigenous people. At night, a spectacular performance takes place. Helmed as a "journey into the birthplace of the Huichol world," the show is complete with vibrant costumes, fire, and acrobatics. Guests can choose from several experience packages, some including dinner and an open bar. Adjacent to the park is an impressive stone sculpture garden with art by some of the region's most famous living artists. Open daily. ⊕ *www.thewirikuta.com*

Nines are positioned higher and farther back from the water. Many will remark that the stretch of 6 to 8 holes on the Arroyo Course is one of the best anywhere, while the 3rd through 5th holes really get your attention on the Mountain Course. No matter the combination of Nines, you won't feel cheated; the conditioning is excellent though expensive. Five sets of tees on every hole accommodate various skill levels. ⊠ *Hwy. 1, Km 7.5, San José del Cabo* ☎ 624/144–5250 ⊕ *www.palmillagc.com* ⬛ *$145–$170* 🏌 *27 holes. Mountain Nine, 3602 yards; Ocean Nine, 3527 yards; Arroyo Nine, 3337 yards. All nines are par 36.*

Puerto Los Cabos Golf Course. This course, one of the area's most popular for visitors, features an unusual combination: one Nine was designed by Jack Nicklaus and the other by Greg Norman. Eventually each will build a second line to make this into two separate courses. Nicklaus's Nine features more expansive driving areas, whereas the Norman Nine puts more of a premium on driving accuracy. Both feature attractive bunkering and paspalum putting surfaces. ⊠ *Paseo de los Pescadores, San José del Cabo* ☎ 624/173–9400, 877/795–8727 ⊕ *www.questrogolf.com* ⬛ *$195–$270* 🏌 *18 holes, 7461 yards, par 73.*

GUIDED ADVENTURE TOURS

FAMILY

Fodor'sChoice

★

Baja Outback. Baja Outback offers a variety of guided tours that range from four hours to several days long. The routes run through Baja backcountry, where you have the opportunity to explore the Cape's rarely seen back roads while learning desert lore from a knowledgeable guide-cum-biologist. Day trips may include anything from hiking and snorkeling to city tours and turtle release programs (August to November). Baja Outback also offers multiday tour packages designed specially for kids, with boogie boarding and sand castle building. For adventure-driven vacationers, tours include kayaking and stand-up paddleboarding near El Arco. ⊠ *San José del Cabo* ☎ 624/142–9215 ⊕ *www.bajaoutback.com* ⬛ *From $95.*

Baja Wild. Baja Wild has a number of adventure packages including the "Six Day Inn-to-Inn Hiking, Biking, Kayaking, Snorkeling, Surfing, and Whale-Watching Adventure." You'll see the natural side of Cabo, with hikes to canyons, hot springs, fossil beds, and caves with rock paintings. They offer backcountry jeep tours, full-day kayak tours at Cabo Pulmo, and ATV tours in the desert. Private tours are available. ⊠ *Plaza Costa Azul, Hwy. 1, Km 28, San José del Cabo* 🕾 *624/122–0107* ⊕ *www.bajawild.com* ⊠ *Backcountry jeep tours from $500 per vehicle; full-day kayak tours at Cabo Pulmo, $150; half-day ATV tours, $100. Private tours are available for double price.*

FAMILY **Wild Canyon Adventures.** It's all in the name at this outdoor adventure company that offers zip-lining, camel rides, bungee jumping, ATV tours, a giant swing, and a glass-bottom gondola—all of which enter vast El Tule Canyon. ATV tours (and brave hikers) can cross Los Cabos Canyon Bridge, the longest wooden pedestrian bridge in the world, measuring 1,082 feet long. Free transportation is offered from your hotel, but be sure to time your activities properly since the shuttle only runs every 3½ hours. ⊠ *El Tule Bridge, The Corridor* 🕾 *624/144–4433* ⊕ *www.wildcanyon.com.mx* ⊠ *Tours from $110; park entrance $15.*

HORSEBACK RIDING

Cantering down an isolated beach or up a desert trail is one of the great pleasures of Los Cabos (as long as the sun isn't beating down too heavily). The following company has well-fed and well-trained horses. One-hour trips generally cost about $50 per person; two-hour trips about $80.

Bonanza Horseback Riding. One of the best ways to explore the San José estuary, marina, and beach is by horseback. One- or two-hour tours take place daily at 9 am and 5 pm. ⊠ *Blvd. Antonio Mijares, Zona Hotelera* ✛ *Across from Holiday Inn Resort* 🕾 *624/142–2922* ⊠ *From $40.*

FAMILY **Cuadra San Francisco Equestrian Center.** The Cuadra San Francisco Equestrian Center offers trail rides and lessons on 50 beautiful and extremely well-trained horses. Trail rides go into the hills overlooking the Cabo Real property or to the San Carlos arroyo; both focus on the flora as much as the riding. Trips are limited to 20 people, with one guide for every six or seven participants. Cuadra also specializes in private trail rides. Note that you must query them for rates, but expect to pay close to $70 per hour. ⊠ *Hwy. 1, Km 19.5, across from Casa del Mar and Las Ventanas al Paraíso hotels, San José del Cabo* 🕾 *624/144–0160* ⊕ *www.loscaboshorses.com.*

Rancho Collins Horses. Horses are available for rent near the Playa Médano hotels, in the arroyo just east of Club Cascadas, near Villa del Arco, for about $30 per person for a one-hour ride. 🕾 *624/113–3075.*

SPORTFISHING CONSERVATION

For decades, anglers wanted their trophies, a photo of themselves with their fish, and a sign showing the weight of the vanquished. Then came the realization that the fish didn't need to be killed, and the conservation movement began encouraging a "catch-and-release" program, returning to the water whatever wasn't to be eaten. In recent years, the world's sportfishing factions have been battling Mexico's powerful commercial union because the Mexican government enacted a law that would enable Mexico's many commercial longliners, as well as gillnet and seiner boats, to fish very close to Mexico's coast, practices that would quickly decimate the fragile fish stocks off Mexico's west coast and into the Sea of Cortez. For more information, go to ⊕ www.seawatch.org. The Billfish Foundation is leading the fight against the newest Mexican shark regulation, which would allow boats within 24 km (15 miles) of the Sea of Cortez and 32 km (20 miles) of Baja's west coast, and does not restrict by catch. It supports a bill in Mexico's congress at this writing that would roll the no-commercial-fishing zones back to 80 km (50 miles) offshore, and to 161 km (100 miles) off the coast of Los Cabos. A 2009 study conducted by the foundation concluded that sportfishing provides, directly or indirectly, 24,000 jobs and an annual $630 million to Los Cabos' economy. More info can be found at ⊕ www.billfish.org.

KAYAKING

One of the most popular, practical, and eco-friendly ways to explore the pristine coves that dot Los Cabos' western shoreline is by kayak. Daylong package tours that combine kayaking with snorkeling cost anywhere from $70 to $150. Single or double kayaks can be rented by the hour for $20 to $25.

Baja Wild. For a combined kayak and snorkeling trip, try Baja Wild. Daylong outdoor trips include surfing; hiking; ATV; and whale-watching trips (November through April), as well as baby sea turtle release excursions (September through November). All trips include transportation, equipment, and lunch; you can substitute scuba diving for snorkeling. ⊠ *Plaza Costa Azul, Hwy. 1, Km 28, s/n Local 5, San José del Cabo* ☎ *624/122–0107* ⊕ *www.bajawild.com* ⌂ *$150.*

SCUBA DIVING

Expert divers head to the **Gordo Banks** (100–130 feet, also known as the Wahoo Banks), which are 13 km (8 miles) off the coast of San José. The currents here are too strong for less experienced divers. This is the spot for hammerhead sharks—which are not generally aggressive with divers—plus many species of tropical fish and rays, and, if you're lucky, dolphins. Fall is the best time to go.

The Corridor has several popular diving sites. **Bahía Santa Maria** (20–60 feet) has water clear enough to see hard and soft corals, octopuses, eels, and many tropical fish. **Chileno Reef** (10–80 feet) is a protected

finger reef 1 km (½ mile) from Chileno Bay, with many invertebrates, including starfish, flower urchins, and hydroids. The **Blowhole** (60–100 feet) is known for diverse terrain—massive boulders, rugged tunnels, shallow caverns, and deep rock cuts—which house manta rays, sea turtles, and large schools of amberjacks and grouper.

SPORTFISHING

The waters off Los Cabos are home to more than 800 species of fish—a good number of which bite all year-round. It's easy to arrange charters online, through hotels, and directly with sportfishing companies along the docks at Marina Cabo San Lucas. Indeed, to select a company yourself, consider hanging out at the marina between 1 pm and 4 pm when the boats come in, and asking the passengers about their experiences. Rather than book through an independent agent roaming the marina, it's best to reserve through a reputable company in an actual office. ■TIP➜ **Do not give a deposit to any agent walking along the marina since there is no guarantee someone will be there the next day to follow through.** Cheaper boats often have engine trouble at sea, resulting in passengers switching to a lower-category vessel without financial compensation. Yes, you might get an incredible deal from an independent agent, but you get what you pay for.

Prices range from $250 or $350 a day for a *panga* (small skiff) to $600 to $2,700 a day for a larger cruiser with a bathroom, a sunbathing deck, air-conditioning, and possibly a few other amenities. The sky's the limit with the larger private yachts (think 80 feet); it's not unheard of for such vessels to cost $6,000 or $10,000 a day. No matter what you pay, rates should include a captain and crew, tackle, bait, drinks, and sometimes lunch. If you plan to spend a full day at sea, it's best to purchase an all-inclusive package rather than a bare-bones trip lacking in services. Factor in the cost of a fishing license (about $18), required for all passengers over 18 years of age regardless if he or she is fishing. Fishing licenses can be purchased for about half the price through the CONAPESCA website (⊕ *www.conapescasandiego.org*). Most hotels in San José will arrange fishing trips. All of the Corridor hotels work with fishing fleets anchored at the Cabo San Lucas marina and a few with boats in Puerto Los Cabos, so any one of them can help you set up your fishing trips. Note that some hotels send customers to the company with the highest commission, so double-check recommendations and do your research. The major drawback of arranging a fishing trip from one of the Corridor hotels is the travel time involved in getting down to the water. It takes up to half an hour or more to reach the docks from Corridor hotels, and most boats depart at 6:30 am.

Gordo Banks Pangas. The *pangas* (small fishing boats) of Gordo Banks Pangas are near some of the hottest fishing spots in the Sea of Cortez: the Outer and Inner Gordo banks. The pangas accommodate up to three. Their cruisers accommodate up to five. ⊠ *La Playa near San José del Cabo, San José del Cabo* ☎ *624/142–1147, 619/488–1859 in U.S.* ⊕ *www.gordobanks.com* 🖃 *Pangas from $250; cruisers from $380 per day.*

SURFING

You can rent a board right at the beach at Costa Azul in San José del Cabo, or at the Cabo Surf Hotel, and paddle right into the gentle, feathering waves at the Old Man's surf spot. If you're at the intermediate level or above, walk a short distance eastward to La Roca (The Rock) break. Big waves are best left to the experts up north, in Todos Santos.

Fodor's Choice ★ **Costa Azul Surf Shop.** For epic surfing tips, rentals, and lessons, head to Costa Azul Surf Shop. They have the best quiver in Los Cabos with more than 150 hand-shaped boards from their popular Olea line. They also offer paddleboards, boogie boards, and snorkel gear. Private, two-hour lessons include transportation, the surfboard rental, a rash guard, and bottled water. All instructors are CPR certified and have 25 years of surfing experience. ⊠ *Hwy. 1, Km 28, San José del Cabo* ☎ *624/142–2771, 624/142–4454* ⊕ *www.costa-azul.com. mx* ⌦ *Rentals, $25 per day, $20 per day for 4 days or more; private lessons $150.*

Mike Doyle Surf School. The Mike Doyle Surf School is the top "surfer-friendly" location in all of Los Cabos. If you stay at the Cabo Surf Hotel where Mike Doyle is located, you can check the surf conditions from the restaurant, bar, pool, or even from your balcony. The school has more than 100 rental boards, from foam boards and short boards to longboards and stand-up paddleboards. There are five surf instructors available at the shop for lessons. ⊠ *Cabo Surf Hotel, on the beach at the bottom of the steps, just below the 7 Seas restaurant, San José del Cabo* ☎ *624/172–6188, 858/964–5117 in U.S.* ⊕ *mikedoylesurf-school.com* ⌦ *From $30 for 2-hr rentals; $79 group rate lessons; $109 for private instruction.*

WALKING TOURS

Land's End Tours. One of the best ways to experience Los Cabos in a single day is through Land's End photo city tour. The outing covers the top attractions of Cabos San Lucas, the Corridor, and San José del Cabo; photographs of your adventure are captured throughout the tour and sent to you within one week by email. Tour highlights include San José's historical center, a boat trip to the arch, a visit to a glass-blowing factory, tequila tasting, shopping, and snorkeling. The six-hour tour begins at 8:15, and the price includes entrance fees, a tour guide, lunch, transportation, and photographs. Tours are offered every day except Wednesday and Sunday. Land's End hosts city tours of Todos Santos on Wednesday and Saturday. ⊠ *San José del Cabo* ☎ *624/123–4962* ⊕ *www.landsendtours.com* ⌦ *$72 without lunch; $87 with lunch.*

Continued on page 63

SPORTFISHING

By Larry Dunmire

Cabo San Lucas is called both the Marlin Mecca and Marlin Capital of the World for good reason. Thanks to the warm waters of the Sea of Cortez, the tip of the Baja Peninsula has one of the world's largest concentrations of billfish. And, no matter what time of year you visit, there's a great chance—some locals say a 90% one—you'll make a catch, too.

More than 800 species of fish swim off Los Cabos, but anglers pursue only about half a dozen types. The most sought-after are the huge blue or black marlin, which have been known to fight for hours. The largest of these fish—the so-called granders—weigh in at 1,000 pounds or more. The more numerous, though smaller (up to 200 pounds), striped marlin are also popular catches.

Those interested in putting the catch-of-the-day on their table aim for the iridescent green and yellow dorado (also called mahi-mahi), tuna, yellowtail, and wahoo (also known as ono)—the latter a relative of the barracuda that can speed along at up to 50 mph. Also gaining popularity is light-tackle fly-fishing for roosterfish, jack crevalle, and pargo from small boats near the shore.

Something's always biting, but the greatest diversity of species inhabit Cabo's waters from June through November, when sea temperatures climb into the high 80s.

(above) A billfish catch in progress

WHAT TO EXPECT

You don't need to be experienced or physically strong to sportfish. Your boat's captain and crew will happily help you along, guiding you on how to properly handle the equipment.

Some of the larger boats have the so-called fighting chairs, which resemble a dentist's chair, firmly mounted to the deck. These rotate smoothly allowing you to follow the movement of a hooked fish and giving you the support you need to fight with a large black or blue marlin for an extended period of time.

Experienced fishermen sometimes forego chairs for the stand-up technique using a padded harness/fighting belt that has a heavy-duty plastic-and-metal rod holder connected to it. Though physically demanding—especially on the arms and lower back—this technique often speeds up the fight and is impressive to watch.

FISHING TWO WAYS

Most of Cabo's boats are equipped for the more traditional heavy-duty sportfishing using large, often cumbersome rods and reels and beautiful, colorful plastic lures with hooks. A modified form of fly-fishing is gaining popularity. This requires a finessed fly-casting technique and spot-on timing between crew and the fisherman. It utilizes ultra-lightweight rods and reels, relatively miniscule line, and a technique known as bait and switch.

You attract fish as near to the back of a boat as possible with hook-less lures. As the crew pulls in the lures, you cast your fly (with hooks) to the marlin. Fights with the lighter equipment—and with circle hooks rather than regular ones—are usually less harmful, enabling more fish to be released.

(top) Sportfishing in Los Cabos—one man's catch

CONSERVATION IN CABO

You're strongly encouraged to use the less-harmful circle hooks (shaped like an "O"), as opposed to J-hooks, which do terrible internal damage. It's now common to release all billfish, as well as any dorado, wahoo, or tuna that you don't plan to eat. Folks here frown on trophy fishing unless it takes place during an official tournament. Instead, quickly take your photos with the fish, then release it.

The Cabo Sportfishing Association has a fleet-wide agreement that no more than one marlin per boat be taken per day. Usually all are released, denoted by the "T" flags flown from a boat's bridge as it enters the marina.

The few marlin that are brought in are hoisted and weighed, photographed, and then put to good use—taken to be smoked or given to needy locals. You can ask the crew to fillet the tastier species right on your boat, and you can usually arrange for the fish to be smoked or vacuum-packed and frozen to take home. Many restaurants, especially those found marina-side in Cabo San Lucas, will gladly prepare your catch any way you like. You hook it, they cook it.

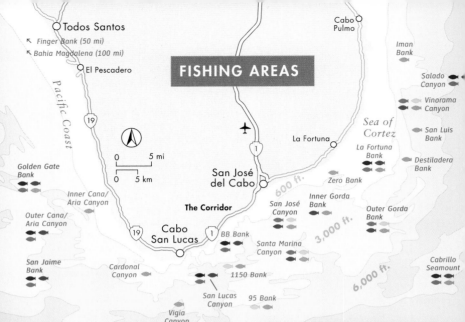

FISHING AREAS

Todos Santos
Finger Bank (50 mi)
Bahia Magdalena (100 mi)
El Pescadero

Cabo Pulmo

Iman Bank

Salado Canyon

Vinorama Canyon

Pacific Coast

19

Sea of Cortez

La Fortuna

San Luis Bank

La Fortuna Bank

0   5 mi
0   5 km

Golden Gate Bank

San José del Cabo

Zero Bank

Destiladera Bank

Inner Cana/ Aria Canyon

The Corridor

San José Canyon

Inner Gorda Bank

Outer Gorda Bank

Outer Cana/ Aria Canyon

Cabo San Lucas

19   1

BB Bank

Santa Marina Canyon

Cabrillo Seamount

San Jaime Bank

Cardonal Canyon

1150 Bank

San Lucas Canyon

95 Bank

Vigia Canyon

600 ft.
3,000 ft.
6,000 ft.

	FISH	AVAILABILITY
	Billfish*	Year around
	Yellowfin Tuna	Year around
	Dorado	July–December
	Wahoo	Year around
	Yellowtail	January–May
	Reef fish**	March–December

*Billfish include marlin, sailfish, and swordfish.

**Reef fish include roosterfish, cabrilla, sierra, pargo, and dog snapper.

For more information on fishing locations, check out BajaDirections.com.

Although there are many great fishing areas amid the underwater canyons and seamounts off the Baja coast, there are four major spots within 40 to 50 km (25 to 30 miles) of Cabo. From north to south these banks are the Golden Gate, San Jaime, the Gordo Banks (outer and inner), and the San José Canyon. All are within an hour or so of the Marina Cabo San Lucas, if you've chartered one of the faster boats. Farther north, about 80 km (50 miles) on the Pacific side above Todos Santos, is the Finger Bank. Also on the Pacific side, more 160 km (100

miles) north of Cabo, is Bahia Magdalena (Mag Bay), where the waters teem with marlin and game fish, and experienced anglers have been known to catch and release as many as 67 billfish in one day.

CABO SAN LUCAS

BOATING

The themes of Los Cabos boat tours vary, but all tours follow essentially the same route: through Bahía Cabo San Lucas, past El Arco and the sea-lion colony, around Land's End into the Pacific Ocean, and then eastward through the Sea of Cortez along the Corridor. Costs run about $80 per person; all tours include an open bar and some offer lunch and snorkel tours. Many of these operators offer whale-watching trips as well.

Cabo Adventures. Cabo Adventures has a luxury day sailing trip and a sunset sailing trip on deluxe Beneteau sailboats, during which the crew will teach you some basic sailing maneuvers, or you can simply sit back and enjoy the scenery—the boats pass Lover's Beach and El Arco. The four-hour trip includes food, drinks, snorkel gear, and stand-up paddleboards. ⊠ *Blvd. Paseo de la Marina, Lot 7, Marina San Lucas* ☎ *624/173–9500, 866/393–5255* ⊕ *www.cabo-adventures. com* ⊑ *$109.*

Oceanus. The double-decker party boat *Oceanus* has snorkel cruises from 10:30 am to 2 pm and a sunset cruise with a live band that leaves at 5 pm (6 pm in summer) from the main dock in Cabo San Lucas. You can rent the *Oceanus* for birthdays, weddings, and other special occasions. Deep discounts can be found when booking online. ⊠ *Blvd. Marina, Marina San Lucas* ☎ *624/143–1059, 624/143–3929* ⊕ *www. oceanusloscabos.com.mx* ⊑ *From $65.*

Pisces Luxury Yachts. Pisces Luxury Yachts has charters starting at $1,880 for 2½-hour sunset excursions on their smallest 48-foot yacht, *Listo,* which holds up to eight passengers . The full-day, all-inclusive rate runs about $3,300 and climbs to $220,000 for six nights on their 163-foot mega yacht. Photos and descriptions of the 10 yachts in their luxury fleet are available on their website. ⊠ *Barcos Piscis, S.A. de C.V., Cabo Maritime Center Marina 8-6, Marina San Lucas* ☎ *624/143–1288* ⊕ *www.piscesyachts.com.*

FOUR-WHEELING

Riding an ATV across the desert is a thrill, but it is one of the more dangerous things you can do in this area. As fun as these tours may be, it is worth thinking about the destruction these vehicles cause to the fragile desert terrain. Additionally, many of the companies do not have insurance, and will make you sign explicit release-of-liability forms before going. They do issue helmets, goggles, and handkerchiefs to protect you from the sand and dust.

When ATV trips are properly conducted, they can be safe and fun. The most popular trip passes first through Cabo San Lucas, continues through desert cactus fields, and arrives at a big play area of large sand dunes with open expanses and specially carved trails, at the foot of **El Faro Viejo**, the old lighthouse. You can reach frighteningly high speeds as you descend the tall dunes. Navigating the narrow trails in the cactus fields is exciting but not for the fainthearted or steering-impaired. Another favorite trek travels past interesting rock formations, little creeks, and the beach on the way to a small mountain village called **La Candelaria.**

A three-hour trip costs about $120 for a single or $140 for a double (two people sharing an ATV) and includes boxed lunches and drinks. Trips to La Candelaria include lunch and cost about $120 for a single and $150 for a double. Wear tennis shoes, clothes you don't mind getting dirty, and a long-sleeve shirt or sweatshirt for afternoon tours in winter.

GOLF

Greens fee prices quoted include off- and high-season rates and are subject to frequent change.

Cabo del Sol Desert Course. The sister to the Ocean Course, the Desert Course designed by Tom Weiskopf sits on the other side of the Corridor away from the water and features an inland desert motif complete with artistic bunkering. Don't be fooled; the layout here is still very good. The Desert Course is very playable, yet from the back tees it may be even harder than the Ocean Course. The attractive layout includes one of the area's longest par-5 holes at 625 yards. Taylormade rental clubs are available for $75. Special rates are available if you play both this and the Cabo del Sol Ocean Course. ⊠ *Hwy. 1, Km 10.3, Cabo San Lucas* ☎ *624/145–8200, 877/703–4394* ⊕ *www.cabodelsol.com* ⌂ *$180–$235* ⚑ *18 holes, 7049 yards, par 72.*

Fodor's Choice ★ **Cabo del Sol Ocean Course.** The Ocean Course has been named one of the top courses in the world by numerous publications as it combines the best of ocean and desert golf. Designer Jack Nicklaus brags that it has the best three finishing holes in the world. On the par-3 17th hole, you drive over an ocean inlet with waves crashing below. The par-4 18th hole is a mirror image of the 18th at Pebble Beach, California. Seven holes are seaside, with the 5th and 17th named as one of the "Top 500 Holes in the World" by *Golf World.* Taylormade clubs are available to rent for $75. The Ocean Course is easily the priciest public-access course in the region, but is generally considered to be the best. ⊠ *Hwy 1, Km 10.3, Cabo San Lucas* ☎ *624/145–8200* ⊕ *www.cabodelsol.com* ⌂ *$175–$375* ⚑ *18 holes, 7091 yards, par 72.*

GUIDED TOURS

Cabo Adventures. With a wide variety of unusual activities Cabo Adventures is a unique adventure operator. Along with its popular Cabo Dolphins program are the four-hour Desert Safaris, which take you into the Sierra Mountains by Swiss-made Unimog to commune with camels, of all things! They also offer zip-lining, mountain biking, whale shark tours, and flyboards (like water jetpacks). ⊠ *Blvd. Paseo de la Marina, Marina San Lucas* ☎ *624/173–9500, 888/526–2238* ⊕ *www.cabo-adventures.com* ⌂ *From $85 per person.*

Horseback riding along stretches of desolate Los Cabos beaches is a treat not to be missed.

KAYAKING

In Cabo San Lucas, Playa Médano is the best beach for kayaking. A number of companies located along El Médano near the Baja Cantina Beachside, at the bottom of Cabo Villas, offer kayak rentals, and there are guided tours that go out to Lover's Beach to view El Arco, and around the Land's End Rocks. Rates are generally uniform from one operator to the other.

Tio Sports. Tio Sports was one of the original water-sports companies on El Médano Beach more than 30 years ago, and is still a major operator with a sports palapa located on the beach at the ME Cabo Resort, plus stands and offices throughout Los Cabos. It provides aquatic tours, kayak rentals, stand-up paddleboards, and packages that include scuba and snorkeling. ⊠ *Playa Médano, Marina San Lucas* ☏ *624/143–3399* ⊕ *www.tiosports.com* ✉ *From $25.*

SCUBA DIVING

Generally, diving costs about $70 for one tank and $95 for two, including transportation. Equipment rental, dives in the Corridor, and night dives typically cost extra. Full-day trips to Gordo Banks and Cabo Pulmo cost about $220, including transportation, food, equipment, and two tanks. Most operators offer two- to four-day package deals.

Most dive shops have courses for noncertified divers; some may be offered through your hotel. Newly certified divers may go on local dives no more than 30 to 40 feet deep. Divers must show their C-card (diver certification card) before going on dives with reputable shops. Many operators offer widely recognized Professional Association of Diving Instructors (PADI) certification courses, which usually take place in training pools for the first couple of lessons.

At sites in **Bahía San Lucas** near El Arco, you're likely to see colorful tropical fish traveling confidently in large schools. Yellow angelfish, green and blue parrot fish, red snappers, perfectly camouflaged stonefish, and long slender needlefish share these waters. Divers regularly see stingrays, manta rays, and moray eels. The only problem with this location is the amount of boat traffic. The sound of motors penetrates deep into the water and can slightly mar the experience. **Neptune's Fingers** (60–120 feet) is a long rock formation with abundant fish. About 150 feet off Playa del Amor, **Pelican Rock** (25–100 feet) is a calm protected spot where you can look down on Sand Falls (underwater cascades that drop into a 1,200 foot canyon) discovered by none other than Jacques Cousteau. **The Point** (15–80 feet) is a good spot for beginners who aren't ready to get too deep. The Shipwreck (40–60 feet), an old Japanese fishing boat, is close to Cabo San Lucas, near The Cape Hotel.

> **MATANCITAS MAN**
>
> The remains of pre-Hispanic Indians, found in the giant sand dune region near the current Cabo San Lucas Lighthouse, were given the name of Matancitas Man by archaeologists. These people were precursors to the Pericú Indians that lived in the Cape when explorer Hernán Cortés arrived in 1535.

OPERATORS

Fodor's Choice
★

Amigos del Mar. The oldest and most complete dive shop in Los Cabos area is Amigos del Mar. Its dive boats range from a 25-foot runabout to a 31-foot custom dive boat. The staff is courteous and knowledgeable, and all the guides speak English. ⊠ *Blvd. Marina, Plaza Galicota, across from Finisterra Hotel, Marina San Lucas* ☎ *624/143–0505, 513/898–0547 in U.S.* ⊕ *www.amigosdelmar.com* ⊒ *2-tank dives from $90; equipment rental $35.*

Manta Scuba. This centrally located PADI 5-star outfit makes trips locally in the Corridor, as well as to Cabo Pulmo, Gordo Banks, and East Cape. ⊠ *Plaza Gali, Blvd. Marina 7D Local 37 Int., Marina San Lucas* ☎ *877/287–1120, 624/144–3871* ⊕ *www.caboscuba.com* ⊒ *2-tank dives from $95; equipment rental $35.*

Solmar V. Find luxury on the über-comfortable live-aboard dive boat *Solmar V*, which takes nine-day remote diving trips to Socorro islands (November–June) for giant mantas, humpback whales, dolphins, tuna, and shark. They also have trips to Guadalupe (August–October) for great-white-shark cage diving. Air is surface supplied so you don't need to be a certified diver to enjoy the Guadalupe trip. There are also five-day trips out of Ensenada, northern Baja. Twelve cabins with private baths serve a maximum of 20 passengers. This is one of Cabo's top diving experiences, so book well in advance. ⊠ *Cabo San Lucas* ☎ *866/591–4906 toll-free in U.S., 310/455–3600* ⊕ *www.solmarv.com* ⊒ *$3,095–$4,299.*

Mutual curiosity between a scuba diver and a gentle whale shark (*Rhincodon typus*)

SPORTFISHING

Most vendors are stationed at the Marina Cabo San Lucas. Ships depart from sportfishing docks at the south end of the marina, near the Puerto Paraíso Mall, or from the docks at the Wyndham Hotel. It's very important to get specific directions and departure times, since it's hard to find your spot at 6:30 in the morning.

Gaviotas Sportfishing Fleet. The Gaviotas Sportfishing Fleet has charter cruisers and super- *pangas* from 26 feet to 43 feet. ⊠ *Docked between Gates 2 and 3 across from the Marina Fiesta Hotel, office at Villa Serena RV Park, Marina San Lucas* ☎ 624/132–7637 ⊕ *www.gaviotassport-fishingfleet.com* ✆ *From $755.*

Minerva's Baja Tackle. Renowned tackle store Minerva's Baja Tackle and Sportfishing Charters has been around for more than 40 years and has its own fleet with four sportfishing charter boats from 31 feet to 33 feet. ⊠ *Madero between Blvd. Marina and Guerrero, Marina San Lucas* ☎ 624/143–1282 ⊕ *www.minervas.com* ✆ *From $764, all-inclusive.*

Fodor's Choice ★ **Picante Fleet.** One of the top sportfishing fleets, Picante Fleet offers a wide selection of 20 well-equipped, top-of-the-line, 31-foot to 68-foot Cabo sport fishers. If you prefer smaller boats, there's the Picantito fleet, with a trio of 24-foot Shamrock walk-around boats. These are primarily used for fishing close to shore. Picante offers trips and boats that vary in size and price. ⊠ *Puerto Paraíso Mall Local 39-A, near Harley-Davidson Store, Cabo San Lucas* ☎ 624/143–2474, 714/442–0644 in U.S. ⊕ *www.picantesportfishing.com* ✆ *From $325; up to $3,850 for 8 hrs.*

Fodor'sChoice   **Pisces Sportfishing Fleet.** Some of Cabo's top hotels use the extensive
★   range of yachts from Pisces Sportfishing Fleet. The fleet includes the
usual 31-foot Bertrams, but also has a sizable fleet of 50- to 70-foot
Viking, Mikelson, Hatteras, and Ocean Alexander yachts with tuna
towers, air-conditioning, and multiple staterooms. Pisces also has luxury yachts up to 120 feet in length. Chartering a 31-foot Bertram is
all-inclusive for up to six people, and trips last for around eight hours.
✉ *Blvd. Marina, Marina San Lucas* ☎ *624/143–1288, 877/286–7938
toll-free in U.S.* ⊕ *www.piscessportfishing.com* ✉ *From $445; Ber-
tram charter $695, all-inclusive.*

WHALE-WATCHING

The gray whale migration doesn't end at Baja's Pacific lagoons. Plenty
of whales of all sizes make it down to the warmer waters off Los
Cabos and into the Mar de Cortés. To watch whales from the shore,
go to the beach at the Solmar Suites, The Grand Solmar, Sandos Finisterra, or any Corridor hotel, or the lookout points along the Corridor highway. *Virtually all of the companies listed in "Boating" offer
whale-watching tours (about $80–$100 depending on size of boat and
length of tour) from Cabo San Lucas.*

EAST CAPE

If you have your own transportation, it is well worth driving out to
Cabo Pulmo, about 65 km (40 miles) northwest of San José del Cabo.
Here you can rent snorkel gear and a kayak or arrange a dive or fishing
trip with one of the operators in this tiny, super- *tranquilo* village. In
these incredible waters, you'll be able to check out everything from
the smallest sea horse to a giant black sea bass.

Getting Here: To reach Cabo Pulmo from the airport in San José (SJD),
follow Highway 1 north to La Paz, past Caduano, Mira Flores, and
Santiago turnoffs. Upon reaching the village of Las Cuevas, turn right
toward La Ribera/Cabo Pulmo (if you cross the bridge, you've gone
too far). Follow the road and turn right just prior to entering La
Ribera. Continue along the Cabo Pulmo road south until the pavement ends, and drive another 10 km (6 miles) on the dirt road to the
village of Cabo Pulmo. You know you've arrived once you reach the
Cabo Pulmo Dive Center housed in a two-story blue building.

SCUBA DIVING

Fodor'sChoice   **Parque Nacional Marino Cabo Pulmo.** This 25,000-year-old coral reef has
★   been legally protected since 1995 and is home to more than 2,000 different kinds of marine organisms—including more than 230 species of
tropical fish and a dozen kinds of petrified coral. The area is renowned
among diving aficionados, whose favorite months to visit are June and
July, when visibility is highest. The park isn't difficult to access. Head
southwest from La Ribera and it's just 8 km (5 miles) from the end
of the paved road; it's bordered by Playa Las Barracas in the north

Continued on page 72

A WHALE'S TALE
by Kelly Lack and Larry Dunmire

Seeing the gray whales off Baja's western coast needs to be on your list of things to do before you die. "But I've *gone* whale watching," you say. Chances are, though, that you were in a big boat and might have spotted the flip of a tail 100 yards out. In Baja your vessel will be a tiny panga, smaller than the whales themselves; they'll swim up, mamas with their babies, coming so close that you can smell the fishiness of their spouts.

QUICK FACTS

Scientific name:
Eshrichtius robustus

Length: Up to 50 feet

Weight: Up to 90,000 pounds (45 tons)

Coloring: Gray and white, usually splotched with lighter growths and barnacles

Life span: 50 years

Reproduction: One calf every 2 years; calves are generally 15 feet long at birth, weighing up to 1,500 pounds (¾ ton)

Current population: More than 22,000 gray whales are alive today

Grey Whales Guerrero Negro

WHEN TO GO

Gray whales and tourists both head south to Baja around December—the whales in pods, the snowbirds in RV caravans—staying put through to April to shake off the chill of winter. So the beaches, hotels, restaurants, and bars during whale-watching season will be bustling. Book your room two to three months ahead to ensure a place to stay. The intense experience that awaits you at Magdalena Bay, San Ignacio, or Scammion's Lagoon is worth traveling in high season.

THE GRAY WHALE:
Migrating Leviathan

Yearly, gray whales endure the longest migration of any mammal on earth—some travel 5,000 miles one way between their feeding grounds in Alaska's frigid Bering Sea and their mating/birthing lagoons in sunny Baja California. The whales are bottom-feeders, unique among cetaceans, and stir up sediment on the sea floor, then use their baleen—long, stiff plates covered with hair-like fibers inside their mouths—to filter out the sediment and trap small marine creatures such as crustaceanlike Gammarid amphipods.

DID YOU KNOW?

Gray whales' easygoing demeanor and predilection for near-shore regions makes for frequent, friendly human/whale interactions. Whalers, however, would disagree. They dubbed mother grays "devilfish" for the fierce manner in which they protect their young.

Though the average life span of a gray whale is 50 years, one individual was reported to reach 77 years of age—a real old-timer.

WHALE ADVENTURES

Cabo Expeditions (*www.caboexpeditions. com.mx*) was the first with whale watching tours more than 15 years ago. The staff is well-trained, and director Oscar Ortiz believes not only in seeing the whales, but also saving them. Last year his Zodiacs rescued two grays from entanglement in giant fishing nets. Boats depart from the Cabo San Lucas Marina, near Dock M.

You've seen whales, but how about swimming with them? **Baja AirVentures** (*www. bajaairventures.com*) arranges weeklong trips to Bahia de los Angeles where you can swim with whale sharks from mid-August to mid-November.

You can fly from San Diego to the secluded Sea of Cortez fishing village, then take pangas out to Las Animas Wilderness Lodge, where you stay in spacious, comfortable yurts.

WHALE NURSERIES: THE BEST SPOTS FOR VIEWING

If you want an up-close encounter, head to one of these three protected spots where the whales gather to mate or give birth; the lagoons are like training wheels to prep the youngsters for the open ocean.

Laguna Ojo de Liebre (Scammon's Lagoon). Near Guerrero Negro, this lagoon is an L-shaped cut out of Baja's landmass, protected to the west by the jut of a peninsula.

Laguna San Ignacio. To reach the San Ignacio Lagoon, farther south than Scammon's, base yourself in the charming town of San Ignacio, 35 miles away. This lagoon is the smallest of the three, and along with Scammon's, has been designated a U.N. World Heritage site.

Bahía de Magdalena. This stretch of ocean, the farthest south, is kept calm by small, low-lying islands (really just humps of sand) that take the brunt of the ocean's waves. Very few people overnight in nearby San Carlos; most day-trip in from La Paz or Loreto.

WHAT TO EXPECT

The experience at the three lagoons is pretty standard: tours push off in the mornings, in *pangas* (tiny, low-lying skiffs) that seat about eight. Wear a water-resistant windbreaker—it will be a little chilly, and you're bound to be splashed once or twice.

The captain will drive around slowly, cutting the motor if he nears a whale (they'll never chase whales). Often the whales will approach you, sometimes showing off their babies. They'll gently nudge the boat, at times sinking completely under it and then raising it up a bit to get a good, long scratch.

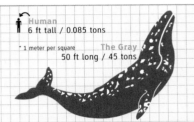

Human
6 ft tall / 0.085 tons

1 meter per square   The Gray
50 ft long / 45 tons

3

IN FOCUS A WHALE'S TALE

Baja whale watching, gray whale

CLOSE UP

An Underwater Paradise

One of Baja's true gems is Cabo Pulmo, the raw, unspoiled national marine preserve along the Sea of Cortez. More than 8 km (5 miles) of nearly deserted rocky beach border the only living coral-reef system on the Sea of Cortez. Several dive sites reveal hundreds of species of tropical fish, large schools of manta rays, and a sea-lion colony. This is a nearly perfect place for scuba diving and snorkeling.

The village of Cabo Pulmo has 100 or so residents, depending on the season. Power comes from solar panels, and drinking water is trucked in over dirt roads.

The town has two small general stores and three restaurants. Cabo Pulmo is a magnet for serious divers, kayakers, and windsurfers and remains one of southern Baja's natural treasures.

and Bahía Los Frailes to the south. It can also be reached by the well-maintained dirt road running along the coast from San José del Cabo. It'll take you three hours or more this way, but the coast along this route is unmatched. (Though, if it's raining, stick to the paved route.) There are two main dive centers, **Cabo Pulmo Dive Center** and **Cabo Pulmo Sport Center**, offering full gear rentals, kayaks, snorkel gear, and sportfishing tours. ⊠ *Hwy. 1, Km 31, Cabo Pulmo* ☎ *624/130–0195* ⊕ *www.cabopulmopark.com* ☜ *$5.*

OPERATORS

Cabo Pulmo Dive Center. Cabo Pulmo Dive Center provides some of the more exceptional dives in the area, and has everything you need, including certification classes (multiday). This 5-star PADI certified outfit is a local family-run shop. It's right on the beach and offers full diving services, as well as cheap rooms from $100 per night. ⊠ *Hwy. 1 at La Ribera turnoff, at the end of the road, in 2-story blue building, Cabo Pulmo* ☎ *624/141–0726* ⊕ *www.cabopulmo.com* ☜ *Diving $105; snorkeling $50.*

Cabo Pulmo Sport Center. Cabo Pulmo Sport Center has snorkeling, diving, and fishing tours. The center has a couple of simple casitas for rent ($90 per night) should you decide to extend your stay. ⊠ *Hwy. 1 at La Ribera turnoff, at end of road in palapa, Cabo Pulmo* ☎ *624/157–9795* ⊕ *www.cabopulmosportcenter.com* ☜ *$45.*

WHERE TO EAT

Updated by
Marlise Kast-
Myers & Chris
Sands

Prepare yourself for a gourmand's delight. The competition, creativity, selection, and, yes, even the prices are utterly beyond comprehension. From elegant dining rooms to casual seafood cafés to simple *taquerías,* Los Cabos serves up anything from standard to thrilling fare.

Seafood is the true highlight here. Fresh catches that land on the menus include dorado (mahimahi), *lenguado* (halibut), *cabrilla* (sea bass), *jurel* (yellowtail), wahoo, and marlin. Local lobster, shrimp, and octopus are particularly good. Fish grilled over a mesquite wood fire is perhaps the most indigenous and tasty seafood dish, while the most popular may be the tacos *de pescado* (fish tacos): traditionally a deep-fried fillet wrapped in a handmade corn tortilla, served with shredded cabbage, cilantro, and salsas. Beef and pork—commonly served marinated and grilled—are also delicious. Many restaurants import their steak, lamb, duck, and quail from the state of Sonora, Mexico's prime pastureland, and also from the United States, though many of the high-end spots are only using local ingredients.

In San José, international chefs prepare excellent Continental, French, Asian, and Mexican dishes in lovely, intimate restaurants, and it's where the major portion of the area's explosion in new eateries has occurred. Following in the footsteps of Northern Baja's Valle de Guadalupe, several restaurants on the outskirts of San José del Cabo are offering farm-to-table cuisine, as well as cooking courses and tours. This organic movement has spread from the farmers' market in San José del Cabo to the luxury resorts along the coast that rely on the farms for their daily menu. The Corridor is the place to go for exceptional (and expensive) hotel restaurants, while intense competition for business in Los Cabos means many restaurants go through periodic remodels and reinvention, the Corridor restaurants included. With San José emerging as the hotbed of culinary activity, it's fair to say that Cabos San Lucas lags somewhat behind. But Cabo has comfort food covered, with franchise eateries from McDonald's, Subway, Johnny Rocket's, Domino's, and Ruth's Chris Steak House.

PLANNING

EATING OUT STRATEGY

Although Mexicans often prefer dining late into the evening, be warned that if you arrive at restaurants in Los Cabos after 10 pm, you're taking your chances. Most places are open year-round, sometimes closing for a month in the middle of the hot Baja summer, and many Los Cabos restaurants close one night a week, typically Sunday or Monday.

PRICES

Restaurants in Los Cabos tend to be pricey, even by U.S. standards. Some add a fee for credit card usage. If you wander off the beaten path—often only a few blocks from the touristy areas—you can find inexpensive, authentic Mexican fare (though still more expensive than elsewhere in Mexico), although many of these spots may not accept credit cards. It has been stated in reviews where this applies.

WHAT IT COSTS IN DOLLARS			
$	$$	$$$	$$$$
At Dinner	under $12	$12–$20	$21–$30	over $30

Restaurant prices are the average cost of a main course at dinner or, if dinner is not served, at lunch.

Use the coordinate (✛ 1:B2) at the end of each listing to locate a site on the corresponding Where to Eat maps. Restaurant reviews have been shortened. For full information, visit Fodors.com.

RESERVATIONS

Reservations are mentioned when essential, but are a good idea during high season (mid-November to May). Restaurant websites are common, and many let you make online reservations.

SMOKING AND DRINKING

Mexican law prohibits smoking in all enclosed businesses, including restaurants. The drinking age here is 18. Establishments do ask for IDs.

TIPPING

You won't find much consistency in tipping expectations among Los Cabos restaurants. Some upscale places automatically add a 15% service charge (or even up to 18%) to the bill—look for the word "*servicio*"—but no one will object if you leave a few pesos more for good service. If a service charge is not included in your bill, a tip of 15% is common.

WHAT TO WEAR

Dress is often casual. Collared shirts and nice slacks are fine at even the most upscale places. In formal restaurants, men must wear closed-toe shoes, so leave the flip-flops behind. Shirts and shoes (or sandals) should be worn any time you're away from the beach.

SAN JOSÉ DEL CABO

Updated
by Marlise
Kast-Myers

San José's downtown is lovely, with adobe houses fronted by jacaranda trees. Entrepreneurs have converted many of the old homes into stylish restaurants, and new and inventive cuisine abounds—fitting for a town with an art district that is burgeoning as well. Boulevard Mijares is San José's Restaurant Row, so simply meander down the main boulevard to find one that will thrill your taste buds and delight your senses. New, organic-focused restaurants are pushing the culinary scene to the outskirts of San José del Cabo. These farm-to-table finds are tucked into green valleys, creating an oasis just beyond the cactus-lined dusty roads of Puerto Los Cabos.

$$
MODERN
MEXICAN
Fodor'sChoice
★

×**Acre.** Not one, but 25 acres are what you'll find at this farmland dining experience where design, sustainability, and modern cuisine intersect. Beyond the palm-tree forest is the main restaurant where a reed pergola casts linear shadows onto concrete floors. **Known for:** quality local ingredients; global cuisine with Mexican fusion; live music Thursday–Monday nights. $ *Average main: $17 ⊠ Rincon De Las Animas, Calle Camino Real s/n, San José del Cabo ☎ 624/171–8226 ⊕ www.acrebaja.com ✛ 1:D3.*

$$
AMERICAN

×**Baja Brewing Company.** Baja's popular brewery is right in the middle of San José del Cabo. Fun and upbeat, this brewpub has great music and serves up filling pub meals. **Known for:** wood-fired pizza; brewery tours; Baja beer on tap. $ *Average main: $15 ⊠ Morelos 1277, between Comonfort and Obregón, Centro ☎ 624/146–9995, 624/142–1292 ⊕ www.bajabrewingcompany.com ✛ 1:C2.*

$
AMERICAN

×**Buzzard's Bar & Grill.** Fronted by miles of secluded East Cape beach, this casual seaside cantina (with cheap cervezas) gets rave reviews from locals who make the 10-minute drive out of San José del Cabo. The palapa restaurant serves up hefty, reasonably priced New York steaks; seafood entrées, such as coconut shrimp; breakfast burritos; hefty build-your-own burgers; and house flan. **Known for:** giant burritos; coconut shrimp with piña colada dipping sauce; laid-back bar with sandy floor. $ *Average main: $9 ⊠ Old East Cape Rd., Laguna Hills ✛ Follow signs from San José del Cabo to Puerto Los Cabos and La Laguna ☎ 624/113–6368 ⊕ www.buzzardsbar.com ⊟ No credit cards ⊘ Closed Aug. and Sept. No dinner Sun. ⌗ Cash only ✛ 1:D3.*

$$$$
ECLECTIC
Fodor'sChoice
★

×**Casiano's.** "No menu, no rules" is the way chef Casiano Reyes describes the spontaneous cuisine at this creative spot where a changing palette of local ingredients appears on a free-form menu. Once you're seated, you'll be presented with a little tablet in a bowl that impressively morphs into a hand towel once your waiter adds water. **Known for:** three- or five-course tasting menu; creative fine dining; perfectly seared fillet. $ *Average main: $80 ⊠ Calle Manuel Doblado 16, Local B-3, Col. Center between Blvd. Antonio Mijares and Av. Centenario, Centro ☎ 624/142–5928 ⊕ casianos.com ⊘ Closed Sun. No lunch ✛ 1:D2.*

$$$
MODERN
MEXICAN
Fodor'sChoice
★

×**Don Sanchez.** Canadian chef-owner Tadd Chapman brings contemporary Baja cuisine to San José's main street in a fine dining setting. Brick pillars, white linens, and a wine wall comprised of nearly 300 blends make up the more formal dining area. **Known for:** butter-poached lobster with chayote pearls; fine wine and hospitality; modern Mexican menu. ⑤ *Average main: $30 ⊠ Blvd. Mijares s/n Edificio Eclipse Int 3, Centro* ☎ *624/142–2444* ⊕ *www.donsanchezrestaurant.com* ✛ *1:D3.*

$ ✕ **El Ahorcado.** By day it looks like a hole-in-the-wall, but when the
MEXICAN   sun goes down, the rummage-sale-meets-taco-stand atmosphere of this open-air local favorite truly comes to life. Get beyond the ghoulish silhouette logo—*ahorcado* means "hangman" in Spanish—and you'll find that the food is pretty good. **Known for:** outstanding tacos; reasonable prices; authentic Mexican experience. ⑤ *Average main: $5 ⊠ Paseo Pescadores at Marinos, San José del Cabo* ☎ *624/172–2093, 624/125–7264* ▭ *No credit cards* ✆ *Closed Mon. No lunch* ⌒ *Cash only* ✛ *1:A2.*

$ ✕ **El Marinero Borracho.** This two-story palapa restaurant, named "The
MEXICAN FUSION   Drunken Sailor," is always packed with locals and tourists alike. It's no wonder: the location across from the marina is the perfect spot to watch the sunset while enjoying a ginger mint mojito or tamarind margarita. **Known for:** unique ceviches menu; best Los Cabos dessert: avocado-lime chocolate cream pie; sunset view. ⑤ *Average main: $9 ⊠ Near Hotel El Ganzo, Calle Cabrilla, next to Jansens Bait and Tackle, Marina* ☎ *624/105–6464* ⊕ *www.ohnicnic.wix.com/the-drunken-sailor* ✆ *Closed Mon.* ✛ *1:D3.*

$$ ✕ **Flora's Field Kitchen.** This alfresco dining experience is built right in
AMERICAN   the center of the self-sustaining "Flora Farm." It's a charming oasis
Fodor'sChoice   featuring a restaurant, gift shop, cooking school, organic market, and
★   culinary cottages (private homes), all under the Flora Farm brand. **Known for:** wood-fired pizzas; farm setting with live music; produce raised on-site. ⑤ *Average main: $18 ⊠ Flora Farms, Las Animas Bajas* ☎ *624/355–4564* ⊕ *www.flora-farms.com* ✆ *Closed Mon. and daily 2:30–5 pm* ✛ *1:D4.*

$ ✕ **French Riviera Bakery.** The scent of fresh-baked French baguettes, and
CAFÉ   picture-perfect display of croissants, éclairs, colorful candies, and ice creams greet you at this café-bistro just off San José del Cabo's main square. In the creperie area, the cook tucks delicate crepes around eggs and cheese, ground beef and onions, or shrimp and pesto. **Known for:** organic local coffee; chocolate truffles; scrumptious breakfast crepes. ⑤ *Average main: $10 ⊠ Manuel Doblado at Av. Hidalgo, Centro* ☎ *624/130–7864* ✛ *1:D2.*

$$ ✕ **Habanero's Gastro Grill and Tequila Bar.** This gastro grill and tequila
MEXICAN FUSION   bar features a menu created by celebrity Chef Tadd Chapman and his mother Christine. Opt for lunch specialties of octopus tacos and grilled veggie ciabatta, and for dinner, try the fish-fillet wrapped shrimp with squid ink risotto, or the panko-crusted rice cakes topped with pulled pork. **Known for:** best key lime pie you've ever had; tequila pairings; outstanding brunch menu. ⑤ *Average main: $16 ⊠ Blvd. Mijares s/n, Int. 4, Plaza Las Misiones, Centro* ☎ *624/142–2626* ⊕ *www.habanerosgastrogrill.com* ✛ *1:D5.*

$$ ✕ **La Dolce.** This popular Italian restaurant right in the center of San José
ITALIAN   on the town's *zócalo* (square) is known for authentic and affordable Italian fare. Locals and visitors alike flock to this reasonably priced perennial favorite for antipasti and wood-fired-oven pizzas, a never-ending selection of pastas, and steaks and seafood dishes. **Known for:** authentic northern Italian cuisine; handmade pizza baked with mesquite

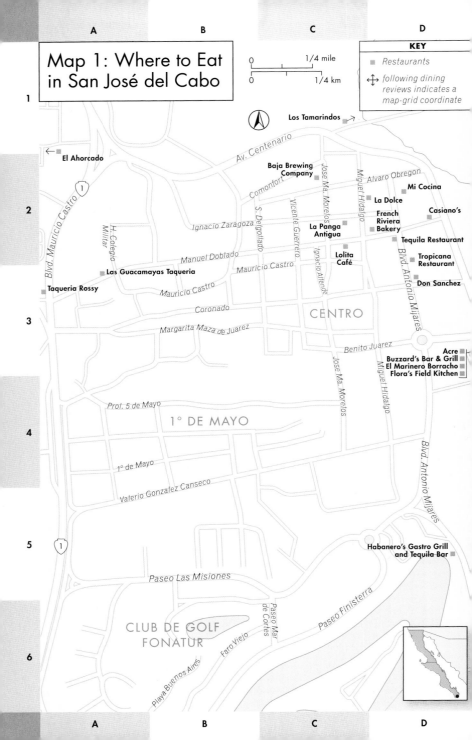

Map 1: Where to Eat in San José del Cabo

KEY
- Restaurants
- ⟷ *following dining reviews* indicates a map-grid coordinate

Los Tamarindos →

Av. Centenario

← El Ahorcado

Baja Brewing Company

Comonfort

Jose Ma. Morelos

Miguel Hidalgo

Alvaro Obregon

Mi Cocina

La Dolce

French Riviera Bakery

Casiano's

Ignacio Zaragoza

S. Delgollado

Vicente Guerrero

La Panga Antigua

Tequila Restaurant

H. Colegio Militar

Manuel Doblado

Ignacio Allende

Lolita Café

Tropicana Restaurant

Las Guacamayas Taqueria

Mauricio Castro

Blvd. Antonio Mijares

Don Sanchez

Taqueria Rossy

Mauricio Castro

Coronado

CENTRO

Margarita Maza de Juarez

Benito Juarez

Acre

Buzzard's Bar & Grill

El Marinero Borracho

Flora's Field Kitchen

Jose Ma. Morelos

Miguel Hidalgo

Prol. 5 de Mayo

1° DE MAYO

1° de Mayo

Blvd. Antonio Mijares

Valerio Gonzalez Canseco

Habanero's Gastro Grill and Tequila Bar

Paseo Las Misiones

Paseo Mar de Cortes

Paseo Finisterra

CLUB DE GOLF FONATUR

Playa Buenos Aires

Faro Viejo

Blvd. Mauricio Castro

wood; great Caesar salad. $ *Average main: $12* ⊠ *Av. Zaragoza at Av. Hidalgo, Plaza Jardin Mijares, Centro* ☎ *624/142–6621* ⊕ *www. ladolcerestaurant.com* ⊘ *Closed Mon.* ✛ *1:D2.*

$$$
MEXICAN

⤬ **La Panga Antigua.** A 170-year-old wooden *panga* (small skiff) hangs above the door at this seafood-heavy, atmospheric restaurant located in San José's oldest mission. The setting is a series of tropical patios, one with a faded mural, another with a burbling fountain, romantically lighted by dim fixtures, and a view of the stars above. **Known for:** magical setting and on-point presentation; innovative contemporary Mexican cuisine; veggies from their organic farm in Pescadero. $ *Average main: $30* ⊠ *Av. Zaragoza 20, Centro* ☎ *624/142–4041* ⊕ *www. lapangaantigua.restaurant* ✛ *1:C2.*

$
MEXICAN

⤬ **Las Guacamayas Taqueria.** Massive globes of 15 types of margaritas and a Mexican guitarist singing American covers makes this a magnet for tourists, but it also draws locals. If you're looking for cheap and delicious Mexican food, you've come to the right place. **Known for:** outstanding marinated pork tacos; great prices; live music and outdoor seating. $ *Average main: $9* ⊠ *Calle Paseo de los Marinos, near corner of Pescadores, Centro* ☎ *624/109–5473, 624/109–5993 cell* ✛ *1:A3.*

$
CAFÉ
Fodor'sChoice
★

⤬ **Lolita Café.** In a relaxing garden filled with retro decor, waiters in mesh trucker hats and pearl-button shirts deliver remarkable urban Mexican cuisine with a dash of grandma's secret recipes. Under the shade of a mango tree, start with the trio of salsas infused with orange and chipotle, served with a basket of freshly fried tortilla chips. **Known for:** delightful breakfast under the shade of a mango tree; yummy churros and gourmet coffees; fresh squeezed juices and healthy smoothies. $ *Average main: $8* ⊠ *Manuel Doblado 24, between Hidalgo and Morelos, Centro* ☎ *624/130–7786* ⊘ *Closed Mon. and Tues. No dinner* ✛ *1:C2.*

$$
MEXICAN FUSION

⤬ **Los Tamarindos.** A former sugarcane mill dating back to 1888, this quaint restaurant is surrounded by farmland that provides organic fruits and vegetables to many of Cabo's top eateries. Wildflowers in mason jars and hand-painted clay dishes set the scene at this rustic spot where the menu is based on the season's harvest. **Known for:** four-hour cooking classes ($95); true farm-to-table dining experience; home-made herbal oil on breads and meats. $ *Average main: $20* ⊠ *Calle Animas Baja, Las Animas Bajas* ☎ *624/105–6031* ⊕ *www.lostamarindos.mx* ⊘ *Closed Tues.* ✛ *1:C1.*

$$$
ECLECTIC

⤬ **Mi Cocina.** At this outdoor restaurant at Casa Natalia boutique hotel, fire bowls glow on the dining terrace, which is surrounded by palm trees and gentle waterfalls, blending the four elements: earth, wind, fire, and water. Tables are spaced far enough apart so that you don't have to share your whispered sweet nothings with neighbors. **Known for:** Mexican dishes with a European twist; adjoining oyster and martini bar; exceptional chicken with chocolate salsa. $ *Average main: $25* ⊠ *Casa Natalia, Blvd. Mijares 4, Centro* ☎ *624/146–7100* ⊕ *www. casanatalia.com* ⊘ *Closed Tues.* ✛ *1:D2.*

$
MEXICAN

⤬ **Taqueria Rossy.** Don't be fooled by the bare-bones atmosphere: Taqueria Rossy serves some of the best tacos in San José. Fish tacos are the thing at this no-frills joint brimming with local families who munch on everything from peel-and-eat shrimp to ceviche and chocolate clams. **Known for:** $2 tacos and $3 margaritas; large condiment bar for dress-your-own taco; best taqueria in town. ⓢ *Average main: $5* ⌂ *Hwy. 1, Km 33, Centro* ☎ *624/142–6755* ✛ *1:A3.*

$$$
ECLECTIC
✕**Tequila Restaurant.** A beautifully redone adobe home sets the stage for this classy dining experience on an open courtyard under the stars. A lengthy tequila list tempts diners to savor the finer brands of Mexico's national drink, and an

> ### MORE ON TEQUILA
>
> The real stuff comes from the Tequila region in mainland Mexico, but Los Cabos folks are producing their own spirits; look for the labels from private local distilleries. Tequila brands offered with Los Cabos labels are Cabo Wabo, Hotel California tequila, Mexita, and Las Varitas brand.

extensive wine cellar will give you plenty of choices for what to sip as you sup. **Known for:** succulent rack of lamb; Mediterranean, Asian, and Mexican influences; beautiful garden setting. ⓢ *Average main: $25* ⌂ *Manuel Doblado 1011, Centro* ☎ *624/142–1155* ⊕ *www.tequilarestaurant.com* ✛ *1:D2.*

$$
INTERNATIONAL
✕**Tropicana Restaurant.** Reminiscent of an old colonial hacienda, this two-story restaurant draws a crowd with its live music, Sunday brunch, and large menu ranging from fresh seafood to imported steaks. The front sidewalk seating is a great place to survey the world going by. **Known for:** live music Thursday–Sunday; hacienda-style dining room; flavorful chicken enchiladas. ⓢ *Average main: $20* ⌂ *Tropicana Inn, Blvd. Mijares 30, Centro* ☎ *624/142–4146* ⊕ *www.tropicanainn.com.mx* ✛ *1:D2.*

THE CORRIDOR

Updated by Marlise Kast-Myers

Dining along the Corridor between San José del Cabo and Cabo San Lucas used to be restricted to the ever-improving hotel restaurants. But with the addition of the Tiendas de Palmilla shopping center, just across from the One&Only Palmilla resort, top-notch eateries are establishing a new dining energy along this stretch of highway, giving drivers along the Corridor a tasty reason to slow down, and maybe even stop.

$$$$
CONTEMPORARY
✕**Cocina De Autor.** Led by two-Michelin-starred chef Sidney Schutte, the signature restaurant at Grand Velas is turning heads for its 10-course tasting menu that's as impressive on presentation as it is on taste. Each bite is a mini-explosion in your mouth—not to be confused with molecular gastronomy (according to the chef himself). **Known for:** 10-course tasting menu; European techniques; reservations required. ⓢ *Average main: $170* ⌂ *At Grand Velas, Carretera Transpeninsular, Km 17.3, The Corridor* ☎ *624/104–9826* ⊕ *www.loscabos.grandvelas.com* ⊙ *No breakfast or lunch* ✛ *2:C4.*

$$$$
SEAFOOD
✕**Cocina del Mar.** Argentinean chef Guillermo Gomez delivers an elevated culinary experience to Cocina del Mar, the elegant restaurant in the exquisite Esperanza Resort. Using daily market ingredients and focusing on simple seafood, Gomez presents inventive dishes such as lobster fettuccine, steamed clams with chorizo, or the impressive salt-crusted totuava. **Known for:** romantic location on the cliff; delicious

banana soufflé; whole fish encased in salt and herbs. $ *Average main: $50* ⊠ *Hwy. 1, Km 7, at Esperanza Resort, The Corridor* ☎ *624/145–6400* ⊕ *www.esperanzaresort.com* ⊘ *No lunch* ✥ *2:D2.*

$
MODERN
MEXICAN
FAMILY

⤬ **El Merkado.** At this glorified food court, more than 20 culinary offerings are at your disposal, ranging from Mexican and Greek to Spanish and Italian. Mom and dad can savor wine, cheese, or tapas, while the little ones can dig into gourmet hot dogs, creamy gelato, or treats from the candy shop. **Known for:** multitude of choices; reasonable prices; great sushi. $ *Average main: $8* ⊠ *At Koral Center, Cerro Colorado, Carretera Transpeninsular, Km 24.5, The Corridor* ☎ *624/137–9834* ⊕ *www.elmerkado.mx* ✥ *2:B5.*

$$$$
MEXICAN

⤬ **El Restaurante at Las Ventanas.** It's well known that Las Ventanas is one of the best hotels in Mexico, and the on-site dining likewise does not disappoint. Chef Fabrice Guisset has unveiled a new Mexican menu that pays homage to the country's culinary traditions, with a focus on family recipes. **Known for:** gourmet tacos; traditional Mexican dishes from around the country; nightly live music. $ *Average main: $50* ⊠ *Hwy. 1, Km 19.5, The Corridor* ☎ *624/144–2800* ⊕ *www.rosewoodhotels. com/en/lasventanas* ✥ *2:C4.*

$$$
MEXICAN FUSION

⤬ **Manta.** Dine with ubercool people at Manta, The Cape's culinary centerpiece by Chef Enrique Olvera. Sip a cocktail in the sunken lounge bar, and move on over to the terrace with views of El Arco and surfers in action. **Known for:** globally inspired Mexican cuisine; remarkable sunset views of El Arco; local ingredients from Baja Califonia Sur. $ *Average main: $30* ⊠ *The Cape, Carretera Transpeninsular, Km 5, Misiones del Cabo, The Corridor* ☎ *624/163–0000* ⊕ *www.mantarestaurant.com* ⊘ *No breakfast or lunch* ✥ *2:C2.*

$$
SUSHI

⤬ **Nick-San-Palmilla.** For fresh, inventive sushi, there's no question that the Nick-San franchise corners the market, and this outpost in the Tiendas de Palmilla shopping mall wins the prize. Pair each of your selections with wine or sake, and let chef Eddie Carvajal choose from the vast menu. **Known for:** great lobster roll and ahi tostada; sushi with Mexican twist; refreshing blackberry margarita. $ *Average main: $18* ⊠ *The Shoppes at Palmilla, Hwy. 1, Km 27.5, The Corridor* ☎ *624/144–6262* ⊕ *www.nicksan.com* ✥ *2:B5.*

$$$
ASIAN FUSION

⤬ **Pitahayas.** Chef Volker Romeike blends Asian and Polynesian ingredients with local products for a menu that showcases well-executed Pacific Rim fusion. Above the beach in the Sheraton's Hacienda del Mar resort in Cabo del Sol, Pitahayas is set under a soaring palapa overlooking the rollicking surf. **Known for:** Mexican Asian fusion; open bar Fridays 9 pm–1 am for $30; large martini menu. $ *Average main: $30* ⊠ *Sheraton Hacienda del Mar, Hwy. 1, Km 10, The Corridor* ☎ *624/145–8010* ⊕ *www.pitahayas.com* ✥ *2:C3.*

$$$
INTERNATIONAL

⤬ **Puerta Vieja.** Puerta Vieja translates into "Old Door," and the beautiful door you enter through, imported from India, is indeed over 160 years old. Though Puerta Vieja serves lunch, we suggest dinner at sunset, when the view of El Arco is the most impressive. **Known for:** tasty lobster chowder; savory chocolate cheesecake; reasonably priced seafood and steak. $ *Average main: $30* ⊠ *Hwy. 1, Km 6.5, The Corridor* ☎ *624/104–3252, 624/104–3334* ⊕ *www.puertavieja.mx* ✥ *2:C2.*

4

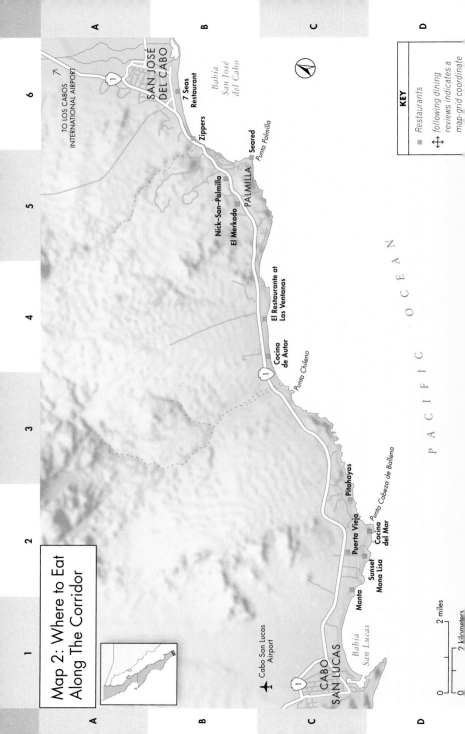

Map 2: Where to Eat Along The Corridor

TO LOS CABOS INTERNATIONAL AIRPORT

SAN JOSÉ DEL CABO

7 Seas Restaurant

Zippers

Seared

Bahía San José del Cabo

Punta Palmilla

PALMILLA

Nick–San–Palmilla

El Merkado

El Restaurante at Las Ventanas

Cocina de Autor

Punta Chileno

Pitahayas

Puerta Vieja

Cocina del Mar

Punta Cabeza de Ballena

Sunset Mona Lisa

Manta

Cabo San Lucas Airport

CABO SAN LUCAS

Bahía San Lucas

P A C I F I C   O C E A N

KEY

Restaurants

↔ *following dining reviews indicates a map-grid coordinate*

2 miles

2 kilometers

$$$$ ✕**Seared.** Opened by three-Michelin-starred chef Jean-Georges Vong-
STEAKHOUSE erichten, this signature restaurant at One&Only Palmilla is one of
Fodor's Choice the priciest spots in Los Cabos, but it's also one of the best. Boasting
★ hand-selected cuts of steak and freshly caught Pacific seafood, the menu
showcases everything from Wagyu to Kobe beef. **Known for:** fine cuts
of beef; elaborate wine list; remarkable appetizers. ⑤ *Average main:*
$100 ✉ One&Only Palmilla, Carretera Transpeninsular, Km 7.5, The
Corridor ☎ *624/146–7000* ⊕ *www.oneandonlyresorts.com* ✛ *2:B5.*

$$$ ✕**7 Seas Restaurant.** It's quite soothing to sit in this restaurant at Cabo
ECLECTIC Surf Hotel, at the ocean's edge under the shade of a palapa while watch-
ing the surfers. For breakfast munch on their *machaca con huevos*
(eggs scrambled with shredded beef) washed down with a fresh-fruit
smoothie. **Known for:** gluten-free and vegetarian options; inventive sea-
food cuisine with eclectic style; regional organic vegetables. ⑤ *Average*
main: $22 ✉ Cabo Surf Hotel, Acapulquito Beach, Km 28, The Cor-
ridor ☎ *624/142–2666* ⊕ *www.7seasrestaurant.com* ✛ *2:B6.*

$$$ ✕**Sunset Mona Lisa.** Stunning views of El Arco from cocktail tables
ITALIAN along the cliffs make this restaurant just outside of Cabo San Lucas
the best place to toast the sunset. If the breeze is still, stay outside
and enjoy dining alfresco; if not, move into the candlelit dining room
under a palapa. **Known for:** Champagne bar with fire pits; sunset
views of El Arco; house-made pastas. ⑤ *Average main: $30 ✉ Hwy.*
1, Km 5.5, The Corridor ☎ *624/145–8160* ⊕ *www.sunsetmonalisa.*
com ✛ *2:C2.*

$$ ✕**Zipper's.** Popular with the surfing crowd, this palapa-covered joint
AMERICAN is right on Cabo Azul beach, just south of San José del Cabo. Though
FAMILY their burger is the reason to come, the aroma of grilling lobster and
tacos, and a sound track of surf tunes are why many return. **Known for:**
fried fish and large portions; live bands playing rock classics; incred-
ible burger. ⑤ *Average main: $12 ✉ Hwy. 1, Km 28.5, The Corridor*
☎ *624/172–6162* ✛ *2:B6.*

CABO SAN LUCAS

Updated by   Cabo San Lucas is known for its rowdy nightlife, and, though much of
Chris Sands   the fine-dining scene has moved to the Corridor and San José, there are
still some solid choices in Cabo. A pedestrian walkway lined with res-
taurants, bars, and shops anchored by the sleek Puerto Paraíso mall
curves around Cabo San Lucas harbor, itself packed with yachts. The
most popular restaurants, clubs, and shops are along Avenida Cárdenas
(the extension of Highway 1 from the Corridor) and Boulevard Marina,
paralleling the waterfront.

$$$ ✕**Alcaravea Gourmet.** Alcaravea Gourmet has come a long way from
ITALIAN its humble beginnings as a tiny, off-the-beaten-path bistro, and is now
considered one of Cabo's top stops for Italian and Mediterranean style
cuisine. Enter through a flower-and-vine-garlanded opening into an
intimate dining area. **Known for:** excellent $10 lunch deal; delicious
pescado con champiñones; top-tier rib-eye steak. ⑤ *Average main: $25*
✉ *Zaragoza at 16 de Septiembre, Centro* ☎ *624/143–3730* ⊙ *Closed*
Sun. ✛ *3:B4.*

CLOSE UP

Budget Bites

Street stands offer low-cost fine food. If there's a crowd of locals, it's probably fresh and prepared well. Best bets include quesadillas, fish tacos, corn on the cob, and *tortas* (sandwiches). Some restaurants have a *comida corrida* (prepared lunch special), a three-course meal that consists of soup or salad, an entrée with rice and vegetables, coffee, and a small dessert. It's not gourmet, but you'll be sated, and at a reasonable price.

In Cabo San Lucas, head for the taco stands in the couple of blocks behind Squid Roe and Avenida Cárdenas, and the backstreets inland from the marina.

The best tacos in Cabo can be found off Highway 1, just outside Cabo San Lucas between Cabo Cielo and the Go-Kart track, at **Asi y Asado** (⊠ *Hwy 1, Km 3.8* 🕾 *624/105–9500* ⊕ *www. asiyasado.com*). There are more than 20 types of tacos, including marinated skirt steak, grilled octopus, and smoked tuna, but it's the Vampiros, served in a hard corn shell and filled with cheese and the meat of your choice, that takes the prize. Pair with made-to-order juices, such as watermelon or lime with pineapple or cucumber.

With branches in both San José and Cabo San Lucas, **Los Claros** (⊠ *Zaragoza at 16 de Septembre in Cabo San Lucas and at Blvd. Antonio Mijares 1092 in San José* 🕾 *624/131–5090*) is the place for a quick taco fix; $2 (fish and shrimp) or $5 (lobster) gets you some serious tacos, while $6 will buy you a killer breakfast. Two-for-one margaritas are served all day, and five beers (Corona or Pacifico) can be had for $10.

At **Pollo de Oro** (⊠ *Morelos at Av. Cárdenas* 🕾 *624/143–0310*), a half-chicken meal costs about $8.

For inexpensive Mexican eateries close to the marina and hotels, try the juice stands.

Tortas El Champions – Rico Suave (⊠ *Av. Cárdenas between Av. Hidalgo and Calle Guerrero* 🕾 *624/143–1043*) makes great smoothies with yogurt, as well as cheese tortas.

In San José del Cabo, **Taqueria Rossy** (⊠ *Hwy. 1, Km 33* 🕾 *624/143–6755*) is a no-frills joint brimming with locals who sink their teeth into fish tacos ($1–$3) piled high with avocados, chilies, cabbage, onions, and an assortment of spicy salsas.

$$$
EUROPEAN

✕**Alexander Restaurant.** Ideally located along Cabo San Lucas's busy marina walkway, Alexander's is where Switzerland meets México. Pull up a chair at one of the sidewalk tables and start with a meat-and-cheese fondue, a treat for which Swiss chef and owner Alex Brulhart is known. **Known for:** Alex Brulhart meat-and-cheese fondue; incredible flambéed tequila shrimp; delicious duck à l'orange. ⑤ *Average main: $30* ⊠ *Plaza Bonita, Cabo San Lucas Marina, Marina San Lucas* 🕾 *624/143–2022* ⊕ *www.alexandercabo.com* ✚ *3:B4.*

$$$
AMERICAN

✕**Baja Brewing Company.** A branch of the established San José del Cabo microbrewery, the beers are brewed in San José, meaning what you get here is "20 minutes fresh." No quibbles with the system; the eight house brews and seasonal additions are a flavorful change from the ubiquitous Tecate. The location of this outpost on the rooftop of the Cabos Villas resort on Médano Beach, however, ups the ante with a semi-open-air venue and view of the ocean. **Known for:** ocean views; open-air dining; fresh brews. $ *Average main: $25 ✉ Cabo Villas Beach Resort & Spa, Callejon del Pescador, Playa El Médano* ☎ *624/143–9199* ⊕ *www.bajabrewingcompany.com* ✛ *3:C4.*

$$
MEXICAN
✕ **Baja Cantina Marina.** This large, casual, sportfishing-oriented cantina, just around the corner from the Tesoro Los Cabos Resort, draws crowds with its all-day drink specials. Boasting a top marina location near L-M-N Dock, an excellent view of the sportfishing and mega yachts, $2 cervezas all day, affordable eats, and American sports on multiple TVs, it's a favorite of the sportfishing deckhands and boat captains. **Known for:** late-night DJs and dancing; all-day drink specials; budget-friendly eats. $ *Average main: $20 ✉ Cabo San Lucas Marina, Dock L-M-N, Marina San Lucas* ☎ *624/143–1111* ⊕ *www.bajacantinamarina.com* ✛ *3:B5.*

$$$$
ECLECTIC
✕ **Bar Esquina.** Set in Cabo San Lucas's boutique Bahia Hotel, Bar Esquina is making a name for itself as Medano Beach's best new restaurant. Whether you're craving eggs Benedict in the morning to help you absorb last night's party, pizza or ceviche, or a burger while you lie by the pool, La Esquina is the spot to fit your mood. **Known for:** delicious tuna tartare; live music five nights a week; eggs Benedict after a night out. $ *Average main: $35 ✉ Bahia Hotel & Beach House, Av. El Pescador, Playa El Médano* ☎ *624/143–1890* ⊕ *www.bahiacabo.com or www.baresquina.com* ✛ *3:C3.*

$
CAFÉ
✕ **The Cabo Coffee Company.** Many of the area's best restaurants source their coffee blends from Cabo Coffee Company. The café, just off the Plaza Amelia Wilkes town square, serves up a wide array of espresso drinks made from organic beans grown in Oaxaca's cloud forest. **Known for:** local hangout; free Wi-Fi; tasty fresh pastries. $ *Average main: $3 ✉ Calle Miguel Hidalgo at Francisco I. Madero, Centro* ☎ *624/105–1754* ⊕ *www.cabocoffee.com* ✛ *3:A5.*

$
MEXICAN
✕ **California Ranch Market.** In addition to its great selection of beer and wines, as well as organic and frozen foods, healthy and low-calorie offerings, and cheese, California Ranch Market is also highly affordable. This corner shop carries familiar products and brands from the United States, and a second location has been added at The Shoppes at Palmilla. **Known for:** excellent prices; extensive beer and wine selection; healthy and organic options. $ *Average main: $5 ✉ Blvd. Marina at Camino del Cerro, at the western end of Marina San Lucas, Cabo San Lucas* ☎ *624/143–1947* ⊕ *californiaranchmarket.com* ⊗ *Closed Sun.* ✛ *3:B6.*

$$
MEXICAN
✕ **Canela Restaurant and Bar.** Canela offers contemporary Mexican fare, as well as a generous selection of American-style burgers and sandwiches. The bi-level space near the marina is filled with traditional arts and crafts, and its walls are lined with tequila bottles. **Known for:** inexpensive breakfasts ($3–$5); cruise ship crowd favorite; great place for cocktails. $ *Average main: $14 ✉ Plaza del Sol shopping center, Francisco Madero at Blvd. Marina, Marina San Lucas* ☎ *624/143–7577* ⊕ *www.canelarestaurant.com* ✛ *3:B5.*

$$
MEXICAN
✕ **Crazy Lobster Bar & Grill.** Lobster's the thing here, but daily specials like surf-and-turf combos round out the list. Open for breakfast, lunch, and dinner, this typical Mexican sit-down locale has a happy hour that runs from 8 am to 6 pm—and prices are super cheap. **Known for:** excellent

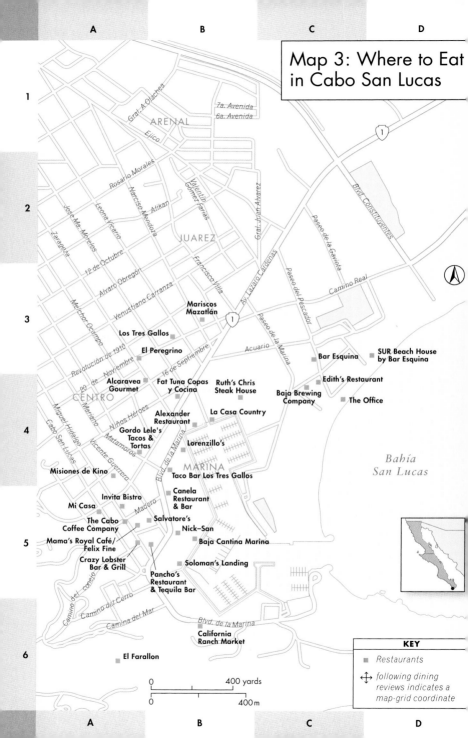

people-watching; open-air dining; incredibly cheap and generous food. $ *Average main: $15* ⊠ *Hidalgo at Zapata, Centro* ☎ 624/143–6535 ⊗ *Closed Sept.* ✛ *3:A5.*

$$$$
MEXICAN
FAMILY

✕ **Edith's Restaurant.** One of the more upscale choices near hectic Médano Beach, Edith's is the sister restaurant to popular The Office on the Beach. The Caesar salad and flambéed banana crepes are prepared table-side at this colorful and popular restaurant. **Known for:** Wally's Special; wine cellar for small private parties; focus on Mexican ingredients. $ *Average main: $50* ⊠ *Camino a Playa El Médano, Playa El Médano* ☎ 624/143–0801 ⊕ *www.edithscabo.com* ⊗ *Closed Sept.* ✛ *3:C4.*

$$$$
SEAFOOD
Fodor's Choice
★

✕ **El Farallon.** Atop a bluff in The Resort at Pedregal, El Farallon provides one of the most breathtaking vantage points in Cabo San Lucas. Chef Gustavo Pinet presents a seafood-heavy menu with a "fresh fish market" displaying the catch of the day. **Known for:** irresistible local chocolate clams; Champagne terrace; dishes come with a tasting of the day's three appetizers. $ *Average main: $125* ⊠ *The Resort at Pedregal, Camino Del Mar 1, Pedregal* ☎ 624/163–4300 ⊕ *www.theresortatpedregal.com* ✛ *3:A6.*

$$
INTERNATIONAL

✕ **El Peregrino.** The name of this restaurant in Spanish means "The Pilgrim," and refers to the power and breadth of knowledge available to intrepid travelers. Fortunately, one needn't be particularly intrepid to find the place, though it is a bit off the beaten track. **Known for:** excellent international fare; cozy dining space; popular slow-cooked barbecue short rib. $ *Average main: $20* ⊠ *Calle Ignacio Zaragoza at 20 de Noviembre, Centro* ☎ 624/688–4872 ✛ *3:B3.*

$$$
SEAFOOD

✕ **Fat Tuna Copas y Cocina.** The latest venture from Nick-San founder Angel Carbajal is a sleek, contemporary restaurant occupying three levels, the uppermost of which is a private rooftop event space. Carbajal's mastery of seafood-focused fare is still much in evidence at Fat Tuna, but the locally celebrated chef has also added steak, pasta dishes, and pizza to his repertoire, including an exquisite, thinly sliced Wagyu rib eye with ponzu and sesame oil pearls, and a decadent lobster Stroganoff over linguine. **Known for:** celebrated chef Angel Carbajal; great service; decadent lobster Stroganoff. $ *Average main: $27* ⊠ *Blvd. Lázaro Cárdenas, between Zaragoza and Morelos, Centro* ☎ 624/143–4740 ✛ *3:B4.*

$
MEXICAN

✕ **Gordo Lele's Tacos & Tortas.** If you're looking for some entertainment to go along with your tacos or *tortas* (sandwiches), listen for the blaring Beatles' tunes at Gordo Lele's, then watch owner Javier Reynoso don his Beatles wig and sing along to "I Want to Hold Your Hand" or "Let It Be." The walls here are filled with Fab Four photos and album covers. Javier's tacos and tortas are made with loving care, and his fans can have two or three ham-and-cheese tortas for what would be the price of one anywhere else, plus an assortment of generously sized tacos. **Known for:** delicious affordable tortas; generously sized tacos; Beatles decor. $ *Average main: $4* ⊠ *Matamoros, between Lázaro Cárdenas and Niños Héroes, Centro* ☎ 624/134–3677 ▭ *No credit cards* ✛ *3:B4.*

$$$
ITALIAN
FAMILY

✕ **Invita Bistro.** Go for the delicious complimentary focaccia bread, stay for the fine wines, family-style fare, and charming views of downtown Cabo San Lucas. Chef and co-owner Antonello Lauri shows off his Roman heritage on the menu at Invita, which is overflowing with traditional Italian favorites like the filling eggplant Parmesan made from recipes passed down from his grandmother. **Known for:** views of town square; serious about their wines; traditional Italian recipes. ⑤ *Average main: $25 ⊠ Calle Miguel Hidalgo, Centro ✛ Across from Plaza Amelia Wilkes ☎ 624/143–1386 ⊕ www.invitabistro.com ✛ 3:A5.*

$$$
STEAKHOUSE

✕ **La Casa Country.** For a good steak in a rustic atmosphere accented by wood tables and leather stools, head to La Casa Country. Serving breakfast, lunch, and dinner with sports games playing on oversize TVs in the background, La Casa is the spot for toothsome carne at reasonable prices, and a wide variety of Mexican fare. **Known for:** marina views; abundant steak options; generous breakfast menu. ⑤ *Average main: $21 ⊠ Cabo San Lucas Marina, next to Puerto Paraiso, Marina San Lucas ☎ 624/105–1999 ✛ 3:B4.*

$$$$
SEAFOOD

✕ **Lorenzillo's.** Gleaming hardwood floors and polished brass give a nautical flair to this second-floor dining room, where fresh lobster is king. Lorenzillo's has long been a fixture in Cancún, where lobster is raised on the company's farm. **Known for:** Xtabentun cocktail with Mayan liqueur, anise, honey; specialty flaming coffee cocktails; pirate- and marine-themed entrées. ⑤ *Average main: $60 ⊠ Av. Cárdenas at Marina, Marina San Lucas ☎ 624/105–0212 ⊕ www.lorenzillos.com.mx ✛ 3:B4.*

$$$
MEXICAN
Fodor's Choice
★

✕ **Los Tres Gallos.** A romantic courtyard shaded by fruit trees, classic *rancheras* (Mexican folk music), and traditional preparations of regional Mexican specialty dishes are the hallmarks at Los Tres Gallos. Discover their delicious heritage dishes such as *cochinita pibil* (slow-roasted pork) and molcajetes filled with flank steak, shrimp, chorizo, nopal, and panela cheese. **Known for:** old-fashioned charm; delicious flan for dessert; tribute to stars of Mexico's golden age of cinema. ⑤ *Average main: $25 ⊠ Calle Leona Vicario at 20 de Noviembre, Centro ☎ 624/130–7709 ⊕ www.lostresgallos.com ✛ 3:B3.*

$
MEXICAN

✕ **Mama's Royal Café.** Claiming to have "the best damn breakfast restaurant in the entire country," Mama's is a casual, lively, indoor-outdoor spot in Cabo San Lucas that serves up bountiful plates of omelets and poached eggs with avocado and ham, and finger-licking fried potatoes. Mama's lives up to their claim of having the "World's Best French Toast"—a treasure stuffed with cream cheese, strawberries, mangoes, bananas, and pecans, and topped with orange liqueur. **Known for:** "World's Best French Toast"; homemade salsas; fresh-squeezed juices. ⑤ *Average main: $10 ⊠ Hidalgo at Zapata, Centro ☎ 624/143–4290 ⊕ www.mamasroyalcafeloscabos.com ☾ Closed Sept. ✛ 3:A5.*

$$
SEAFOOD

✕ **Mariscos Mazatlán.** Ask a local where he or she goes for dinner, and they inevitably mention Mariscos Mazatlán. The crowds of Mexicans lunching at this simple seafood restaurant lend credibility to the claim, as do the huge stuffed fish mounted on the colorfully painted walls. **Known for:** affordable authentic cuisine; local favorite; delicious seafood. ⑤ *Average main: $20 ⊠ Narciso Mendoza at 20 de Noviembre, Arenal ☎ 624/143–8565 ✛ 3:B3.*

$$
MEXICAN
FAMILY

✕ **Mi Casa.** One of Cabo San Lucas's top restaurants is in a cobalt-blue adobe building painted with murals. Interior decorations range from Day of the Dead statues and silver crosses and hearts, to T-shirts and tequilas. **Known for:** regional Mexican specialties; must-try mole poblano; live mariachi band. $ *Average main: $20* ✉ *Av. Cabo San Lucas at Lazaro Cardenas, Centro* ☎ *624/143–1933* ⊕ *www.micasarestaurant.com.mx* ⊘ *No lunch Sun.* ✛ *3:A5.*

$$ ✕ **Misiones de Kino.** You may feel like you discovered a well-kept secret
MEXICAN when you find this palapa-roof house with adobe walls, just a few blocks off the main strip and around the corner from the Mar de Cortez Hotel. Sit on the front patio or in a backyard hut strung with weathered lanterns and photographs of the Mexican Revolution. **Known for:** second menu with pasta and Italian options; cabrilla con salsa de frambuesa; camarón coco. $ *Average main: $17* ✉ *Calle Vicente Guerrero at 5 de Mayo, Centro* ☎ *624/105–1408* ⊕ *www.misionesdekino.com* ⊘ *Closed Sun.* ✛ *3:A4.*

$$$ ✕ **Nick-San.** Nick-San may very well be Cabo San Lucas's top restaurant.
SUSHI Owner Angel Carbajal is an artist behind the sushi counter (he also
Fodor's Choice has his own fishing boats that collect fish each day), and his creative
★ fusion menu of Japanese and Mexican cuisines truly sets his masterpieces apart. **Known for:** tuna specialties; reservations recommended; divine sauce on the cilantro sashimi. $ *Average main: $22* ✉ *Plaza de la Danza, Blvd. Marina, next to Tesoro Los Cabos Hotel, Marina San Lucas* ☎ *624/143–2491* ⊕ *www.nicksan.com* ✛ *3:B5.*

$$$ ✕ **The Office.** At least once during your visit to Los Cabos, you should
MEXICAN visit The Office, the original breakfast spot on Médano Beach's sandy shore. The Office screams "tourist-trap," bedecked with tiki torches and colorful rainbow tablecloths, but it's all in good fun, and it's always packed with revelers enjoying the near-perfect views of El Arco. **Known for:** strong Mexican coffee; views of El Arco; Cabo breakfast staple. $ *Average main: $30* ✉ *Playa El Médano* ☎ *624/143–3464* ⊕ *theofficeonthebeach.com* ⊘ *Closed Aug. and Sept.* ✛ *3:C4.*

$$$ ✕ **Pancho's Restaurant & Tequila Bar.** Owner Juan Calderoni has an enor-
MEXICAN mous collection of tequilas, and an extensive knowledge of the stuff.
FAMILY His restaurant is something of a tequila museum, with a colorful array of hundreds of the world's top tequilas—many no longer available—displayed behind the bar. **Known for:** nearly 500 types of tequila; Oaxacan decor; private tequila tastings. $ *Average main: $30* ✉ *Calle Hidalgo, between Zapata and Camino del Conejo, Centro* ☎ *624/143–2891, 624/143–0973* ⊕ *www.panchos.com* ✛ *3:A5.*

$$$$ ✕ **Ruth's Chris Steak House.** If you need a break from tacos and have a
STEAKHOUSE hankering for a steak like they cook 'em back home, Ruth's Chris at the Puerto Paraíso mall facing the marina is your best bet. It's known for its wide range of meaty cuts from fillets to porterhouse, and also serves veal, chicken, fish, and lamb. **Known for:** mouthwatering steak; range of cuts; specialty cocktails. $ *Average main: $60* ✉ *Puerto Paraíso, 1st fl., Marina San Lucas* ☎ *624/144–3232* ⊕ *www.ruthschris.com* ✛ *3:B4.*

$$ ✕ **Salvatore's.** The local gringo cadre has nothing but *bueno* things to
ITALIAN say about this affordable and dependable little Italian spot, located by the pool at the Siesta Suites Hotel in downtown Cabo San Lucas. Baked rigatoni, osso buco, chicken parmigiana, lasagna, and lamb ravioli are just some of the many Italian staples offered at this funky little spot. **Known for:** large portions; reasonably priced; tasty traditional Italian cuisine. $ *Average main: $15* ✉ *Zapata between Guerrero and Hidalgo, Centro* ☎ *624/105–1044* ⊘ *No lunch Sun.* ✛ *3:A5.*

4

$$
SEAFOOD
FAMILY
✕**Solomon's Landing.** Chef and owner Brian Solomon runs one of the most popular restaurants on the Cabo San Lucas Marina, supplementing great seaside views with first-class service and an enormous range of quality food and beverage. Fresh local seafood is the specialty of the house, but pastas, steaks, and traditional Mexican favorites are also staples of the lunch and dinner menus. **Known for:** live music and dancing on Friday; monthly food and wine events; fresh local seafood. Ⓢ *Average main: $20* ⊠ *Cabo San Lucas Marina, behind Tesoro Los Cabos Resort, Marina San Lucas* ☎ *624/143–3050* ⊕ *www.solomonslandingcabo.com* ✛ *3:B5.*

$$
SEAFOOD
✕**SUR Beach House by Bar Esquina.** Less than two blocks from its affiliate restaurant Bar Esquina at Bahia Hotel & Beach House, SUR is a picturesque mix of casual chic appointments and breezy seaside ambience set on Playa El Médano. The specialties of *la casa* are pan-Pacific fusions featuring fresh local seafood, from ceviches and sushi to tacos and Peruvian-style *tiraditos* (raw fish similar to crudo). **Known for:** pan-Pacific fusions; morning yoga classes and SUP board rentals; Peruvian-style tiraditos. Ⓢ *Average main: $20* ⊠ *Playa El Médano, at Calle Cormoranes, Playa El Médano* ✛ *Next to The Sand Bar* ☎ *624/143–1890* ⊕ *www.surcabo.com* ✛ *3:D3.*

$
MEXICAN
✕**Taco Bar Los Tres Gallos.** The recently launched comfort food arm of acclaimed Mexican restaurant Los Tres Gallos showcases plenty of delicious taco options, as well as old-school Mexican cocktails seldom seen anymore outside Mexico City's traditional cantinas. Vegetarian tacos are available, as are burgers for homesick gringos. **Known for:** vegetarian options; old-school Mexican cocktails; American-style hamburgers. Ⓢ *Average main: $5* ⊠ *Plaza del Sol, Blvd. Marina, Local 15 and 16, Marina San Lucas* ☎ *624/172–0042* ✛ *3:B4.*

5

WHERE TO STAY

Updated
by Marlise
Kast-Myers

Expect high-quality accommodations wherever you stay in Los Cabos—whether at a huge resort or a small bed-and-breakfast. Much of the area's beaches are now backed by major properties, all vying to create the most desirable stretch on the sand. For the privilege of staying in these hot properties, you'll pay top dollar—and more for oceanfront rooms with incredible views.

Prices at accommodations off the beach reflect the popularity of the area and may surprise travelers used to spending much less in other areas of Mexico—even in the hot summer months which are, technically, the low season.

Sprawling Mediterranean-style resorts of generally 200 to 400 rooms dominate the coastline of Los Cabos, especially on the 29-km-long (18-mile-long) Corridor, but also on the beaches in Cabo San Lucas and San José (the town of San José is not on the coast, but inland just a bit). Currently Los Cabos has over 63 hotels with more than 16,000 rooms. By 2019, the destination plans to add 5,000 more hotel rooms with the grand openings of Nobu Hotel, Ritz Carlton, Montage, Cachet Corazon, Villa La Valencia, Garza Blanca, Grand Solmar, Vidanta, Solaz, Le Blanc, The Hard Rock Hotel, Four Seasons Resort, Park Hyatt, and Riu.

Los Cabos resorts are known for their lavish pools and lush grounds in addition to their beachfront access, although the majority of beaches on the densely developed coastline, with the notable exception of Playa Médano in Cabo San Lucas, can have an oddly deserted appearance because of the dangerous currents in the water and the predominance of luxurious pools.

Many of the resorts along the Corridor offer all-inclusive plans if you want to check into your hotel and stay put for the duration of your stay. Choosing that option means you'll have little reason to venture out and taste some of the diverse and remarkable food available in this region. These huge resorts offer high-quality facilities and pleasant service, to be sure, but guests looking to get a feel for the local culture may find the generic, chain-hotel atmosphere frustrating. For those wanting less Westernized slickness, and a more intimate experience of Mexican hospitality, checking into one of the many excellent smaller properties is the way to go.

If you're inclined to go beyond the beach-and-party vibe of Cabo San Lucas, it's well worth spending time in Todos Santos *(see Los Cabos Side Trips chapter)* and San José del Cabo. Both towns offer exceptional independent hotels and inns, as well as burgeoning art scenes, great restaurants, and ambience you won't find elsewhere.

PLANNING

WHEN TO GO
With its growing popularity, Los Cabos has a high season that seems to keep gaining months. It's been said that high season is now mid-November through May, though the crowds are a bit more manageable in October and after mid-April. Summers can be scorchers in this desert landscape, reaching temperatures in the 90s and above. No matter what time of year you visit, rain is pretty unlikely. Los Cabos gets most of its rain—about 15 days—between August and September, so book accordingly. Book your trip early—as many as six months in advance for top holidays such as Thanksgiving, Christmas, New Year's, and Easter, and at least three months in advance for other high-season stays. Note that during holidays, a seven-night minimum stay is required at most high-end resorts.

WHAT TO EXPECT
Bargains here are few; rooms generally start at $200 a night and can climb into the thousands. For groups of six or more planning an extended stay, condos or villas can be a convenient and economical option, though you should always book early.

Hotel rates in Baja California Sur are subject to a 16% sales tax. Service charges (at least 12%) and meals generally aren't included in hotel rates, except at some all-inclusive resorts. Several of the high-end properties include a daily service charge in your bill; be sure you know the policy before tipping (though additional tips are always welcome). We always list the available facilities, but we don't specify extra costs; so always ask about what's included.

CHOOSING THE RIGHT REGION
San José del Cabo is the closest to the international airport, and it's here that you'll be farthest from the crowds that gravitate toward downtown Cabo San Lucas's fiesta atmosphere. These towns have retained their Mexican colonial roots and are the most charming of Los Cabos region. Some boutique hotels and bed-and-breakfasts lie in or near the town centers of these very walkable towns, and others are more remote. For high-season stays, try to make reservations at least three months in advance, and six months in advance for holidays. Precious few lodgings serve travelers on a budget.

The Corridor—the stretch that connects San José with Cabo San Lucas—is booming with megaresorts. These microcosms contain two or more hotels, throughout which golf courses, private villas, and upscale condo projects are interspersed. ■ TIP→ **If you are planning a vacation in Los Cabos, do keep in mind that most of the beaches at the resorts along the Corridor are not swimmable.**

Cabo San Lucas continues its meteoric climb into the five-star stratosphere. Nearly every hotel in Cabo has undergone some kind of renovation following the 2014 Hurricane Odile. When Casa Dorada Resort opened, smack in the middle of busy El Médano Beach, it raised the bar in regards to rooms, services, and pampering, and The Resort at Pedregal and Grand Solmar Land's End have set a new high standard.

The rate of development in the area is astonishing, and begs the question of sustainability. As developable space in Los Cabos region diminishes and becomes prohibitively expensive, the newest expansions are moving beyond the Sea of Cortez coastline north of San José del Cabo, known as the "East Cape," and north of Cabo San Lucas along the Pacific coast. For years, building restrictions have been discussed, but money talks in every language. The only "restrictions" seem to be how much actual land is left.

ALL ABOUT ALL-INCLUSIVES

All-inclusives are like all-you-can-eat buffets—with all the positive and negative aspects included. You fork over the cash and just have at it, from the food and drink to an expansive pool complex and often water sports and excursions, too. You might consider this as one way for first-time visitors (especially families) to experience Los Cabos and not break the bank. The all-inclusive concept has come a long way since Club Med launched the concept decades ago. These days, all-inclusive properties are becoming more and more sophisticated, offering an impressive array of restaurants, bars, activities, and entertainment—and often striving to keep some local flavor present in the process. Note that while some all-inclusives offer endless complimentary amenities, others have a list (in fine print) of what you'll be billed for in the end.

WEDDINGS

If you decide to get married in Los Cabos, you'll be able to enjoy nuptials with friends and family in a gorgeous setting, and there'll be no worries about heading out for the honeymoon the morning after—you're already there. Los Cabos has a bevy of choices, and prices, for dream destination weddings. If money is no object, look into the big-name properties such as One&Only Palmilla, Las Ventanas al Paraíso, Esperanza, The Resort at Pedregal, Grand Velas, and the Marquis Los Cabos, where celebs often say "I do." Palmilla and Grand Velas even have official Directors of Celebrations to assist. At Las Ventanas, the Romance Director has an entire program dedicated to dream weddings, offering everything from a fireworks display to a ring bearer on horseback. But the true champion of weddings has got to be the Dreams Los Cabos property, where as many as five couples get hitched each week. *For more information on planning a wedding, civil ceremony, or civil union in Los Cabos, see Weddings in the Experience chapter.*

PRICES

WHAT IT COSTS IN DOLLARS			
$	$$	$$$	$$$$
Hotels	under $200	$200–$299	$300–$399	over $399

Hotel prices are the lowest cost of a standard double room in high season.

CABOS WITH KIDS

If you're heading down to Los Cabos with the little ones in tow, you're in luck, because many properties are kid-friendly. Unless they are adults-only properties, most of them welcome children with Kids' Clubs. *The properties that go out of their way to provide entertainment for kids are marked with "Family" in this chapter.* Many of the independent hotels listed don't restrict children, but their size and arrangement suggest more adult-oriented accommodations. We've mentioned these factors in our reviews.

CABO CONDOS

If you're planning to stay a week or more, renting a condo can be more economical and convenient than a hotel. Los Cabos has countless condominium properties, ranging from modest homes to ultraluxurious villas in such exclusive areas as Palmilla near San José del Cabo and the hill-clinging Pedregal neighborhood above Cabo San Lucas and its marina. Many private owners rent out their condos, either through the development's rental pool or property management companies. The price is the same for both, but with the latter you might get a better selection.

Nearly all condos are furnished and have a fully equipped kitchen, a television, bed and bath linens, laundry facilities, and maid service. Most are seaside and range from studios to three-bedroom units. A minimum stay of one week is typically required, though rules can vary by property. Start the booking process at least four months in advance, especially for high-season rentals.

CONTACTS

Cabo Homes and Condos. ☎ 866/321–CABO(2226) in U.S. ⊕ *www.cabohomesandcondos.com.*

Cabo Villas. Offering private villa vacation rentals, Cabo Villas represents several high-end homes at five-star properties throughout Los Cabos. ☎ 855/745–2226 in U.S. and Canada ⊕ *www.cabovillas.com.*

OUR REVIEWS

Use the coordinate (✛ 1:B2) at the end of each listing to locate a site on the corresponding maps. Hotel reviews have been shortened. For full information, visit Fodors.com.

SAN JOSÉ DEL CABO

If being in Mexico (and not in the thick of a hopping resort scene) is more your speed, Cabo San Lucas's sister city San José del Cabo is the place to base your stay. Its downtown, with century-old buildings and many elevated sidewalks, is a delight to explore on foot. Plaza Mijares, the open and popular *zócalo,* is graced by a fountain, lighted at night, and a stage where live music takes place frequently for the crowds who gather to stroll, enjoy ice cream, and relax after the heat of the day has let up. Several streets fronting the square are pedestrian-only, giving this historic downtown a lush and leisurely feel. Just beyond the center of town, and a bit farther south, is the ever-expanding Zona Hotelera, where a dozen or so hotels, timeshares, and condo projects face the long stretch of beach on the Sea of Cortez. Closer to the marina at Puerto los Cabos, the boutique El Ganzo Hotel and chain resorts like Secrets and JW Marriott have staked their claim, with plans for further development past La Playita.

$$$$
RESORT

⬛ **Cabo Azul Resort.** On the beach in San José del Cabo, this chic, white-washed property is peaceful from the moment you walk through the 20-foot antique door to a waterfall wall and Indian marble floors which lead to a breathtaking lobby centered by a circular rope structure dropping 1,200 feet from the ceiling. **Pros:** huge villas; sophisticated and elegant property; kids' club and designated pool for children. **Cons:** spotty Internet; beach not safe for swimming; not all rooms have ocean views. ⑤ *Rooms from: $450* ✉ *Paseo Malecón, Zona Hotelera* ☎ *624/163–5100, 877/216–2226 in U.S.* ⊕ *www.caboazulresort.com* ⇱ *346 rooms* ⑩ *No meals* ✚ *1:C5.*

$$
HOTEL
Fodor's Choice
★

⬛ **Casa Natalia.** An intimate, graceful boutique hotel, Casa Natalia is in the heart of San José's downtown and opens onto the zócalo. **Pros:** oasis in the heart of downtown; fantastic complimentary breakfast for superior rooms; lovely pool area. **Cons:** no bathtubs in the standard rooms; occasional noise from music and fiestas on Plaza Mijares. ⑤ *Rooms from: $245* ✉ *Blvd. Mijares 4, Centro* ☎ *624/146–7100* ⊕ *www.casa-natalia.com* ⇱ *19 rooms* ⑩ *Breakfast* ✚ *1:C2.*

$
HOTEL

⬛ **Encanto Inn & Suites.** In the heart of San José's Historic Arts District, this gorgeous and comfortable inn has two separate buildings—one looks onto the verdant gardens and pool; the other one, across the street, is in a charming, historic building with a narrow courtyard. **Pros:** Mexican-hacienda feeling; excellent location; pet friendly. **Cons:** staffing is minimal; no on-site parking; some rooms get street noise. ⑤ *Rooms from: $183* ✉ *Calle Morelos 133, Centro* ☎ *624/142–0388* ⊕ *www.elencantoinn.com* ⇱ *25 rooms* ⑩ *Breakfast* ✚ *1:C1.*

$$
RESORT
FAMILY

⬛ **Holiday Inn Resort Los Cabos.** As the last property in San José del Cabo's Hotel Zone, the familiar Holiday Inn brand here gets high marks for its attentive, friendly, old-world Mexican attitude among the staff members. **Pros:** Chiqui Kids' Club (ages 5–12); adults-only pool; free Wi-Fi. **Cons:** rooms tend to be basic; food is run-of-the-mill buffet-style restaurants; dated style. ⑤ *Rooms from: $235* ✉ *Blvd. Mijares at Paseo San José, cul-de-sac at end of Hotel Zone, Zona Hotelera* ☎ *624/142–9229* ⊕ *www.holidayinnresorts.com/loscabos* ⇱ *397 rooms* ⑩ *All-inclusive* ✚ *1:D4.*

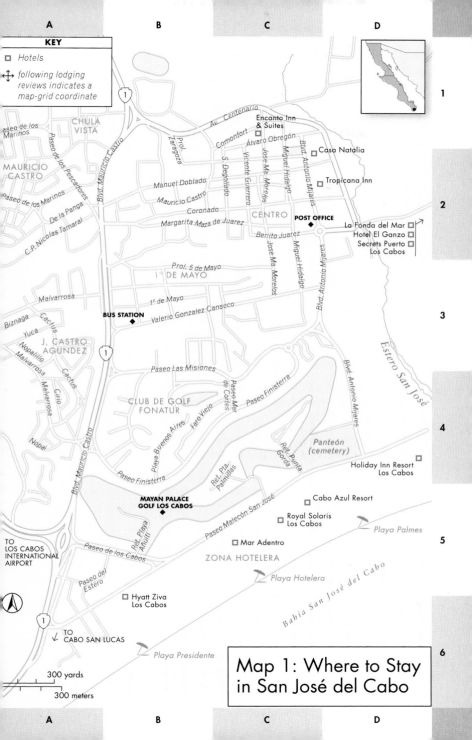

Map 1: Where to Stay in San José del Cabo

$$$$ ⬚ **Hotel El Ganzo.** Expression reins at this boutique hotel with an uber-
HOTEL   chic vibe where guests can interact with artists-in-residence, musicians,
and filmmakers in a creative and luxurious setting. **Pros:** an outlet for
artists; free beach cruisers to explore the cactus gardens; horseback riding and estuary kayak tours. **Cons:** must spend a minimum of $30 to use
the beach club; service does not match the price; no children under 18.
⑤ *Rooms from: $400* ⊠ *Tiburón s/n, La Playita, Marina* ☎ *624/104-*
9000 ⊕ *www.elganzo.com* ⤴ *70 rooms* ⦿ *No meals* ✛ *1:D2.*

$$$ ⬚ **Hyatt Ziva Los Cabos.** This resort is great for both families and
RESORT   couples looking for a complete getaway, featuring 592 suites, eight
FAMILY   restaurants ranging from French to Italian and Spanish to Japanese,
Fodor'sChoice   seven bars, four pools (including an adults-only option), and a Kids'
★   Club. **Pros:** great à la carte restaurant selection; spacious suites; Kids'
Club and adjacent water park offer diversion for little ones. **Cons:**
resort's size is a bit overwhelming; slow elevator; 30% of rooms lack
ocean views. ⑤ *Rooms from: $390* ⊠ *Paseo Malecon, Lote 5, Zona*
Hotelera ☎ *624/163–7730* ⊕ *loscabos.ziva.hyatt.com/en/hotel/home.*
html ⤴ *592 rooms* ⦿ *All-inclusive* ✛ *1:B6.*

$ ⬚ **La Fonda del Mar.** If you're looking for a peaceful back-to-nature
B&B/INN   retreat, check out this hotel on a long, secluded beach that straddles
the line between desert and ocean. **Pros:** beautiful beachfront property;
excellent full breakfast included in room rate; solar-powered. **Cons:**
located past La Playita which is far from town; no hot water or TVs;
payment is cash only; shared shower facilities. ⑤ *Rooms from: $120*
⊠ *Old East Cape Rd., La Playita* ✛ *Follow the signs to El Encanto de*
La Laguna or ask for directions to Buzzard's since many locals refer
to the hotel by the bar's name ☎ *624/145–2139 cell, 624/113–6368*
restaurant ⊕ *www.buzzardsbar.com* ▭ *No credit cards* ⤴ *4 rooms*
⦿ *Breakfast* ✛ *1:D2.*

$$$ ⬚ **Mar Adentro.** Despite the lack of signage out front, this place is
HOTEL   easy to spot as the only stark white resort in San José del Cabo, and
with its enormous water courtyard that reflects colors of the setting
sun. **Pros:** reasonably priced menu at Origin Restaurant; impressive
minimalist design; on-site cinema. **Cons:** form over function; non-
swimmable beach; two hotel towers closest to the beach are privately
owned. ⑤ *Rooms from: $350* ⊠ *Paseo Malecón San José Lote 8, Zona*
Hotelera ☎ *624/104–9999* ⊕ *www.maradentrocabos.com* ⤴ *250*
rooms ⦿ *No meals* ✛ *1:C5.*

$ ⬚ **Royal Solaris Los Cabos.** Royal Solaris was the first all-inclusive in
RENTAL   Los Cabos, and it runs smoothly like the established property it is,
FAMILY   with plenty of entertainment options and sports activities offered. **Pros:**
Kids' Club 9–5; climbing wall and mini water park; best value of the
all-inclusives. **Cons:** the accommodations and food only adequate;
not romantic; timeshare salespeople are pushy. ⑤ *Rooms from: $190*
⊠ *Paseo Malecon, Lote 10, Colonia Campo de Golf, Zona Hotelera*
☎ *624/145–6800, 877/270–0440 in U.S.* ⊕ *www.hotelessolaris.com*
⤴ *390 rooms* ⦿ *All-inclusive* ✛ *1:C5.*

$$$$ ⬚ **Secrets Puerto Los Cabos.** The first of the all-inclusive chains to reach
RESORT   La Playita, this adults-only resort has swim-up rooms, ocean views,
seven restaurants, and a 13,000-square-foot Spa by Pevonia. **Pros:**

nightly entertainment shows; plenty of activities; caters to adults. **Cons:** beach not swimmable; annoying timeshare pitches; no kids under 18. ⑤ *Rooms from: $550* ✉ *Av. Paseo de los Pescadores s/n, La Playita* ☎ *624/144–2600* ⊕ *www.secretsresorts.com* ⇄ *500 rooms* †⊙| *All-inclusive* ✛ *1:D2.*

$ ⌂ **Tropicana Inn.** It's not on the beach, but this hotel in a quiet enclave
HOTEL   along one of San José's main boulevards is a delightful, reasonable find. **Pros:** lively on-site restaurant and bar; rooms are immaculate; small on-site spa. **Cons:** positioned as adult escape but kids are allowed; poor views and lighting in some rooms. ⑤ *Rooms from: $113* ✉ *Blvd. Mijares 30, Centro* ☎ *624/142–1580* ⊕ *www.tropicanainn.com.mx* ⇄ *40 rooms* †⊙| *Breakfast* ✛ *1:D2.*

THE CORRIDOR

Even before the Corridor had an official name or even a paved road, the few hotels here were ritzy and elite; one even had its own private airstrip. As the saying goes, the more things change, the more they stay the same—developers have deliberately kept this area high-end and private. The Corridor is the most valuable strip of real estate in the region, with guard-gated exclusivity, golf courses, luxury developments, and unsurpassed views of the Sea of Cortez.

$$ ⌂ **Cabo Surf Hotel.** Professional and amateur surfers alike claim the
HOTEL   prime ocean-view rooms in this small hotel on the cliffs above Playa
Fodor's Choice   Costa Azul that has successfully blended surfing and pampering into
★   one property. **Pros:** blends surfing and pampering; hotel guests receive discount on surf lessons and rental; free yoga on weekends. **Cons:** traffic from the highway can be noisy; usually full as wedding parties tend to book the entire hotel. ⑤ *Rooms from: $279* ✉ *Hwy. 1, Km 28, The Corridor* ☎ *624/142–2676, 858/964–5117 in U.S.* ⊕ *www.cabosurf. com* ⇄ *36 rooms* †⊙| *No meals* ✛ *2:B6.*

$$$$ ⌂ **The Cape.** Of all the draws of this 2015 Thompson Hotel—from the
HOTEL   architectural masterpiece by Javier Sanchez to the breathtaking views of El Arco—perhaps the greatest appeal is the integration of nature like the spa set in natural rock formation or the boulders, cacti, and native plants that dot the grounds where two black buildings house sleek, modern rooms. **Pros:** great surf spot out front ; unbelievable view of the arch; beautifully designed. **Cons:** not ideal for children; pool area can get loud on weekends. ⑤ *Rooms from: $534* ✉ *Carretera Transpeninsular, Km 5, The Corridor* ☎ *624/163–0000* ⊕ *www.thompsonhotels. com* ⇄ *161 rooms* †⊙| *No meals* ✛ *2:C2.*

$$$ ⌂ **Casa del Mar Golf Resort & Spa.** Operating as both condos and a resort,
HOTEL   this hacienda-style gated community has guest rooms with white marble floors, dark beamed ceilings, and teak furnishings along with views of the sea and a beautiful white-sand beach. **Pros:** generous complimentary perks; great breakfast buffet and poolside service; intimate and peaceful atmosphere. **Cons:** hotel's 50 rooms are surrounded by 220 timeshare condos; undertow at beach; pushy timeshare pitch. ⑤ *Rooms from: $350* ✉ *Hwy. 1, Km 19.5, The Corridor* ☎ *624/145–7700* ⊕ *www. casadelmar.com.mx* ⇄ *50 rooms* †⊙| *No meals* ✛ *2:C4.*

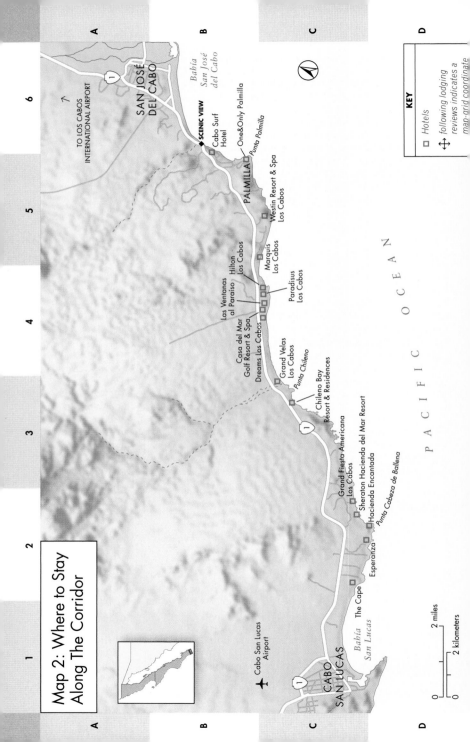

Map 2: Where to Stay Along The Corridor

TO LOS CABOS INTERNATIONAL AIRPORT

SAN JOSÉ DEL CABO

Bahía San José del Cabo

◆ SCENIC VIEW

Cabo Surf Hotel

One&Only Palmilla

Punta Palmilla

PALMILLA

Westin Resort & Spa Los Cabos

Marquis Los Cabos

Hilton Los Cabos

Paradisus Los Cabos

Las Ventanas al Paraíso

Casa del Mar Golf Resort & Spa

Dreams Los Cabos

Grand Velas Los Cabos

Punta Chileno

Chileno Bay Resort & Residences

Grand Fiesta Americana Los Cabos

Sheraton Hacienda del Mar Resort

Hacienda Encantada

Punta Cabeza de Ballena

Esperanza

The Cape

Cabo San Lucas Airport

Bahía San Lucas

CABO SAN LUCAS

P A C I F I C   O C E A N

KEY

□ *Hotels*

↔ *following lodging reviews indicates a map-grid coordinate*

2 miles

2 kilometers

A B C D — 1 2 3 4 5 6

$$$$
HOTEL
FAMILY

Chileno Bay Resort & Residences. Set on the protected cove of Chileno Bay, one of the best spots for snorkeling and swimming in Los Cabos, this 60-room hotel opened in 2017, and has hit the mark with families seeking personalized, informal service. **Pros:** ideal for families; pristine beaches with tranquil waters; infinity pool and oceanfront hot tubs. **Cons:** beach can get crowded with nonguests; construction along Corridor; no meal plans. $ *Rooms from: $430* ⌧ *Carratera Transpeninsular, Km 15, The Corridor* ☎ *884/207–9354* ⊕ *chilenobay.aubergeresorts. com* ⤳ *60 rooms* � ⃝ *No meals* ⊕ *2:C3.*

$$$$
RESORT
FAMILY

Dreams Los Cabos. This casual, unfussy resort is touted as a romantic getaway, but with an average of five weddings a week, it's more a destination for families and wedding parties with guests of all ages in attendance. **Pros:** Explorer's Club for kids; golf concierge; plenty to entertain. **Cons:** resort can sometimes feel overrun with children; food is abundant but cuisine is only average; $15 daily charge for Internet access. $ *Rooms from: $400* ⌧ *Hwy. 1, Km 18.5, The Corridor* ☎ *866/237–3267, 624/145–7600* ⊕ *www.dreamsresorts.com* ⤳ *308 suites* � ⃝ *All-inclusive* ⊕ *2:C4.*

$$$$
RESORT
Fodor's Choice
★

Esperanza. One of the most exquisite resorts in Los Cabos, focused on privacy and impeccable service, and home to one of the best spas in the region, Esperanza is true luxury. **Pros:** most private property in Los Cabos; two secluded white-sand beaches; casitas have ocean views and renovated interiors. **Cons:** the high cost of incidentals can get exhausting; wind can be fierce on the rocky cliffs. $ *Rooms from: $750* ⌧ *Hwy. 1, Km 7, Punta Ballena, The Corridor* ☎ *624/145–6400, 866/311–2226 in U.S.* ⊕ *www.esperanzaresort.com* ⤳ *57 rooms* � ⃝ *Breakfast* ⊕ *2:C2.*

$$$$
RESORT

Grand Fiesta Americana Los Cabos. The dramatic lobby of this all-inclusive resort is eight stories above the beach, and every room looks out onto the Sea of Cortez. **Pros:** every room has an ocean view; discounts to the spa and golf course; complimentary minibar and free kids' club. **Cons:** rocky beach; service is notoriously spotty; slow elevators. $ *Rooms from: $450* ⌧ *Cabo del Sol, Hwy. 1, Km 10.3, The Corridor* ☎ *624/145–6200, 866/927–7666* ⊕ *www.fiestamericanagrand.com* ⚑ *Jack Nicklaus Ocean Golf Course at Cabo del Sol* ⤳ *235 rooms, 14 suites* � ⃝ *All-inclusive* ⊕ *2:C2.*

$$$$
RESORT
Fodor's Choice
★

Grand Velas Los Cabos. With a curved, half-moon layout that ensures ocean views for all rooms, this luxury resort does not cut the usual "all inclusive" corners: instead the Grand Velas offers an excess of everything, from its spacious rooms (1,180-square-feet), each with an outdoor Jacuzzi, minibar, walk-in closet, and views of the ocean and three pools, to top-notch dining options, premium drinks, and excellent service. **Pros:** coolest Kids-and-Teens' clubs in Cabo; 2-Michelin-star chef at Cocina de Autor; tequila and mezcal tasting room. **Cons:** restaurants require reservations; rocky beach; construction in Corridor. $ *Rooms from: $800* ⌧ *Carretera Transpeninsular, Km 17.3, The Corridor* ☎ *624/104–9800* ⊕ *www.loscabos.grandvelas.com* ⤳ *304 rooms* � ⃝ *All-inclusive* ⊕ *2:C3.*

$$$$
RESORT

Hacienda Encantada. Despite the enormous size of this timeshare-resort hybrid, there are only 222 rooms, meaning guests are treated to 1,400-square-foot hacienda-styled suites. **Pros:** outstanding views; excellent taco bar; all-inclusive package includes dining at marina

5

The Esperanza resort boasts two secluded white-sand beaches.

restaurants. **Cons:** beach not swimmable; extra charge for premium alcohol, certain menu items, and room service; noisy golf carts putt around the property. $ *Rooms from: $400* ⊠ *Carretera Transpeninsular, Km 7.3, The Corridor* ☎ *624/163–5555, 877/797–0519 in U.S.* ⊕ *www.haciendaencantada.com* ➡ *222 rooms* ⦿ *All-inclusive; No meals* ✚ *2:C2.*

$$$
RESORT
FAMILY

⚏ **Hilton Los Cabos.** Rooms are spacious at this hacienda-style Hilton built on one of the Corridor's few swim-friendly beaches. **Pros:** 24-hour gym; 20% discount on greens fees; great cocktail bar. **Cons:** spa services are not up to par with the rest of the resort; $10 charge for Wi-Fi per day; one side of the pool is reserved for Vista Club members. $ *Rooms from: $350* ⊠ *Hwy. 1, Km 19.5, The Corridor* ☎ *624/145–6500, 800/HILTONS* ⊕ *www.hiltonloscabos.com* ➡ *322 rooms, 53 suites* ⦿ *No meals* ✚ *2:C4.*

$$$$
RESORT
Fodor's Choice
★

⚏ **Las Ventanas al Paraíso.** From the moment your private butler greets you with a foamy margarita and escorts you to the spa for a welcome massage, you know you're in for some serious pampering and a special experience. **Pros:** exceptional service; stellar dining and wine/tequila selection; experiences include whale safaris, magic show dinners, and more. **Cons:** there can be a four- to eight-night minimum depending on the season and holiday; 35% tax and gratuity added to every bill; dangerous riptides. $ *Rooms from: $950* ⊠ *Hwy. 1, Km 19.5, The Corridor* ☎ *624/144–2800, 888/ROSEWOOD in U.S.* ⊕ *www.lasventanas.com* ➡ *83 rooms* ⦿ *No meals; All meals; Some meals* ✚ *2:C4.*

$$$$
RESORT

⚏ **Marquis Los Cabos.** Stunning architecture, a property-wide art collection of unique pieces, noticeable attention to detail, and loads of luxurious touches make the Marquis a standout. **Pros:** tranquillity prevails for complete escape; exceptional full-service spa; five on-site restaurants. **Cons:** busy wedding venue; surf is unswimmable; open to nonguests for a fee. ⑤ *Rooms from: $592* ✉ *Carretera 1, Km 21.5, The Corridor* ☎ *624/144–2000, 877/238–9399* ⊕ *www.marquisloscabos.com* ⤴ *232 rooms* ⊗ *All-inclusive* ✛ *2:C5.*

$$$$
RESORT
Fodor's Choice
★

🏨 **One&Only Palmilla.** Built in 1956 by the son of the then-president of Mexico, and refreshed with multi-million-dollar renovations in 2015, the One&Only was the first resort in Los Cabos area, and it retains an old-world ambience and elegance, superior attention to detail and service, and its position as one of the most exclusive luxury resorts in the region. **Pros:** flawless service and amenities; complimentary tequila and snacks delivered daily by personal butler; notable dining options. **Cons:** prices are high; often boisterous groups mar the otherwise genteel atmosphere. ⑤ *Rooms from: $900* ✉ *Hwy. 1, Km 27.5, The Corridor* ☎ *624/146–7000, 866/829–2977 in U.S.* ⊕ *www.oneandonlyresorts.com* 🏌 *Jack Nicklaus–designed 18-hole course* ⤴ *176 rooms* ⊗ *No meals* ✛ *2:B5.*

> ## SURFING IN STYLE
>
> One&Only Palmilla offers guests a range of five-star surf tours with the acclaimed company Tropic Surf—the pioneer in "luxury surfing." Regardless of age or ability, guests can paddle into Cabo's best breaks in style, all with an emphasis on service, luxury, water safety, and improvement.

$$$$
RESORT

🏨 **Paradisus Los Cabos.** Remodeled for two years post–hurricane Odile, this former Meliá Cabo Real property now has fabulous rooms decorated in beachy tones of turquoise and gold, with private terraces overlooking the ocean or gardens as well as swim-up rooms, part of the Royal Service section open to adults only. **Pros:** near golf courses; decent rates; swimmable beach with man-made cove. **Cons:** Gastro Bar not part of all-inclusive plan; slippery pool area; loud music at pool carries into some rooms. ⑤ *Rooms from: $400* ✉ *Hwy 1, Km 19.5, The Corridor* ☎ *624/144–2218, 888/741–5600* ⊕ *www.melia.com* ⤴ *350 rooms* ⊗ *All-inclusive* ✛ *2:C4.*

$$
RESORT
FAMILY

🏨 **Sheraton Hacienda del Mar Resort.** Small domes and barrel tile roofs top eight buildings at this lovely, hacienda-style resort in the Cabo Del Sol development. **Pros:** rooms are serene and quiet; access to amazing golf courses; children under 17 stay free. **Cons:** beach is not usually good for swimming; thin walls; daily Internet fee. ⑤ *Rooms from: $220* ✉ *Cabo del Sol, Hwy. 1, Km 10, The Corridor* ☎ *624/145–8000, 800/325–3535 in U.S.* ⊕ *www.sheratonloscabos.com* 🏌 *All Cabo del Sol's courses are available to guests* ⤴ *270 rooms* ⊗ *No meals* ✛ *2:C2.*

$$
RESORT
FAMILY

🏨 **Westin Resort & Spa, Los Cabos.** Built by prominent Mexican artist Javier Sordo Madaleno, the colorful design and architecture reflecting the famous Arco (arch) makes this Westin more memorable than some of the others in the Corridor. **Pros:** good children's center; great gym with yoga and Pilates classes; multiple pools including an adults-only option; every room has an ocean view. **Cons:** it's a trek from the parking lot and lobby to the rooms and pools; lots of groups; daily Internet surcharge. ⑤ *Rooms from: $239* ✉ *Hwy. 1, Km 22.5, The Corridor* ☎ *624/142–9000, 888/625–5144 in U.S.* ⊕ *www.starwood.com/westin* ⤴ *147 rooms* ⊗ *No meals* ✛ *2:C5.*

5

One&Only Palmilla is a stunning seaside resort.

CABO SAN LUCAS

In Cabo San Lucas, there's a massive hotel on every available plot of waterfront turf. A pedestrian walkway known as the Marina Golden Zone is lined with restaurants, bars, and shops. It's anchored by the sleek Puerto Paraíso mall that curves around the entire perimeter of Cabo San Lucas harbor, itself packed with wall-to-wall sportfishing and pleasure yachts. Unfortunately, a five-story hotel complex at one edge of the harbor blocks a small portion of the water view and sea breezes from the town's side streets, but it can't be denied that Cabo is a carnival and a parade, all at once. The short Pacific coast beach just over the rocky hills at the west end of the marina has a more peaceful ambience, though monstrous hotel projects have gobbled up much of the sand here, too. If being right on the water isn't a primary concern, it is well worth checking out some of the smaller, independently owned hotels sprinkled around the downtown area. Several offer gracious, hacienda-style accommodations with a personal touch that huge hotels cannot match. For a tranquil setting close enough to all the action, opt for one of the resorts near Land's End.

$
B&B/INN
Fodor's Choice
★

The Bungalows Hotel. If solitude and a reasonable room rate are more important than being in the center of the action, Bungalows is your place. **Pros:** oasis-like property; excellent value; outstanding breakfasts. **Cons:** noise from traffic and surrounding neighborhood; a bit off the beaten path; 10 blocks to beach. *§ Rooms from: $165 ⊠ Blvd. Miguel Angel Herrera, Arenal ☎ 624/143–0585 ⊕ www.thebungalowshotel. com ➟ 16 rooms ⊙ Breakfast ✛ 3:A5.*

$
B&B/INN
Fodor's Choice
★

🏠 **Casa Bella.** The Ungson family had been in Cabo for more than four decades before turning their home across from Plaza San Lucas into the classiest and friendliest inn in the neighborhood. **Pros:** property feels totally secluded; private home ambience; stunning bathrooms, some with gardens. **Cons:** no TVs or phones in the rooms; some street noise; not kid friendly. $ *Rooms from: $160* ✉ *Calle Hidalgo 10, Centro* ☎ *624/143–6400, 818/392–8874 In U.S.* ⊕ *www.casabellahotel.com* ⤳ *14 rooms* ‖ *Breakfast* ✛ *3:A5.*

$$$$
RESORT
FAMILY

🏠 **Casa Dorada Los Cabos Resort & Spa.** Through the dramatic entry on the stone facade you'll find this seven-floor, all-suites combination hotel-timeshare has it all. **Pros:** beautifully appointed rooms; ocean views from every room; located at the heart of Playa Médano. **Cons:** noise from bars and clubs on beach in front of the hotel; timeshare sales-people are aggressive; extra charge for Wi-Fi. $ *Rooms from: $626* ✉ *Playa Médano, Av. del Pescador, Playa El Médano* ☎ *624/163–5757, 866/448–0151 toll-free in U.S.* ⊕ *www.casadorada.com* ⤳ *186 suites* ‖ *No meals* ✛ *3:C3.*

$$$$
RESORT
FAMILY

🏠 **Grand Solmar Land's End Resort & Spa.** Architecture melds perfectly with natural surroundings as luxury villas dramatically hug cliff and sea and subterranean stone passages open to infinity pools framed by cactus gardens and raked sand. **Pros:** ocean views; as close to El Arco as you can get; villas give a sense of home and isolation. **Cons:** beach not safe for swimming; hefty charge for in-room coffee, water, and Wi-Fi; also a timeshare. $ *Rooms from: $676* ✉ *Av. Solmar 1A, next to Solmar Resort, Centro* ☎ *624/144–2500* ⊕ *www.grandsolmarresort. com* ⤳ *263 rooms* ‖ *All-inclusive; No meals* ✛ *3:D6.*

$
HOTEL

🏠 **Hotel Mar de Cortez.** Another one of Cabo's original hotels, Hotel Mar is just four blocks from the marina, a block from the main square, near *muchos* restaurants, bars, clubs, and shopping. **Pros:** clean rooms and pleasant surroundings; good value; free Internet. **Cons:** noisy air-conditioning units; surrounding streets are busy and loud; spotty Wi-Fi. $ *Rooms from: $85* ✉ *Av. Lazaro Cardenas, between Vin-cente Guerrero and Matamoros, Cabo San Lucas* ☎ *624/143–0032, 800/347–8821 in U.S.* ⊕ *www.mardecortez.com* ☾ *Closed Sept.* ⤳ *104 rooms* ‖ *Breakfast* ✛ *3:A4.*

$
HOTEL

🏠 **Los Milagros.** A mosaic sign (crafted by co-owner Ricardo Rode) near the entrance hints at the beauty inside this small stylish inn offering a relaxed atmosphere and boutique feel without the boutique cost. **Pros:** quiet inn located close to everything in Cabo; one room is accessible to travelers with disabilities; free Wi-Fi and TVs in every room. **Cons:** air-conditioning units in rooms can be loud; pool is small and not heated; daily fee for parking in private lot. $ *Rooms from: $85* ✉ *Matamoros 116, Cabo San Lucas* ☎ *718/928–6647 in U.S., 624/143–4566* ⊕ *www. losmilagros.com.mx* ⤳ *12 rooms* ‖ *No meals* ✛ *3:A4.*

$$
RESORT

🏠 **Marina Fiesta Resort & Spa.** Though this colonial-style building is not ocean-side, most rooms have a pleasant view of the cloverleaf-shape pool and the yacht-filled marina. **Pros:** close to popular bars and shops; walking distance to Playa Médano; all-inclusive plan gives access to restaurants on marina. **Cons:** aggressive timeshare salespeople; no ocean views; center rooms are dated. $ *Rooms from: $257* ✉ *Marina,*

5

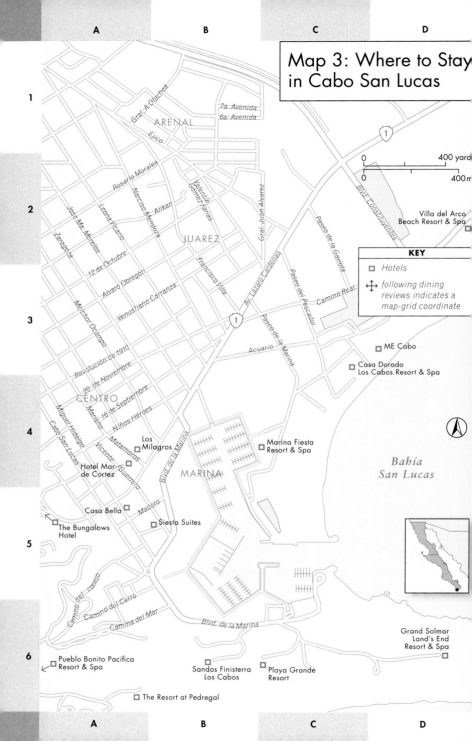

Map 3: Where to Stay in Cabo San Lucas

ARENAL

7a. Avenida
6a. Avenida

Grsl. A Obregón

Efico

Rosario Morales

Narciso Mendoza

Atikan

Valentín Gómez Farías

JUAREZ

Grsl. Juan Alvarez

Paseo de la Gaviota

José Ma. Morelos

Leona Vicario

12 de Octubre

Alvaro Obregón

Francisco Villa

Av. Lázaro Cárdenas

Paseo del Pescador

Camino Real

Zaragoza

Melchor Ocampo

Venustiano Carranza

Revolución de 1910

20 de Noviembre

CENTRO

16 de Septiembre

Mariano

Niños Héroes

Paseo de la Marina

Acuario

Miguel Hidalgo

Cabo San Lucas

Vicente Guerrero

Matamoros

Blvd. de la Marina

MARINA

Los Milagros

Hotel Mar de Cortez

Casa Bella

Madero

The Bungalows Hotel

Siesta Suites

Camino del Conejo

Camino del Cerro

Camino del Mar

Blvd. de la Marina

Marina Fiesta Resort & Spa

Bahía San Lucas

Villa del Arco Beach Resort & Spa

ME Cabo

Casa Dorado Los Cabos Resort & Spa

Blvd. Constituyentes

KEY

☐ Hotels

⬌ following dining reviews indicates a map-grid coordinate

Grand Solmar Land's End Resort & Spa

Pueblo Bonito Pacifica Resort & Spa

Sandos Finisterra Los Cabos

Playa Grande Resort

The Resort at Pedregal

0   400 yard
0   400 m

Lots 36 and 37, Marina San Lucas ☎ *624/145–6020, 877/243–4880 in U.S.* ⊕ *www.marinafiestaresort. com* ⤳ *155 rooms* ⦿ *All-inclusive; No meals* ✛ *3:B4.*

\$\$\$
RESORT ⏇ **ME Cabo.** In the middle of Médano's most popular beach is the ME, the Meliá brand's posh offering in Cabos San Lucas with its huge pool areas—including the most popular swim-up bar in Cabo—and hot tubs under the palms is a playground for adults (although children are allowed). **Pros:** great for adults and singles; situated on one of the few swimmable beaches in Los Cabos; comfortable rooms with modern amenities. **Cons:** affordable rooms are limited; crowded pool area with loud music; meals not included. ⑤ *Rooms from: $350* ✉ *Playa Médano, Cabo San Lucas* ☎ *624/145–7800, 877/954–8363 in U.S.* ⊕ *www.melia.com* ⤳ *150 rooms* ⦿ *No meals* ✛ *3:D3.*

\$\$
RESORT
FAMILY ⏇ **Playa Grande Resort.** This large, multicolor all-suite hotel complex on the beach looks a bit Las Vegas, even by Cabo standards, but it's got all kinds of activities and facilities, making it a great family vacation option. **Pros:** Playa Grande Spa is huge; putt-putt golf course and play structures; fabulous pools. **Cons:** fitness center and Internet charges apply; getting to and from rooms is time-consuming and confusing; expensive spa services. ⑤ *Rooms from: $200* ✉ *Av. Playa Grande 1, Cabo San Lucas* ☎ *624/145–7524, 800/344–3349 in U.S.* ⊕ *www.sol-mar.com* ⤳ *358 rooms* ⦿ *No meals* ✛ *3:C6.*

\$\$\$\$
RESORT ⏇ **Pueblo Bonito Pacifica Resort & Spa.** Considered a resort within a resort, The Towers at Pacifica, which opened in December 2016, make up the VIP section of the larger property, with a separate lounge bar, premium liquor, and spacious suites with living rooms and modern amenities. **Pros:** adults only; luxurious accommodations and service; beautiful views and cactus gardens. **Cons:** $40 charge for use of beach beds; beach is not swimmable; thin walls. ⑤ *Rooms from: $600* ✉ *Predio Paraiso Escondido, Cabo San Lucas* ☎ *624/142–9696, 800/990–8250 in U.S.* ⊕ *www.pueblobonitopacifica.com* ⤳ *140 rooms, 14 suites* ⦿ *All-inclusive* ✛ *3:A6.*

\$\$\$\$
RESORT
Fodor's Choice
★ ⏇ **The Resort at Pedregal.** The majestic Resort at Pedregal lies on Cabo San Lucas's most coveted parcel of land—an extraordinary, 24-acre site at the southern tip of the peninsula accessible by the private Dos Mares tunnel. **Pros:** every room has a plunge pool; outstanding spa; exceptional service and a staff that calls you by name. **Cons:** Pacific-side beach is not swimmable; not ideal for children; El Farallon restaurant is very expensive. ⑤ *Rooms from: $595* ✉ *Camino del Mar 1, Pedregal* ☎ *624/163–4300* ⊕ *www.theresortatpedregal.com* ⤳ *113 rooms* ⦿ *No meals* ✛ *3:A6.*

\$\$\$\$
RESORT ⏇ **Sandos Finisterra Los Cabos.** One of the first hotels built in Cabo, this all-inclusive resort retains a loyal clientele with great service, property upgrades, and a superb location perched on a hill overlooking the marina and the Pacific. **Pros:** fantastic location; rooms have either bay

A NOTE ON TIMESHARES

For some families who frequently like to get away to resorts, the timeshare concept can be an economical way to vacation. Timeshares are a big business in Los Cabos, and the offers are constant, especially as you walk through the town of Cabo San Lucas. Timeshare representatives at the airport and in many hotel lobbies will try to entice you to attend a presentation by offering free transportation, breakfast, and activities, or even attractive amounts of cash. These salespeople are a major downside to many expensive lodgings where you wouldn't expect to be harassed. Don't feel obligated to accept—presentations often last two hours or more and can be draining. If you're staying in a hotel that has timeshare units, aggressive salespeople may call your room every morning asking you to attend a free breakfast. If you're not interested, ask to be removed from their call list. Or, simply say "I live here," and they'll leave you alone.

or ocean view. **Cons:** beach is not swimmable; pushy timeshare pitch. $ *Rooms from: $500* ⊠ *Blvd. Marina, Cabo San Lucas* ☎ 624/145–6700 ⊕ *www.sandos.com* ⟿ *272 rooms* ⭐ *All-inclusive* ✛ *3:B6.*

$ ⚏ **Siesta Suites.** The owners keep a close eye on this four-story hotel—a
HOTEL calm refuge two blocks from the marina—and dispense great insider advice to visitors. **Pros:** friendly staff; barbecue area to cook catch of the day; quiet, simple, and affordable. **Cons:** limited off-street parking; no elevator; pool is small and is surrounded by tables from Salvatore's restaurant at night. $ *Rooms from: $69* ⊠ *Calle Zapata at Guerrero, Centro* ☎ 624/143–2773, 866/271–0952 *toll-free in U.S.* ⊕ *www. cabosiestasuites.com* ⟿ *5 rooms, 15 suites* ⭐ *No meals* ✛ *3:A5.*

$$ ⚏ **Villa del Arco Beach Resort & Spa.** As with its sister properties del
RESORT Palma and La Estancia, Villa del Arco offers comfortable, stylishly
FAMILY decorated one-, two- and three-bedroom suites and penthouses with all the amenities, including full kitchens, and bustling pools anchored by a pirate ship/restaurant docked within that delights kids of all ages. **Pros:** on-property deli and market; spacious, comfortable rooms; fabulous spa. **Cons:** service can be spotty; limited beach chairs are reserved by early morning; beach vendors can be pushy. $ *Rooms from: $293* ⊠ *Camino Viejo a San José, Km 0.5, Cabo San Lucas* ☎ 624/145–7200, 877/845–5247 *in U.S.* ⊕ *www.villagroupresorts. com* ⟿ *224 rooms* ⭐ *No meals* ✛ *3:D2.*

6

SHOPS AND SPAS

Updated
by Marlise
Kast-Myers

Los Cabos may not have many homegrown wares, but the stores are filled with beautiful and unusual items from all over mainland Mexico. You can find hand-painted blue Talavera tiles from Puebla; blue-and-yellow pottery from Guanajuato; black pottery from San Bartolo Coyotepec (near Oaxaca); hammocks from the Yucatán; embroidered clothing from Oaxaca, Chiapas, and the Yucatán; silver jewelry from Taxco; fire opals from Queretaro; and the fine beaded crafts of the Huichol tribe from Nayarit and Jalisco.

If you're on the hunt for custom or locally made goods, Fábrica de Vidrio Soplado (Blown-Glass Factory) in Los Cabos produces beautiful glassware. Dozens of shops will custom-design gold and silver jewelry for you, fashioning pieces in one to two days. Liquor shops sell a locally produced liqueur called *damiana*, which is touted as an aphrodisiac. A few shops will even create custom-designed bathing suits for you in a day or so. Additionally, national and international artists are opening galleries across the region as part of its burgeoning arts scene in Los Cabos, with many in San José del Cabo's rapidly evolving city center, and even more dotted throughout Todos Santos's historic downtown.

No longer hawking only the requisite T-shirts, belt buckles, and trinkets, Cabo's improved shopping scene has reached the high standards of other Mexican resorts. Its once-vacant streets are today lined with dozens of new shops, from open-air bazaars and souvenir shops to luxury malls and designer boutiques.

PLANNING

HOURS OF OPERATION

Many stores are open as early as 9 am, and often stay open until 9 or 10 pm. A few close for siesta at 1 pm or 2 pm, then reopen at 4 pm. About half of Los Cabos' shops close on Sunday; those that do open usually close up by 2 or 3 in the afternoon.

It's not uncommon to find some shops and galleries closed in San José del Cabo or Todos Santos during the hot season (roughly June to September), though very few shops close in Cabo San Lucas. We've noted this whenever possible; however, some shops simply close up for several weeks if things get excruciatingly slow or hot. In any case, low-season hours are usually reduced, so call ahead during that time of year.

A NOTE OF CAUTION

One of the benefits of traveling in Los Cabos is the low crime rate, thanks in part to the large population of expats and year-round tourists, and the *tranquilo* nature of locals. That being said, it's always wise to pay attention to what's going on when money is changing hands. Some tips: Watch that your credit card goes through the machine only once, so that no duplicates of your slip are made. If there's an error and a new slip needs to be drawn up, make sure the original is destroyed. Don't let your card leave a store without you. One scam is to ask you to wait while the clerk runs next door ostensibly to use another business's phone or to verify your number—but really to make extra copies. Again, this area is refreshingly safe and incident-free compared to many areas on the mainland, but it's always wise to be aware.

BEST LOCAL GIFTS AND SOUVENIRS

Cabo San Lucas is a great shopping town. Works of art by local artists make great treasures to take back home—and galleries will usually ship the items for you. T-shirts, resort wear, and clothing from hip Mexican designers will all compete for space in your suitcase.

If you're looking for something truly authentic and *hecho en Cabo* (made in Cabo), check out the blown glass at the intriguing **Fábrica de Vidrio Soplado**. Other fun souvenirs include the new labels of tequila offered from such outlets as Cabo Wabo, Hotel California in Todos Santos, the Cabo Surf Hotel, and Las Veritas, a popular Cabo dance club and bar.

SENDING STUFF HOME

Many stores and galleries offer shipping services for large or unwieldy items.

For more shipping info, see Travel Smart Los Cabos.

WHAT YOU CAN'T BRING HOME

Don't buy items made from tortoiseshell or any sea turtle products: it's illegal (Mexico's turtle species are endangered or threatened, and these items aren't allowed into the United States, Canada, or the United Kingdom). Cowboy boots, hats, and sandals made from the leather of endangered species such as crocodiles may also be taken from you at customs, as will birds, or stuffed iguanas or parrots. It isn't uncommon for U.S.

Customs agents to seize seashells, so those and all sea creatures are best left where you found them.

Both the U.S. and Mexican governments also have strict laws and guidelines about the import–export of antiquities. Check with customs beforehand if you plan to buy anything unusual or particularly valuable.

American visitors are allowed to bring back up to 100 cigars or $800 worth of Cuban cigars without paying a duty. Mexican cigars without the correct Mexican seals on the individual cigars and on the box may be confiscated. For those 21 and older, U.S. customs allows one liter of alcohol per person to be entered into the U.S. duty-free.

ART WALKS

Thursday art walks happen in downtown San José from November to June. Participating galleries and shops stay open until 9 pm and serve drinks and snacks, and many arrange for special events or openings. There is usually music on Plaza Mijares, and it's not uncommon for the streets to be full of people, locals and tourists alike. "Historic Art District" brochures are in most galleries and shops. ⊕ *www.artcabo.com.*

TIPS AND TRICKS

Better deals are often given to cash customers—even though credit cards are nearly always accepted—because stores must pay a commission to the credit-card companies. If you are paying in cash, it is perfectly reasonable to ask for a 5%–10% discount—though you shouldn't assume you'll be given one.

U.S. dollars are widely accepted in Los Cabos, although most shops pay a lower exchange rate than a bank (or ATM) or *casa de cambio* (money exchange).

Bargaining is common in markets and by beach vendors, who may ask as much as two or three times their bottom line. Occasionally an itinerant vendor will ask for the real value of the item, putting the energetic haggler into the awkward position of offering far too little. One vendor says he asks *norteamericanos* "for twice the asking price, since they always want to haggle." The trick is to know an item's true worth by comparison shopping. It's not necessary to bargain for already inexpensive trinkets like key chains or quartz-and-bead necklaces or bracelets.

HUICHOL SHOPPING TIPS

See also Art of the Huichol special feature in this chapter.

Beaded items: The smaller the beads, the more delicate and expensive the piece. Beads with larger holes are fine for stringed work, but if used in bowls and statuettes cheapen the piece.

Items made with iridescent beads from Japan are the priciest. Look for good-quality glass beads, definition, symmetry, and artful use of color. Beads should fit together tightly in straight lines, with no gaps.

Yarn paintings: Symmetry is not necessary, although there should be an overall sense of unity. Thinner thread results in finer, more costly work. Look for tightness, with no visible gaps or broken threads.

SHOPPING GLOSSARY

bakery: *panadería*	**market:** *mercado*
bookseller: *librería*	**notions store:** *mercería*
candy store: *dulcería*	**perfume store:** *perfumeria*
florist: *florería*	**shoe store:** *zapateria*
grocery store: *abarrotes*	**stationery store:** *papelería*
health-food store: *tienda naturista*	**tobacconist:** *tabaquería*
jewelry store: *joyería*	**toy store:** *juguetería*
laundromat: *lavanderia*	

Paintings should have a stamp of authenticity on the back, including artist's name and tribal affiliation.

Prayer arrows: Collectors and purists should look for the traditionally made arrows of brazilwood inserted into a bamboo shaft. The most interesting ones contain embroidery work, or tiny carved icons, or are painted with copal symbols indicative of their original, intended purpose, like protecting a child or ensuring a successful corn crop.

SAN JOSÉ DEL CABO

Cabo San Lucas's sister city has a refined air, with many shops in old colonial buildings just a short walk from the town's *zócalo* (central plaza). Jewelry and art are great buys—this is where you'll find the best shopping for high-quality Mexican folk art. Many of the most worthwhile shops are clustered within a few of blocks around Plaza Mijares, where Boulevard Mijares and Avenida Zaragoza both end at the zócalo at the center of San José. Thursday nights from November to June are designated Art Nights, when galleries stay open until 9 serving drinks and snacks, with various performances, demonstrations, and dancing.

ART GALLERIES

Casa Dahlia Fine Art Gallery. Casa Dahlia Fine Art Gallery features contemporary artists from Mexico and abroad, and invites visitors to linger in its beautifully renovated historic building. ⊠ *Morelos and Zaragoza, San José del Cabo* ☎ 624/166–0262 *cell, 720/346–3286 in U.S.* ⊕ *www. leahporter.com* ☯ *Closed weekends.*

Frank Arnold Gallery. Frank Arnold Gallery has two big draws: it's arguably the best gallery space in town, in a modern building by local architect Alfredo Gomez; and it holds Frank Arnold's dramatic, widely acclaimed contemporary paintings that have been compared to de Kooning, Gorky, and Hans Hofmann. The gallery also features bronze sculptures and fine art prints. ⊠ *1137 Calle Comonfort, San José del Cabo* ☎ 624/142–4422, *559/301–1148 in U.S.* ⊕ *www.frankarnoldart.com.*

SELF-GUIDED GALLERY WALK IN SAN JOSÉ

A good number of galleries are closed, or have greatly reduced operating hours, during the hottest months of the year, usually late June through September. If there is one gallery you are particularly interested in, it's worth calling ahead to check on hours.

The Thursday art walks start at 5 pm, with galleries open until 9 pm. Start your walk on Hidalgo and Obregón, and wander down Obregón through the six or so galleries scattered on the next two blocks. Turning left on to Guerrero, you'll want to stop in to see **Galería de Ida Victoria**. Turn right out of the galleries and walk a block over to Comonfort, where you'll connect to Morelos in another block to find the galleries in **Casa Paulina** awaiting, and the **Frank Arnold Gallery** a half block farther up on Comonfort. If you're hungry, head to **Baja Brewing Company** on Morelos at Comonfort. Finish up by heading back to the zócalo and wandering among the shops on Plaza Mijares—making sure not to miss **silvermoon gallery**.

Galería Corsica. Galería Corsica is in a spectacularly dramatic space. The gallery, which has two sister galleries in Puerto Vallarta, shows museum-quality fine art with an emphasis on paintings and large, impressive sculpture pieces. ⊠ *Alvaro Obregon 10, San José del Cabo* 🕾 *624/146–9177* ⊕ *www.galeriacorsica.com.*

Galería de Ida Victoria. Galería de Ida Victoria has been designed with skylights and domes to show off the international art contained within its three floors, which includes paintings, sculpture, photography, and prints. ⊠ *Guerrero 1128, between Zaragoza and Obregon, San José del Cabo* 🕾 *624/142–5772* ⊕ *www.idavictoriagallery.com* ⊗ *Closed Sun.*

La Dolce Art Gallery. Near San José's classic cathedral on the zócalo, La Dolce Art Gallery specializes in modern painting styles. ⊠ *Hidalgo between Zaragoza and Obregón, San José del Cabo* 🕾 *624/142–6621* ⊕ *www.alecalderoni.com* ⊗ *Closed Mon.*

Fodor's Choice
★ **Patricia Mendoza Gallery.** Explore works of art by Mexico's top contemporary artists such as Eduardo Mejorada, Javier Guadarrama, Jorge Marín, Victor Mora, Luis Filcer, and Joao Rodriguez, among others. All of the artists represented here are known nationally and internationally in important collections and museums. ⊠ *Obregón at Hidalgo, San José del Cabo* 🕾 *624/158–6497, 624/105–2270* ⊕ *www.patriciamendoza-gallery.com* ⊗ *Closed Sun.*

silvermoon gallery. silvermoon gallery is remarkable in Los Cabos region both for the assortment and the quality of art contained within its walls. Mexican folk art makes up most of the inventory here. Treasures include Carlos Albert's whimsical papier-mâché sculptures, Mata Ortiz pottery from the Quezada family, Huichol yarn "paintings," Alebrijes (colorful wooden animal sculptures) from Oaxaca, and fine jewelry. Owner Armando Sanchez Icaza is gracious and knowledgeable; he knows volumes about the artists whose work he carries. His silversmiths can also make custom jewelry for you within a day or two. ⊠ *Plaza Mijares 10, San José del Cabo* 🕾 *624/142–6077* ⊗ *Closed Sun.*

CLOTHING

Curios 3 Marias. This souvenir shop carries T-shirts, embroidered dresses, and all sorts of other fun goodies, curios, knickknacks, and clothing items to pick up for folks at home. ⊠ *Blvd. Mijares at Manuel Doblado, Centro* ☎ *624/105–2366.*

FOLK ART AND CERAMICS

Curios Carmela. Curios Carmela displays an almost overwhelming array of Mexican textiles, pottery, glassware, hammocks, clothing, and souvenirs, but with a bit of searching you'll find some great bargains. ⊠ *Blvd. Mijares 43, San José del Cabo* ☎ *624/142–1617* ☞ *No sign on the building.*

El Armario. Calling itself "the cutest shop in town," El Amario offers a selection of Mexican folk art, ceramic pottery, candles, clay figurines, and papier-mâché—plus fresh coffee out on the patio. ⊠ *Obregón at Morelos, San José del Cabo* ☎ *624/105–2989* ⊗ *Closed Sun.*

La Sacristia Art & History. La Sacristia has a fine selection of Talavera pottery, traditional and contemporary Mexican jewelry, blown glass, and contemporary paintings. The glassware is incredible. ⊠ *Hidalgo 9, at Alvaro Obregón, San José del Cabo* ☎ *624/142–4007* ⊕ *www.artcabo.com/la-sacristia.html.*

Necri. Known for their hand-painted Talavera pottery from Puebla and Guanajuato, this store also sells ceramics, handicrafts, black pottery, Majolica dinnerware, and pewter pieces. ⊠ *Calle Alvaro Obregón 17, San José del Cabo* ☎ *624/130–7500* ⊕ *www.necri.com.mx* ⊗ *Closed Sun.*

HOME FURNISHINGS

Casa Paulina. More than just an art gallery, Casa Paulina inspires decorating ideas with items for the home. Candles, lamps, chairs, throws, and enormous clay pots are a few of the treasures you might find. ⊠ *Plaza Paulina, Morelos at Comonfort, San José del Cabo* ☎ *624/142–5555* ⊕ *www.casapaulina.com.*

JEWELRY

Artwalk Shop. This small boutique at Casa Natalia has jewelry, handbags, and art made from recycled metals. Artwalk also has a good selection of brass jewelry from Mexico City. ⊠ *Blvd. Mijares 4, at Casa Natalia, San José del Cabo* ☎ *624/146–7100* ⊕ *www.casanatalia.com/artwalk-shop-gallery* ⊗ *Closed Tues.*

MALLS

Plaza Artesanos. With a block of 75 stalls, Plaza Artesanos has a wide selection of handmade crafts and souvenirs, including pottery, jewelry, blankets, clothing, hammocks, leather bags, and even pure Mexican vanilla extract. Don't be afraid to barter by starting at half the asking price and then meeting somewhere in the middle. ⊠ *Blvd. Mijares, between Valerio Gonzalez and Paseo Finisterra, San José del Cabo* ☎ *624/143–7353, 762/105–5384.*

Plaza del Pescador. An outdoor mall conveniently located across the street from San José del Cabo's string of resorts, Plaza del Pescador offers guests an alternative to hotel dining. You'll find everything from sushi and gelato to tapas and a wine bar. Among the 25 shops and restaurants are a bookstore, jewelry store, fitness gym, and coffee shop. ⊠ *Paseo Malecon, Local 21A, across from Cabo Azul Resort, San José del Cabo* ☎ *624/142–3436* ⊕ *www.plazadelpescador.com.*

MARKETS

FAMILY **Farmer's Market** (*San José del Cabo Mercado Organico*). Get your organic fix at the *Mercado Organico* every Saturday 9–3 between November and May. Jewelry, artwork, soaps, fruit, and vegetables are a few of the goodies you'll find here. Food stalls serve everything from tacos to pizza, and entertainment is offered for kids. ⊠ *Margarita Maza de Juarez, between Benito Juarez and Vincente Guerrero Col 8 de Octubre, San José del Cabo* ☎ *624/142–0948* ⊕ *www.sanjomo.com* ⊗ *Closed June–Oct.*

SPAS

Paz Spa. Surrounded by natural stone walls, all of the treatment rooms at Cabo Azul's Paz Spa are named after semiprecious stones such as onyx, pearl, opal, lapis, jade, and amber. Specialties include 50-minute massages to 210-minute complete experiences, as well as exfoliations, wraps, facials, manicure, and pedicure. A terrace suite can accommodate up to four treatments at one time for those looking for group relaxation. Seven other rooms round out the spa itself, and two double cabanas on the beach are available for those seeking the sound of the waves as backdrop to their treatment. Popular therapies include a Papaya Sugar Polish and Shea Butter Massage, as well as an Aloe Cooling Massage. An on-site salon is open Monday to Saturday 9–5. ⊠ *Cabo Azul Resort, Paseo Malecón s/n Lote 11 Fonatur, San José del Cabo* ☎ *624/163–5100* ⊕ *www.caboazulresort.com.*

The Spa at Hyatt Ziva. The concept at Hyatt Ziva's spa is to explore water, earth, and air. Lounge by the communal pool or duck into one of 19 treatment rooms for revitalizing massages, romantic packages, anti-aging facials, detoxifying body wraps, and deep-cleansing scrubs using local, natural ingredients. For those interested in a quick fix, manicures and pedicures are popular, and the on-site salon can help turn a bad-hair day into something grand. ⊠ *Hyatt Ziva Los Cabos, Paseo Malecon s/n Lote 5, San José del Cabo* ☎ *624/163–7730* ⊕ *loscabos.ziva.hyatt.com* 🕮 *Day Pass: $145. Body treatments: $110–$285. Facials: $75–$240.*

SUNDRIES AND LIQUOR

Los Barriles de Don Malaquias. Go beyond Cuervo and Patrón at Los Barriles de Don Malaquias, which specializes in rare tequilas. The tequila selection is complemented by a good collection of Cuban cigars. Owner Rigoberto Cuervo Rosales is often on-site to offer tequila tastings. ⊠ *Blvd. Mijares at Juárez, San José del Cabo* ☎ *624/130–7800.*

The Market. From the maker of Flora Farms, this corner store sells all things organic including fresh fruit, pickled vegetables, soaps, jams, honey, coffee, and body oils. It's a great place to grab a healthy snack or stock up on produce delivered daily from Flora's local farm. ⊠ *Morelos at corner of Alvaro Obregon, San José del Cabo* ☎ *624/142–1665* ⊕ *www.flora-farms.com* ☺ *Closed Sun.*

THE CORRIDOR

There are shopping options along the Corridor—the stretch of land between San José del Cabo to the east and Cabo San Lucas to the west—but the shops cater more to resort guests and American expats than to travelers looking to experience Los Cabos. The closest thing you'll find to a shopping mall here is Las Tiendas de Palmilla, across from Palmilla Resort, with fewer than a dozen shops, galleries, and restaurants. Unless you're in search of something specific at one of the shops on the Corridor, you'll have much more fun shopping in San José del Cabo, Cabo San Lucas, or Todos Santos.

MALLS

Fodor'sChoice **Koral Center** (*El Merkado*). Conveniently located in the Corridor, ★ the Koral Center houses stores, medical facilities, a day spa, and El Merkado—a gourmet food court that converges 20 culinary offerings and the latest in Mexican gastronomy. You'll find everything from tacos and tapas to sushi and an organic market selling local products. ⊠ *Carretera Transpeninsular, Km 24.5, Cerro Colorado, The Corridor* ☎ *624/122–3840* ⊕ *www.koralcenter.com.*

Las Tiendas de Palmilla. Las Tiendas de Palmilla is across from the posh Palmilla Resort. There is a smattering of shops and galleries, a couple of restaurants, a coffee shop, a nice terrace with a peaceful fountain, and a view of the Palmilla development with the Sea of Cortez beyond. **Antigua de México** is a branch of the famous Tlaquepaque store, and shoppers will discover distinctive furniture and bedding supplies, and many Mexican-flavor interior-decorating items. **Pez Gordo Art Gallery** is artist Dana Leib's second location, and offers her pieces, as well as those by other artists. Stop in **Casa Vieja** for beautiful women's apparel by Mexican designers, including Pineda-Covalin—you'll find a wide range of styles in fibers such as cotton, silk, linen, and even cactus. If you need to fuel up during your time here, there's an outpost of popular **Nick-San**, and **Cream Cafe.** ⊠ *Hwy. 1, Km 27.5, The Corridor* ☎ *624/144–6999* ⊕ *www.lastiendasdepalmilla.com.*

SPAS

Fodor'sChoice **One&Only Palmilla Spa.** Therapists lead you through a locked gate into ★ peaceful palm-filled gardens with a bubbling hot tub and a daybed covered with plump pillows. There are 13 private treatment villas for up to two people; 7 are equipped with an outdoor shower, bathtub, and thatched-roof daybed for relaxing in between or after treatments.

Each treatment begins with a Floral Footbath, including the signature Secret Garden Remedy, using oil infused with herbs grown on-site. Achy athletes can opt for the surfers or golfers massage. The spa also boasts a yoga pavilion, juice bar, Amanda George hair salon, and a 1920s-style barber shop for men. For the ultimate in relaxation, try the Baja Deep Tissue Pindas Ritual—two hours that combine a scalp massage, hot stones, and deep pressure. ⊠ *Hwy. 1, Km 27.5, The Corridor* ☎ *624/146–7000* ⊕ *www.palmilla.oneandonlyresorts. com* ✉ *Body treatments: $250–$450. Facials: $175–$250. Mani/Pedi: $55–$150. Parking: Valet (free).*

SOMMA Wine Spa. SOMMA is the only spa of its kind in Mexico, with only seven others throughout the world. The concept spa uses grapes from the up-and-coming Valle de Guadalupe wine region just outside of Ensenada. It's an unusual experience blended with classical treatments, focusing on the calming, cosmetic, and antioxidant properties of grapes and wine, or vinotherapy. It towers high above the Sea of Cortez with 15 treatment rooms, both indoor and open-air, and offers a geothermal hot spring and more than 33 facial and body treatments from a Champagne Mud Wrap to a Le Vine Massage. ⊠ *Fiesta Americana Grand Resort, Hwy. 1, Km 10.3, Cabo del Sol, The Corridor* ☎ *624/145–6287* ⊕ *www.fiestamericanagrand.com/mx-los-cabos/hotel-grand-los-cabos* ✉ *Body treatments: $80–$250. Facials: $170–$234. Mani/Pedi: $40–$60.* ☞ *Parking: Valet and self-parking.*

The Spa at Esperanza. At the exclusive, 17-acre Esperanza Resort between Cabo San Lucas and San José del Cabo the beautiful spa is reached by way of a stone path over a koi pond. At check-in you're presented with an *agua fresca*, a healthy drink made with papaya or mango, or other fruits and herbs. Treatments incorporate local ingredients, tropical fruits, and ocean-based products. Look for such pampering as the papaya-mango body polish, the grated-coconut-and-lime exfoliation, and the four-hands massage. Yoga classes are held at 7:15 and 9 each morning for $35 (free for hotel guests). ⊠ *Esperanza Resort, Hwy. 1, Km 7, The Corridor* ☎ *624/145–6406* ⊕ *www.esperanzaresort. com* ✉ *Body treatments: $160–$335. Facials: $160–$295. Mani/Pedi: $45–$200.* ☞ *Parking: Valet (free).*

The Spa at Las Ventanas al Paraíso. Known for its innovative treatments— nopal (cactus) anticellulite and detox wrap, crystal healing massages, and raindrop therapy, the Spa at Las Ventanas has both indoor and outdoor facilities. Some of the eight treatment rooms have private patios, and the two couples' suites come with a private butler. Healing rituals like the Holistic Twilight Ceremony are performed daily. Salt glows and massages are available in a pavilion by the sea. There are also pampering treatments for kids (Mommy and Me) and couples (Sea and Stars). ⊠ *Las Ventanas al Paraíso Resort, Hwy. 1, Km 19.5, The Corridor* ☎ *624/144–0300* ⊕ *www.lasventanas.com* ✉ *Body treatments: $185–$900. Facials: $220–$410. Mani/Pedi: $45–$145.* ☞ *Parking: Valet (free).*

CABO SAN LUCAS

Cabo San Lucas has the widest variety of shopping options in Los Cabos area, with everything from intriguing Mexican folk art and designer clothing to beer holsters and touristy T-shirts. Bargains on typical Mexican tourist items can be found in the dozens of shops between Boulevard Paseo de la Marina and Avenida Lazaro Cárdenas.

If you get hungry when you're shopping, it's worth trying the inexpensive taco and juice stands tucked into the mini–flea markets that stretch between streets.

Many of the shops in malls like Puerto Paraíso are typical of those you'd find in any mall in the United States—with prices to match. All over the downtown and marina areas, however, are great shops and galleries with unique and compelling items.

ART GALLERIES

Sergio Bustamante. The talented artist from Guadalajara has a shop in the Puerto Paraíso Mall. Bustamante's works initially focused on painting and papier-mâché. His sculptures in resin and bronze, many reflecting animal themes, can be purchased at this wonderful gallery and store. Ceramic sculptures and an extensive line of exquisite jewelry in bronze, gold, and silver, many set with precious and semiprecious stones, are found here as well. Don't balk at the price tags: each piece belongs to a limited edition and is created by hand. ⊠ *Puerto Paraíso Mall, Cabo San Lucas* ☎ *866/300–8030 in U.S., 624/144–4895* ⊕ *www.sergiobustamante.com.mx.*

CLOTHING

Almarte Boutique. This lovely boutique sells designer clothing, silver jewelry, candles, art, books, and even items featured throughout The Resort at Pedregal such as headboards, doors, and tableware. If you've been admiring the glass-blown hearts dangling from leaf-barren Torote Trees throughout Cabo, this is the place to buy them. The women's line of beach-elegant clothing includes linens, silks, hats and loose-knitted flowing wraps. Some of their highly recognized designers include Chan Luu, Gillian Julius, Minnie Rose, Tom Ford, Jade Tribe, and Roberto Tirado. The store is open to the public; simply notify security at the main gate. ⊠ *The Resort at Pedregal, Camino del Mar 1, El Pedregal, Marina San Lucas* ☎ *624/163–4300* ⊕ *www. theresortatpedregal.com.*

Dos Lunas. Dos Lunas is full of trendy, colorful sportswear and straw hats, as well as a large selection of handcrafted accessories, bags, and gifts. ⊠ *Plaza Bonita, Blvd. Marina, Cabo San Lucas* ☎ *624/143–1969* ⊕ *www.loscabos-tourism.com/cabo/doslunas* ⊙ *Closed Sun.*

Pepita's Magic of the Moon. A favorite among locals and Cabo regulars, Magic of the Moon features clothing designed by Pepita Nelson, the owner. If you can't find anything that fits you or your style, she will design an outfit for you and finish it in three days. Also check out the

Continued on page 125

THE ART OF THE HUICHOL

Updated by
Georgia de Katona

The intricately woven and beaded designs of the Huichols' art are as vibrant and fascinating as the traditions of its people, best known as the "Peyote People" for their traditional and ceremonial use of the hallucinogenic drug. Peyote-inspired visions are thought to be messages from God and are reflected in the art.

Like the Lacandon Maya, the Huichol resisted assimilation by Spanish invaders, fleeing to inhospitable mountains and remote valleys. There they retained their pantheistic religion in which shamans lead the community in spiritual matters and the use of peyote facilitates communication directly with God.

Roads didn't reach larger Huichol communities until the mid-20th century, bringing electricity and other modern distractions. The collision with the outside world has had pros and cons, but art lovers have only benefited from their increased access to intricately patterned woven and beaded goods. Today the traditional souls that remain on the land—a significant population of perhaps 6,000 to 8,000— still create votive bowls, prayer arrows, jewelry, and bags, and sell them to finance elaborate religious ceremonies. The pieces go for as little as $5 or as much as $5,000, depending on the skill and fame of the artist and quality of materials.

(left) Huichol yarn painting, National Museum of Anthropology, (top) Huichol art, Puerto Vallarta

UNDERSTANDING THE HUICHOL

When Spanish conquistadors arrived in the early 16th century, the Huichol, unwilling to work as slaves on the haciendas of the Spanish or to adopt their religion, fled to the Sierra Madre. They lived there, disconnected from society, for nearly 500 years. Beginning in the 1970s, roads and electricity made their way to tiny Huichol towns. Today, about half of the population of perhaps 7,000 continues to live in ancestral villages and *rancheritas* (tiny individual farms).

THE POWER OF PRAYER

They believe that without their prayers and offerings the sun wouldn't rise, the earth would cease spinning. It is hard, then, for them to reconcile their poverty with the relative easy living of "free-riders" (Huichol term for non-spiritual freeloaders) who enjoy fine cars and expensive houses thanks to the Huichols efforts to sustain the planet. But rather than hold our reckless materialism against us, the Huichol add us to their prayers.

THE PEYOTE PEOPLE

Visions inspired by the hallucinogenic peyote cactus are considered by the Huichol to be messages from God and to help in solving personal and communal problems. Indirectly, they provide inspiration for their almost psychedelic art. Just a generation or two ago, an-

nual peyote-gathering pilgrimages were done on foot. Today the journey is still a man's chief obligation, but they now drive to the holy site at Wiricuta, in San Luis Potosi State.

SHAMANISM

A Huichol man has a lifelong calling as a shaman. There are two shamanic paths: the path of the wolf, which is more aggressive, demanding, and powerful (wolf shamans profess the ability to morph into wolves); and the path of the deer, which is playful. A shaman chooses his own path.

BEADED ITEMS

The smaller the beads, the more delicate and expensive the piece. Items made with iridescent beads from Japan are the priciest. Look for good-quality glass beads, definition, symmetry, and artful use of color. Beads should fit together tightly in straight lines, with no gaps.

YARN PAINTINGS

Symmetry is not necessary, although there should be an overall sense of unity. Thinner thread results in finer, more costly work. Look for tightness, with no visible gaps or broken threads. Paintings should have a stamp of authenticity on the back, including artist's name and tribal affiliation.

PRAYER ARROWS

Collectors and purists should look for the traditionally made arrows of brazilwood inserted into a bamboo shaft. The most interesting ones contain embroidery work, or tiny carved icons, or are painted with copal symbols indicative of their original intended purpose, for example protecting a child or ensuring a successful corn crop.

Huichol bird, Jalisco

HOW TO READ THE SYMBOLS

Spiders that come out at dawn are thought to welcome the rising sun.

The deer is the animal manifestation of the god Kahumari, who intercedes in heaven on earthlings' behalf.

Anything with horns or antlers symbolizes communion and oneness with God.

Yarn painting

■ The trilogy of corn, peyote, and deer represents three aspects of God. According to Huichol mythology, peyote sprang up in the footprints of the deer. Depicted like stylized flowers, peyote represents communication with God. Corn, the Huichol's staple

Corn symbol

food, symbolizes health and prosperity. An image drawn inside the root ball depicts the essence of God within it.

■ The double-headed eagle is the emblem of the omnipresent sky god.

Peyote

■ A nierika is a portal between the spirit world and our own. Often in the form of a yarn painting, a nierika can be round or square.

■ Salamanders and turtles are associated with rain; the former provoke the clouds. Turtles maintain underground springs and purify water.

■ A scorpion is the soldier of the sun.

Scorpion

■ The Huichol depict raindrops as tiny snakes; in yarn paintings they descend to enrich the fields.

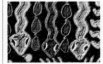

Snakes

Jose Beníctez Sánchez, (1938—2009) may be the elder statesman of yarn painters and has shown in Japan, Spain, the U.S., and at the Museum of Modern Art in Mexico City.

TRADITION TRANSFORMED

The art of the Huichol was, for centuries, made from undyed wool, shells, stones, and other natural materials. It was not until the 1970s that the Huichol began incorporating bright, zingy colors, without sacrificing the intricate patterns and symbols used for centuries. The result is strenuously colorful, yet dignified.

YARN PAINTINGS

Dramatic and vivid yarn paintings are highly symbolic, stylized visions of life.

MASKS AND ANIMAL STATUETTES

Bead-covered wooden or ceramic masks and animal statuettes are other adaptations made for outsiders.

PRAYER ARROWS

Made for every ceremony, prayer arrows send petitions winging to God.

VOTIVE BOWLS

Ceremonial votive bowls, made from gourds, are decorated with bright, stylized beadwork.

WOVEN SHOULDER BAGS

Carried by men, the bags are decorated with traditional Huichol icons.

For years, Huichol men as well as women wore BEADED BRACELETS; today earrings and necklaces are also made.

Diamond-shape GOD'S EYES of sticks and yarn protect children from harm.

People in Glass Houses

The Glass Factory (*Fábrica de Vidrio Soplado*). A beautiful glass mosaic over the entrance to Fábrica de Vidrio Soplado (Blown-Glass Factory) welcomes Los Cabos' most famous artisans every day. Founded in 1988 by engineer Sebastian Romo, the factory uses a glassmaking process close to the one first developed in western Asia 4,000 years ago, later refined into glassblowing during the Roman empire. At the factory, 30 artisans produce more than 500 pieces a day from hundreds of pounds of locally recycled glass. Visitors watch while crushed recycled glass is liquefied in gas-fired ovens and, seconds later, transformed into exquisite figures. Secrets for making the thick glassware's deep blues, greens, and reds—the result of special mixtures of metals and gold—are passed from generation to generation. You are sometimes invited to make your own glassware by blowing through a hollow rod to shape a glob of molten glass at the end. ⊠ *Calle General Juan Álvarez, between Captain Manuel Pineda and 7ª Ave., Centro ⊹ Off the Todos Santos bypass* ☎ *624/143–0255* ⊕ *www.glassfactory.com.mx.*

handmade ceramic jewelry, beaded bustiers, and colorful bathing suits. ⊠ *Madero between Guererro and Blvd. Marina, next to J&J, Cabo San Lucas* ☎ *624/144–6131* ☉ *Closed Sun.*

FOLK ART

Zen-Mar Gallery. This friendly place carries hundreds of masks, Day of the Dead figures, rugs, glassware, bark-paper wall hangings from Puebla, and all sorts of other fun and captivating items. This is one of Cabo's more comprehensive folk-art shops. ⊠ *Cárdenas between Matamoros and Ocampo, Cabo San Lucas* ☎ *624/143–0661.*

FOOD

Cabo Coffee Company. The aroma of roasting coffee lures locals and visitors alike into Cabo Coffee company, where you can also find refreshing smoothies, cookies, and muffins. The organic green coffee beans are flown fresh from Oaxaca, where they are roasted and bagged for sale. The store sells a number of Starbucks-like flavored coffee drinks and chai tea, as well as ice cream. There is also a book exchange with a few good beach reads. ⊠ *Madero at Hidalgo, Cabo San Lucas* ☎ *624/105–1754* ⊕ *www.cabocoffee.com.*

California Ranch Market. The area's best organic grocery store, California Ranch Market, offers a good selection of imported wines, cheeses, and other gourmet delicacies, as well as American food brands. Freshly squeezed juices and handmade paninis are also available. ⊠ *Camino del Cerro at Blvd. Marina, Cabo San Lucas* ☎ *624/143–1947* ⊕ *www. californiaranchmarket.com.*

GIFTS

Waboutique. Associated with the funky Cabo Wabo bar, Waboutique sells memorabilia, excellent tequila, and souvenirs such as baseball hats, shot glasses, and mugs with the Cabo Wabo logo. ⊠ *Calle Guerrero between Madero and Lazaro Cárdenas, Cabo San Lucas* ☎ *624/143–1188* ⊕ *www.cabowabo.com.*

JEWELRY

Diamonds International. Certified master jewelers are on staff at Diamonds International. This store sells impressive diamonds, designer jewelry, and luxury timepieces. A second branch is in the Puerto Paraíso Mall. ⊠ *Corner of Vicente Guerrero and Blvd. Paseo de la Marina, Centro* ☎ *624/145–8812 Vincente Guerrero location, 624/105–0810 Puerto Paraíso Mall* ⊕ *www.diamondsinternational.com.*

Ultrajewels. Rolex, Cartier, Tiffany & Co., Mikimoto, TAG Heuer, Omega, Montblanc, and many other top names are offered at Ultrajewels, often at discounted prices. ⊠ *Blvd. Marina, Malecón corner, Cabo San Lucas* ✛ *Below Lorenzillo's Restaurant* ☎ *624/163–4280* ⊕ *www.ultrajewels.com.*

MALLS

Luxury Avenue. An indoor mall housing luxury boutiques like Coach, Fendi, Montblanc, and Cartier, Luxury Avenue is your one-stop shopping for upscale items in Cabo. It's open daily 10 am–9 pm. There is a second branch in Cancún, Mexico. ⊠ *Av. Lazaro Cardenas, adjacent to Puerto Paraíso Mall, Marina San Lucas* ☎ *624/163–4280* ⊕ *www. luxuryavenue.com.*

Marina Golden Zone. There are a number of shops and attractions at the Marina Golden Zone, made up of Puerto Paraíso Mall, Marina Fiesta Resort, and Luxury Avenue Boutique Mall. The latter is a collection of famous designer boutiques selling Coach, Fendi, Chopard, and Montblanc, all under one roof. It's worth coming here just to stroll along the boardwalk. ⊠ *Marina San Lucas, Cabo San Lucas* ⊕ *www. goldenzonecabo.com.*

Plaza Bonita. Plaza Bonita is a pleasant place to stroll; it's located at the western edge of the marina and has a few shops ranging from leather and clothing to local artwork and souvenirs. You'll also find an ATM, pharmacy, and Starbucks. ⊠ *Blvd. Marina at Av. Cárdenas, Cabo San Lucas.*

Plaza del Sol. This open-air market has vendors selling local souvenirs like sarongs, sombreros, bathing suit cover-ups, and beaded necklaces. It's also home to the popular palapa bar, Uno Mas. ⊠ *Blvd. Paseo at the corner of the marina, next to Cabo Wabo, Marina San Lucas.*

Puerto Paraíso Mall. As Los Cabos continues on its upscale trajectory, it's safe to declare that this region has arrived and the shopping here has gone palatial. There is no better, or more apt, way to describe Puerto Paraíso, the city's thriving, air-conditioned, three-story marble- and glass-enclosed mall. With well more than 100 stores, boutiques, restaurants, galleries, and services, it's quickly becoming the social center of San Lucas. Paraíso offers a dizzying selection of stores. You can have a steak at **Ruth's Chris Steak House;** custom-design your own bikini; shop for beautiful art glass; or rent (or even buy) a Harley-Davidson motorcycle—almost anything is possible in this shopper's paradise. **Sergio Bustamante,** an acclaimed silversmith and sculptor, has a store here, and clothing shops include **Tommy Bahama, Hugo Boss,** and beachwear boutiques such as **Allegra, Azul, Pacific Blue, Tropica Calipso, Beach House,** and **Nautica.** A 10-screen movie-theater complex provides cinematic respite, and, the third floor is home to a play area for children and a small casino. Puerto Paraíso is connected to Luxury Avenue, a string of designer boutiques offering top brands like Cartier, Coach, Fendi, and Montblanc. ⊠ *Av. Cárdenas, Marina San Lucas* ☎ *624/144–3000* ⊕ *www.puertoparaiso.mx.*

> ### DUTY-FREE DELIGHT
>
> **Ultrafemme.** Ultrafemme is the quintessential duty-free shop offering prices that can be up to 30% off designer cosmetic and perfume lines, and name-brand selection of fine jewelry and watches (Rolex, Cartier, and Omega). ⊠ *Luxury Ave. Boutique Mall, Lázaro Cárdenas St., Cabo San Lucas* ☎ *624/163–4280* ⊕ *www.ultrafemme.com.*

SPAS

Aromian Spa at Pueblo Bonito Pacifica. This resort complex on the Pacific side of Cabo is an adults-only property, filled with feng shui design, immaculately kept cactus gardens, and water, water, everywhere. Treatments at the Aromian Spa run the gamut from crystal Reiki healing to a yogurt-and-violets exfoliation, and even spa treatments for kids at their neighboring sister property, Pueblo Bonito Sunset Beach. ⊠ *Pueblo Bonita Pacifica Resort, Predio Paraiso Escondido, Cabo San Lucas* ☎ *624/143–9696* ⊕ *www.pueblobonitopacifica.com* 🗌 *Body treatments: $130–$330. Facials: $90–$275. Hair: $25–$110. Mani/Pedi: $35–$62.*

Luna y Mar Spa. The "Mood and Sea" Spa at The Resort at Pedregal promises a revitalizing escape with treatments based around the themes of moon, sea, and Mexican healing. The 10 treatment rooms in this body-melting spa, easily one of the best in the region, offer guests passage to the ultimate in relaxation. Cascading pools create a soothing sound track to the kneading of top technicians. Beyond body and skin treatments, the facility has a hair and salon, fitness center, and tennis courts. ⊠ *The Resort at Pedregal, Camino Del Mar, Marina San Lucas* ☎ *624/163–4300* ⊕ *www.theresortatpedregal.com* 🗌 *Body treatments: $145–$360. Facials: $175–$240.*

Playa Grande Spa. Playa Grande's spa is known for its thalassotherapy treatments, which come from the practice of using seawater baths and seaweed-based treatments for prevention and curative purposes. Their signature treatment "All in One" combines such techniques as Swedish, deep tissue, hot stone, and bamboo reeds to roll and knead the muscles into a state of extreme relaxation. ⊠ *Playa Grande Resort, Av. Playa Grande 1, Playa Solmar, Cabo San Lucas* ☎ *624/145–7575* ⊕ *www.playagranderesort.com* 🖃 *Body treatments: $175–$250. Facials: $130–$175. Hair: $30–$190. Mani/ Pedi: $30–$60. Waxing: $20–$60.*

TOBACCO AND LIQUOR

J&J Casa de los Habanos. This is the best place to find quality Cuban and international cigars, lighters, and ashtrays as well as tequila and Cuban coffee. You can schedule a tequila tasting or try one of their sturdy margaritas while you shop for cigars. ⊠ *Madero at Blvd. Marina, Cabo San Lucas* ☎ *624/143–6160* ⊕ *www.jnjcabo.com.*

7

NIGHTLIFE

Updated by Marlise Kast-Myers

Crowds roam the main strip of Cabo San Lucas every night from happy hour through last call, staggering home just before dawn. It's not hard to see why this is *the* nightlife capital of southern Baja.

Cabo is internationally famous (or infamous) for being a raucous party town, especially during spring break. Nightlife in San José del Cabo, though, is more about a good drink and conversation.

Between the two towns, the self-contained resorts along the Corridor have a nightlife of their own; you can find a fabulous cocktail at their upscale restaurants and bars.

It's not all about the parties though; enjoying a fine dinner is a time-honored way to spend a Los Cabos evening. During the slow, sweltering months of August and September, some establishments curtail their offerings, or close for a few weeks altogether. Don't fret, though: you'll find nightlife here no matter what season you visit.

PLANNING

WHAT'S WHERE

San José del Cabo: Proprietors here say that you "graduate" to San José del Cabo after you sow the wild oats of your youth in Cabo San Lucas. For a cozy, romantic, and often cultural evening, nothing beats the quieter and more intimate San José nightlife.

The Corridor: This sprawling strip between the two cities is the province of big resorts and their in-house bars. Expect upscale venues (and patrons). A few nightspots not affiliated with any hotel do exist here and are quite popular.

Cabo San Lucas: If Vegas hadn't already co-opted the "what happens here, stays here," mentality, Cabo San Lucas might have snatched it up. You can experience spring break here, even if you went to college 30 years ago. Quiet Cabo nightlife does exist; you just need to look a bit harder.

WHAT TO WEAR

Think casual-classy when taking in dance clubs such as El Squid Roe. For the upscale bars and clubs such as Mandala, you'll feel out of place wearing flip-flops. "Gringo" means less formal. Shorts and T-shirts are acceptable at the Giggling Marlin. "No shoes, no shirt, no service" is always followed here.

WHAT IT COSTS

Baja's very own Tecate can be pricier here than at home. Many places compete for the best happy-hour deals, often about $2 for a cerveza. Margaritas cost around $5. A glass of wine in an upscale venue should run $9 and up. The rowdy beach bars in Cabo San Lucas have waitresses blowing whistles while handing out test tubes of vodka. Don't be fooled—there's a charge and tip behind each offer, so expect to pay around $5 for each. Many places add a 15%–20% tip to your tab. (Look for the word "*servicio*" on your bill.) A big musical event means a nominal cover charge of a few dollars; those are rare.

WHAT'S GOING ON

You'll find copies of Los Cabos publications in hotels, restaurants, and bars all over the city. The most helpful are *Los Cabos Visitors Guide* and *Los Cabos Magazine*. The free English-language newspapers *Gringo Gazette* (⊕ *www.gringogazette.com*) and *Destino: Los Cabos* (⊕ *www.destinomagazine.com*) offer timely and cultural articles on the ever-changing scene. (We especially like the *Gringo Gazette* for its fun-loving, humorous look at expatriate life in Los Cabos.) The English-Spanish *Los Cabos News* (⊕ *www.loscabos-news.com.mx*) is also a good source for local event listings. These publications are available free at many hotels and stores or at racks on the sidewalk.

SAFETY

Nighttime is reasonably safe and secure here. Ask the bar or restaurant to call a taxi for you if you're going far. Taxis aren't cheap, but you shouldn't put a price on getting home safely. All the standard precautions apply: stick to well-lighted areas where people congregate. Wandering dark, deserted streets or lonely stretches of beaches is never wise, nor is staggering home in a state of inebriation.

DRINKING AGE/SMOKING RULES

Mexico's nationwide drinking age is 18. Bars here check IDs at the door if they have any doubts about your age. Consumption of alcohol or the possession of an open beverage container is not permitted on public sidewalks, streets, or beaches (outside of licensed establishments), or in motor vehicles, whether moving or stationary.

Smoking is prohibited in all enclosed businesses, including bars and restaurants. Lighting up is allowed at outdoor-seating areas provided by such venues, but not indoors.

SAN JOSÉ DEL CABO

After-dark action in San José del Cabo caters mostly to locals and tourists seeking tranquillity and seclusion. There are no big dance clubs or discos in San José. What little nightlife there is revolves around restaurants, casual bars, and large hotels. A pre- or post-dinner stroll makes a wonderful addition to any San José evening. When night falls, people begin to fill the streets, many of them hurrying off to evening Mass when they hear the church bells peal from the central plaza.

A number of galleries hold court in central San José del Cabo, creating the **San José del Cabo Art District**. It's just north and east of the town's cathedral, primarily along Obregón, Morelos, and Guerrero streets. On Thursday nights (5–9 pm) from November to June, visit the **Art Walk,** where you can meander around about 15 galleries, sampling wine and cheese as you go.

BARS

Baja Brewing Co. The Baja Brewing Co. serves cold, on-site–microbrewed cerveza and international pub fare. You'll find entrées ranging from ahi tuna quesadillas to basil-and-blue-cheese burgers. Our favorite of the eight beers is the Baja Blond Ale; the BBC also brews Oatmeal Stout, Raspberry Lager, homemade root beer, and a dark, smooth Black Scorpion. If you can't make up your mind, order the sampler. Brewery tours take place weekdays at 4 pm. ⊠ *Morelos 1277 and Obregón, San José del Cabo* ☏ *624/142–1292* ⊕ *www.bajabrewingcompany.com.*

Dvur at Casa Don Rodrigo. Come here for the ambience and cocktails (the food has mixed reviews) like the blackberry mojito or house margarita. Once the home of the owner's grandparents, the building dates back to 1927 and its original brick walls are still intact, adorned with historic family photographs. The courtyard, strung with lanterns and fairy lights, is a pleasant place to enjoy the live mariachi, offered Thursday to Saturday 8–10. ⊠ *Blvd. Antonio Mijares 29, San José del Cabo* ☏ *624/166–9439, 624/142–0418.*

Jazz Tapas Bar. Paying tribute to jazz legends, this bar in Plaza del Pescador combines wine, tapas, and musically inspired artwork in a stylish setting. Try their Tapas Sampler and Big Jazz Mojito while listening to the smooth sounds of the live band, which plays Mondays and Fridays 7:30–10:30 pm. ⊠ *Plaza del Pescador, Paseo Malecon San José, Local 8, across from Cabo Azul Resort, San José del Cabo* ☏ *624/147–0181* ⊕ *www.jazztapasbar.com.*

La Osteria. Live music on Thursdays and Fridays coupled with the refreshing cocktails make this one of the best spots to grab a drink in San José del Cabo. Acoustic guitars add to the quaint atmosphere you'll find in the lantern-lit, stone courtyard. Tapas make a tasty accompaniment to the house sangrias. ⊠ *Alvaro Obregon 1207, across from Salsitas, San José del Cabo* ☏ *624/146–9696* ⊕ *laosteria.restaurantwebexperts.com* ☾ *Closed Sun.*

Shooters. For a gringo-friendly atmosphere where you can order a Budweiser and watch sports on big-screen TVs, head to Shooters, a rooftop bar overlooking the main square. Open daily 9 am–11 pm, breakfast

Hagar's Hangout: Cabo Wabo

According to local lore, in the mid-1980s former Van Halen lead singer Sammy Hagar and a friend were walking along the beach in Cabo San Lucas when they passed a drunk man stumbling. Hagar remarked, "Hey, he's doing the Cabo Wabo." A few years later, in 1990, Hagar and the rest of Van Halen opened the bar called Cabo Wabo—establishing one of the premier stops on the Cabo party circuit. When the group broke up in 1996, all but Hagar sold their shares in the bar.

Mexican and American rock bands perform every night. Almost always packed, the place erupts during Hagar's birthday celebration around October 13, when the legend himself drops in to play. When not on tour,

Hagar stops in at Cabo Wabo up to 10 times throughout the year. Visit the club's website for an events calendar. ⊕ www.cabowabo.com.

Often accompanying Hagar are his musician friends, like Chris Isaak, Kirk Hammett of Metallica, David Crosby, Slash, Rob Zombie, the Cult, and the Sex Pistols.

The lighthouse replica at the entrance makes the bar easy to spot from afar. Designed by architect Marco Monroy, Cabo Wabo has cavernous ceilings and walls adorned with painted zebra stripes and psychedelic neon patterns. Hagar liked Monroy's work so much that he had the bar's design re-created for his set on the Red Voodoo tour.

7

and lunch are both busy times. Be sure to order a 25-peso (just more than $1) beer. ⊠ Manuel Doblado at Blvd. Mijares, San José del Cabo ☎ 624/146–9900 ⊕ www.shootersbar.com.mx.

Tropicana Inn. The Tropicana Inn's bar is a great place to mingle and enjoy live music. Conversation is usually possible on the terrace overlooking the bar and stage, though when a good band gets going, you'll be too busy dancing to talk. Flamenco and mariachi bands play Thursday through Sunday 7:30– 10:30 pm. ⊠ Blvd. Mijares 30, San José del Cabo ☎ 624/142–1580 ⊕ www.tropicanainn.com.mx.

THE CORRIDOR

Nightlife along Highway 1 between San José del Cabo and Cabos San Lucas historically consists of hotel bars in big resorts, most of which are frequented only by their guests. A few stand-alone places have sprung up in recent years, including the chic Privé nightclub. A taxi or car is the best way to reach these places. Because walking home is generally not an option unless you're staying in-house or next door, nightlife ends early out here, with most bars turning off the lights around 10 or 11 pm. Head to Cabo San Lucas if you want to party later.

BARS

Latitude 22+ Roadhouse. This noisy, friendly roadhouse always attracts gringos looking to down a shot of tequila, sip cold beer, and mingle with old or new friends. The menu features good, dependable, and mostly

American fare. From October to June they host live music, ranging in style from pop to blues to country. ⊠ *Hwy. 1, Km 4.5, The Corridor* ☎ *624/143–1516* ⊕ *www.latno2baddays.com* ⊙ *Closed Sun.*

La Vista. As far as posh hotel bars go, it's hard to top the Hilton Los Cabos' La Vista, whose terrace overlooks the Sea of Cortez. There's nothing raucous here, just intimate conversation over wine and cocktails, with complimentary hors d'oeuvres 5–6 pm. ⊠ *Hilton Los Cabos, Hwy. 1, Km 19.5, The Corridor* ☎ *624/145–6500* ⊕ *www.hiltonloscabos.com.*

The Lounge Bar. The name sounds rather utilitarian, but the dim lighting and intimate ambience here are anything but. Enjoy stunning views of El Arco—you are, after all, on the Cabo San Lucas end of the Corridor—at Esperanza's elegant bar and lounge on lush couches. Linger over quiet drinks or smoke a cigar as you listen to the sounds of the ocean. There's live music nightly at 7 pm. ⊠ *Esperanza Resort, Hwy. 1, Km 7, Manzana 10, Punta Ballena, The Corridor* ☎ *624/145–6400* ⊕ *www.esperanzaresort.com.*

Fodor's Choice ★ **The Rooftop.** For drinks with a view of El Arco, head to The Rooftop bar and lounge at Cape Hotel. The sleek setting boasts a beer garden, handcrafted cocktails, and live music at sunset. If it gets too breezy, move to their Glass Box boutique hotel bar specializing in tequilas and mezcals. ⊠ *At The Cape Hotel, Carretera Transpeninsular, Km 5, The Corridor* ☎ *624/163–0000* ⊕ *www.thompsonhotels.com.*

Sunset Point. This casual wine-and-pizza lounge is a colorful rooftop hot spot that shares the same stunning view of famous Los Cabos Arch as its downstairs counterpart, Sunset de Mona Lisa. With a selection of more than 140 wines and Champagnes, complemented by free tapas daily 5–6 pm, this is the place to watch the sun set over light bites and cocktails. ⊠ *At Mona Lisa Sunset Restaurant, near Misiones Condos and Hotel, Carretera Transpeninsular, Km 6.5, Bello Plaza del Rey 7 and 8, The Corridor* ☎ *624/145–8077, 624/145–8260* ⊕ *www.sunsetmonalisa.com.*

Zipper's. Named for the nearby surf break, beachfront Zipper's attracts a mixed crowd of surfers and nonsurfers alike. A good selection of beer, as well as ribs and burgers, is always on hand, with live music weekdays and Sunday. ⊠ *Hwy. 1, Km 28.5, The Corridor* ☎ *624/172–6162.*

CABO SAN LUCAS

The epicenter of Cabo San Lucas nightlife is along the Marina San Lucas and the two streets that run parallel beyond it. You'll walk a gauntlet of servers waving menus in your face, but the sidewalk bars along the marina between Plaza Bonita and Puerto Paraíso are great during happy hour and late into the night. Many bars also serve during the day several times a week when cruise ships are in port.

Watch out for the tequila shooters and Jell-O shots forced upon revelers by merry waiters—they usually cost at least $5 each. Topless bars and "gentlemen's" clubs are abundant (their "showgirls" signs give them away). Single men are often accosted outside San Lucas bars with offers of drugs and sex. Be careful in this area, and be aware that the police may be behind some of these solicitations.

BARS

Baja Brewing Co. The Cabo San Lucas branch of the microbrewery in San José del Cabo shares the same menu and selection of beers on tap. Yet the partially open space atop a seaside hotel lends a decidedly different, relaxed vibe. Perfect after a day at the beach, enjoy live music, ranging from Cuban to rock to funk, Thursday through Saturday. There is a third BBC location on the ground floor of the nearby Cabo Marina's Puerto Paraiso Mall. ⊠ *Rooftop of Cabo Villas, Médano Beach, Cabo San Lucas* ☎ *624/143–9166* ⊕ *www.bajabrewingcompany.com.*

Billygan's Island. The once boisterous Billygan's Island on Médano Beach is now one of the more tame spots on the sand. The bikini dance contests may be a thing of the past, but you can still get great deals on margaritas and buckets of beer (five beers for $12). ⊠ *Médano Beach, Cabo San Lucas* ☎ *624/143–3435, 624/144–3908.*

Blue Marlin Ibiza. Miami meets Cabo at this restaurant, bar, and club with an over-the-top feeling of luxury. White gauze canopies shade plush sun beds and lounge chairs around multiple swimming pools, while DJs spin until 6 pm daily. Their sushi menu pairs well with a fruity cocktail and will help keep the buzz under control. ⊠ *ME Cabo Hotel, Playa Médano, Cabo San Lucas* ☎ *624/145–7800* ⊕ *www.bluemarlinibizaloscabos.com.*

Dos Mares. Sophisticated, tranquil, and comfortable, Dos Mares offers a peaceful, panoramic view of the fishing yachts in the Marina San Lucas. Snack on shrimp, scallops, and oysters while sipping two-for-one margaritas during happy hour 11 am–5 pm. ⊠ *De la Darsena Lote 18 Col. Centro, on Marina boardwalk, near Puerto Paraíso Mall, Marina San Lucas* ☎ *624/143–0582* ⊕ *www.barometro.com.mx.*

Las Varitas. Las Varitas, one of Cabo's most popular clubs, is a branch of La Paz rock club favored by young Mexicans. Local and internationally famous Latin rock bands perform here almost every night, and the establishment even boasts its own label of house tequila. ⊠ *Paseo de la Marina, near corner of Camino Viejo San José, Cabo San Lucas* ☎ *624/143–9999* ☺ *Closed Sun.*

Mango Deck. Feel like getting a little bit rowdy and dancing in the sand? Overlooking the arch, Mango Deck is a happening spot every day of the week, with live music and DJs spinning until 11 pm. ⊠ *At the western end of El Médano Beach, near the Casa Dorada resort, Cabo San Lucas* ☎ *624/143–0901* ⊕ *www.mangodeckcabo.com.*

Nowhere ¿Bar? Local professionals loosen up over beers while exuberant tourists have too much fun at the Nowhere ¿Bar? Two-for-one drinks and a lively dance floor are a big draw here. Reckless gyrating isn't strictly limited to the dance floor, though—don't be at all surprised to see people busting a move on the tables from early evening on. Sushi and tacos are served from adjacent restaurants. ⊠ *Plaza Bonita, Blvd. Marina 17, Cabo San Lucas* ☎ *624/143–4493* ⊕ *www.nowherebar.com.*

The Office. The Office began as a place to rent windsurfing equipment, and expanded into a bar/eatery now famous for its seafood and goblet-size margaritas. Despite the fact that the floor here is the sand, this place is a tad more upscale than the other venues on Médano Beach. On

Thursdays 7–9 pm is a musical show with Mexican folk dancer—a little touristy, but always a crowd-pleaser. There's live music nightly 7–9:45 pm. ⊠ *Médano Beach, between Mango Deck and Billygan's Island, Cabo San Lucas* ☎ *624/143–3464* ⊕ *www.theofficeonthebeach.com.*

Fodor'sChoice
★

Slim's Elbow Room. Slim's calls itself "the world's smallest bar," and you'll be lucky to get a seat at this kitschy four-seat space that plays honky-tonk music and serves $3 beers and tequila shots. Signed dollar bills line the walls and ceiling, and a buzzing, standing crowd loiters out the door and onto the Boulevard Marina sidewalk each evening, vibing off its energy. ⊠ *Plaza de los Mariachis, Blvd. Marina, Cabo San Lucas* ⊕ *www.slimscabo.com.*

Tanga Tanga. Tanga Tanga, which has both an outdoor and indoor bar, is a hot and popular spot for listening to live music, playing pool or darts, and watching sports on big-screen TVs. Local reggae and rock groups play here most afternoons and nights. Margaritas are plentiful, and the wings are extra spicy! ⊠ *Plaza de la Danza, Blvd. Marina, Cabo San Lucas* ☎ *624/144–4501.*

Uno Mas. This tiny palapa bar outside of Cabo Wabo is the type of place you stumble on—and you might wind up stumbling out of it after "una mas" cold one. Grab a bar stool and order your favorite cocktail made with fresh squeezed juice. Pace yourself as these drinks have been known to pack a punch—not to mention the bartender starts shaking 'em up at 10 am. ⊠ *Plaza del Sol, Blvd. Marina, next to Cabo Wabo, Marina San Lucas* ☎ *624/105–1877* ⊕ *www.unomascabo.com.*

DANCE CLUBS

El Squid Roe. Anything goes at this four-story party spot. Waiters dance and gyrate with female patrons, roaming waitresses pour Jell-O shots down your throat, college kids challenge each other to beer-chugging contests, and scantily clad dancers undulate in a makeshift penitentiary. During spring break or high season, more than 3,000 revelers come here on any given night—and many stay until sunrise. Feeling out of place? Head for one of the balconies on the third and fourth floors (which can be reached by elevator) where the scene is a bit less lurid. Around the corner stands the bar's souvenir shop with humorous T-shirts. El Squid Roe also has a full menu, serving pastas, steaks, and salads. ⊠ *Av. Lazaro Cárdenas, between Zaragoza and Morelos, Cabo San Lucas* ☎ *624/143–0655* ⊕ *www.elsquidroe.com.*

Giggling Marlin. Giggling Marlin predates Cabo's tourism explosion, though its gimmicks remain popular. Watch brave (and inebriated) souls be hoisted upside down at the mock fish-weighing scale, or join in an impromptu moonwalk between tables. Many fun (albeit risqué) floor shows relax people's inhibitions. The age of the clientele varies, as does the music, but the dance floor is usually jammed. Daily two-for-one drink specials pack 'em in 9 am–5 pm. The bartender may place a shot of tequila in front of you the minute you sit down—but you'll pay at least $5 if you drink it. Look for Giggling Marlin's drink coupon inside Cabo's free city map. ⊠ *Blvd. Marina at Matamoros, Cabo San Lucas* ☎ *624/143–0606* ⊕ *www.gigglingmarlin.com.*

A Shot of Tequila

What once was the drink of the poor Mexican farmer is now produced en masse and enjoyed internationally, with countless varieties crowding shelves across the world. Unfortunately, lower-quality brands make up the bulk of exports, so if the thought of sipping this heady liquor turns your stomach, take some time to seek out some of a higher quality while you're in Los Cabos.

Tequila must contain at least 51% blue agave, a plant related to the lily. The best tequilas are 100% blue agave. Liquid is distilled from the sap of 7- to 10-year-old plants and fermented. If you buy tequila with a worm, it was probably bottled in the United States, and is likely not a good-quality tequila.

Most of the good stuff is made in the town of Tequila, near Guadalajara. Labels bearing *reposado* indicate up to a year of aging; *añejo,* from one to three years. The longer tequila ages, the smoother it tastes.

Getting your fill of taste-testing is an easy thing to do in Los Cabos, because every bar will have at least a couple of bottles on the shelves, but you should visit at least one establishment that specializes in the good stuff. There are a number of locations in Los Cabos to do so: **Pancho's Restaurant & Tequila Bar** comes to mind, as does the **Tequila & Ceviche Bar** at posh Las Ventanas al Paraíso Resort. **Habanero's** located in San José del Cabo has a tequila pairing course, instructed by certified Tequilier (Tequila Sommelier) Tadd Chapman.

Pancho's might as well be a tequila museum. Hundreds of tequilas are available for tasting, and many of the colorfully named brands up on the shelves are no longer manufactured. Schedule a private tasting, at $50 per person, with Bernard Corriveau, the official "Tequila Ambassador" of Mexico, who will teach you a bit about the history, production process, and art of this complex liquor. Corriveau, appointed a "Maestro Tequilero" by the Consejo Regalador de Tequila (loosely, the industry's Tequila Board), just might be the most knowledgeable person on tequila in Los Cabos. Pancho's holds group tequila tastings in English each Tuesday night at 7 pm.

At Las Ventanas al Paraíso Resort, you can enjoy the small, intimate Sushi, Tequila & Ceviche Bar set off from its lobby. The resort's "Tequileros" conduct the lessons for a maximum of 25 guests where you'll learn the history, classifications, distillation process, and different types of tequila along with the appropriate way to drink it. Of the 160 different varieties available for sampling, some are affordable, while others—the Clase Azul Ultra, aged five years, produced in numbered batches of 200 bottles and $224 per shot—are liquid gold. Other favorites include the Don Julio Real, $74 per shot; the Chinaco Blanco, extra añejo, $18 per shot; the Casa Dragones Joven, $65 per shot; the Gran Centanario Lwyenda, $54 per shot; and the Reserva de la Familia, $32 per shot. Classes are held at a cost of $105 per person. Tequilas are served with ceviche sampler, guacamole, and homemade tortillas chips.

At the **Antigua Los Cabos Museum and Store**, located on the *zócalo* (town square), you can sample various tequilas and other interesting liquors free of charge.

Mandala. At this popular upscale spot, be prepared to wait in line, or pay $200 for a VIP table. Drinks are pricy, but the large dance floor and DJs spinning hip-hop and Latin music just might be worth the disco splurge. ⊠ *Av. Lázaro Cárdenas 1112, Centro* ☎ *624/143–2056* ⊕ *www.mandaladisco.com.*

Rose Bar. Located inside ME Cabo, this bar draws DJs from around the world who come to play their sets and fuel the cozy, neon club. ⊠ *At ME Cabo, on El Médano Beach, Cabo San Lucas* ☎ *624/145–7800* ⊕ *www.melia.com.*

ROCK CLUBS

Cabo Wabo. Depending on when you visit Cabo Wabo, you might just witness a jam session with owner Sammy Hagar and some of his legendary musician friends, who stop by a few times throughout the year. Plan way in advance to attend Hagar's Birthday Bash Week—usually the second week in October—as tickets sell out. The bar's design—high cavernous ceilings, zebra stipes, and psychedelic neon patterns—was re-created for the set of Hagar's Red Voodoo tour. ■TIP→ **Make dinner reservations to avoid the long lines to get in the club.** Lunch and dinner are served with extensive menus, and a taco grill cooks up tasty munchies outside if you wish to cool off after dancing. Shops on-site or at the international airport sell Cabo Wabo souvenir clothing. ⊠ *Calle Guerrero, Cabo San Lucas* ☎ *624/143–1188* ⊕ *www.cabowabo.com.*

SUNSET CRUISES

Several companies run nightly cruises for dinner or drinks that capture stunning sunsets as their vessels round the cape. Stands around the marina act as agents and can book excursions for you, but some manage to rope you into a timeshare visit in the process. Better to book through your hotel's front desk or directly through the company.

Caborey. Caborey offers a nightly 2½-hour sunset-dinner cruise on a three-deck catamaran. The cost is $74 and includes a full prix-fixe dinner with your choice of one of six main courses, an open bar for domestic beverages, and a Las Vegas–style show of Mexican music. Departure time is 6 pm September through April, and 5 pm the rest of the year. Check online for discount tickets. ⊠ *Cabo San Lucas* ☎ *624/105–1976, 866/460–4105 in North America* ⊕ *www.caborey.com* ⌕ *Tours depart from main cruise ship terminal at Cabo San Lucas Marina.*

Tropicat. Jazz plays nightly as passengers aboard the Tropicat watch the sun set over the 65-foot catamaran, which departs at 6 pm September–April and at 5 pm the rest of the year. The two-hour excursion is $75 per person and includes premium wines and hors d'oeuvres. Check online for ticket discounts. The catamaran departs from Dock #4, between the cruise ship pier and the dolphin center. ⊠ *Camino Del Cerro 215 El Pedregal, across from the Electric Company, Cabo San Lucas* ☎ *624/143–3797, 619/446–6339 in U.S.* ⊕ *www.pezgato.com.*

LOS CABOS
SIDE TRIPS

Todos Santos and La Paz

WELCOME TO LOS CABOS SIDE TRIPS

TOP REASONS TO GO

★ **Shopping Todos Santos:** An influx of artisans and craftspeople has turned Todos Santos into the region's snazziest, highest-quality shopping destination.

★ **Lodging Value:** Todos Santos offers a selection of charming inns at just a fraction of the cost—but all at full quality—of Los Cabos hostelries down the coast.

★ **The Aquarium of the World:** Jacques Cousteau christened the Sea of Cortez; La Paz makes the perfect launching point for exploring this body of water's rich marine life.

★ **The Best of Urban Baja:** La Paz is your bet for the urban pleasures of a charming, low-key Mexican city that lines a grand seaside promenade to boot.

★ **A Whale of a Time:** The annual December-through-April migration of gray whales to and from Alaska is visible from various points on the Baja coast and a guaranteed stunner.

In Todos Santos climb the hill north of the bus terminal to reach the original colonial town center with its stupendous views, landmark mission church, and several small inns and galleries. Coming into Todos Santos from the south, Highway 19 parallels area beaches without necessarily hugging the coastline. Roads leading to the shore are in decent shape, but twist and turn at points. Follow the signs; things are well marked.

The focal point of La Paz is the dense grid of streets in the city center, with most sights, lodgings, and restaurants either on the *malecón* (aka Paseo Alvaro Obregón), or a few blocks inland at most. (Remember: The odd curvature of the coast means that you are looking *west* out over the Sea of Cortez here.) The alternative to staying in the city is the 18-km (11-mile) highway leading north from La Paz to its port of Pichilingue, lined with a few small seaside hotels.

1 Todos Santos. Todos outgrew its surfing roots without abandoning them entirely, but you'll more likely come here for its growing number of galleries and craft shops. The arts scene has fueled a rise in gracious small inns, making this popular Los Cabos–area day trip an overnight destination in its own right.

2 La Paz. Don't let La Paz's workaday hustle and bustle fool you. This seaside state capital is one of Mexico's loveliest small cities—you'll be sold after an evening stroll on the oceanfront *malecón*, ice cream cone in hand—and the launching point for Baja's best diving, fishing, and whale-watching excursions.

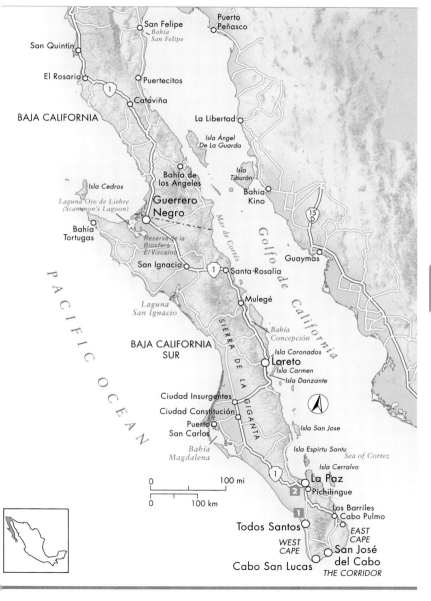

BAJA CALIFORNIA

San Quintín

El Rosario

Cataviña

San Felipe
*Bahía
San Felipe*

Puertecitos

Puerto
Peñasco

La Libertad

*Isla Ángel
De La Guarda*

Bahía de
los Angeles

Isla Cedros

*Laguna Ojo de Liebre
(Scammon's Lagoon)*

Guerrero
Negro

*Isla
Tiburón*

Bahía
Kino

Bahía
Tortugas

*Reserva de la
Biosfera
El Vizcaíno*

Mar de Cortés

Golfo de California

15
D

San Ignacio

Santa Rosalía

Guaymas

*Laguna
San Ignacio*

Mulegé

BAJA CALIFORNIA
SUR

SIERRA DE LA GIGANTA

*Bahía
Concepción*

Isla Coronados

Loreto

Isla Carmen

Isla Danzante

Ciudad Insurgentes

Ciudad Constitución

Puerto
San Carlos

*Bahía
Magdalena*

Isla San Jose

Isla Espirtu Santu

Sea of Cortez

Isla Cerralvo

La Paz

Pichilingue

Los Barriles
Cabo Pulmo

Todos Santos

*EAST
CAPE*

*WEST
CAPE*

Cabo San Lucas

San José
del Cabo

THE CORRIDOR

100 mi

100 km

8

Updated by
Chris Sands

At the risk of sounding glib, we might suggest that you skip Los Cabos altogether. The highlights of your visit to the far southern tip of the Baja peninsula may include two very un-Cabo-like destinations. One is objectively a small community; the other is actually the region's largest city, but will always be an overgrown small town at heart.

Their tranquil, reverent names—Todos Santos ("all saints") and La Paz ("peace")—are the first hint that you have left the glitz of Los Cabos behind, and that it's time to shift gears and enjoy the enchantment of Mexico. As an added bonus, both are positioned in such a way on the peninsula that you can enjoy beautiful sunsets over the sea. (Los Cabos gives you only ocean sun *rises*.)

The appeal of Todos Santos is becoming more well known, as a growing number of expats—American and European alike—move to the area. There's a lot to love here: the surf on the Pacific, just a couple of miles west of town, is good; weather is always a bit cooler than in Los Cabos; and the lush, leisurely feel of this artsy colonial town— think a smaller version of central Mexico's San Miguel de Allende—is relatively undisturbed by the many tourists who venture up from Los Cabos for the day. Todos Santos has always been the quintessential Los Cabos day trip, especially for the myriad cruise passengers who call there. As the town's tourism offerings grow, it's becoming a destination in its own right. Break the typical pattern of day-tripping to Todos Santos and spend at least one night here amid the palms, at one of the small pleasant inns.

La Paz plants itself firmly on the Sea of Cortez side of the Baja peninsula. A couple of hours north of Los Cabos, it remains slightly outside the Cabo orbit, and it has always attracted visitors (and an expanding expat population) who make La Paz their exclusive Baja destination. Of course, 200,000-plus Paceños view their city as being the center of the universe, thank you very much. (La Paz is the capital of the state of Baja California Sur and Los Cabos is in *their* orbit.) In addition to many urban trappings, La Paz offers a growing number of outdoor-travel options. This city on the water has become all about what's in the water. Sportfishing and scuba diving are big here, and La Paz is now a major launching point for whale-watching excursions.

WHAT IT COSTS IN DOLLARS				
	$	$$	$$$	$$$$
Restaurants	under $12	$12–$20	$21–$30	over $30
Hotels	under $150	$150–$250	$251–$350	over $350

Restaurant prices are the average cost of a main course at dinner or, if dinner is not served, at lunch. Hotel prices are the lowest cost of a standard double room in high season.

Restaurant and hotel reviews have been shortened. For full information, visit Fodors.com.

TODOS SANTOS

73 km (44 miles) north of Cabo San Lucas, 81 km (49 miles) south of La Paz.

From the hodgepodge of signs and local businesses you see on the drive into Todos Santos, south on Highway 19, it appears that you're heading to the outskirts of a typical Baja town. But climb the hill to its old colonial center with its mission church and blocks of restored buildings, and the Todos Santos that is gaining rave reviews in tourism circles is revealed.

Todos Santos was designated one of the country's Pueblos Mágicos (Magical Towns) in 2006, joining 110 other towns around Mexico chosen for their religious or cultural significance. Pueblos Mágicos receive important financial support from the federal government for development of tourism and historical preservation. Architects and entrepreneurs have restored early 19th-century adobe-and-brick buildings around the main plaza of this former sugar town and have turned them into charming inns, whose hallmark is attentive service at prices far more reasonable than a night in Los Cabos. A good number of restaurateurs provide sophisticated, globally inspired food at hip eateries.

Todos Santos has always meant shopping, at least since about three decades ago when the first U.S. and Mexican artists began to relocate their galleries here. Day-trippers head up here from Los Cabos, enjoying lunch and a morning of shopping. The growing number of visitors who buck that trend and spend a night or two here leave feeling very satisfied indeed.

Los Cabos visitors typically take day trips here, though several small inns provide a peaceful antidote to Cabo's noise and crowds. El Pescadero, the largest settlement before Todos Santos, is home to ranchers and farmers who grow herbs and vegetables. Business hours are erratic, especially in September and October.

Highway 19, now upgraded to four lanes, connects Todos Santos south with Cabo San Lucas and north with La Paz, making the drive easier than ever. Nonetheless, we recommend making the trip before dark; the occasional cow or rock blocks the road. Autotransportes Aguila provides comfortable coach service over a dozen times a day in both directions between Los Cabos (San José and San Lucas) and La Paz, with an intermediate stop in Todos Santos. Plan on an hour from La Paz or Cabo San Lucas and 90 minutes from San José del Cabo. Ecobaja Tours offers scheduled shuttle service ($20 one-way) four times daily between Todos Santos and Los Cabos Airport, 90 minutes away.

Baja California Sur State Tourist Office. The Baja California Sur State Tourist Office is in La Paz about a 10-minute drive north of the *malecón* (seaside promenade). It serves as both the state and city tourism office. There's also an information booth on the malecón (no phone) that can give you info on La Paz and surrounding areas. Both offices and the booth are open weekdays 8–3. ⊠ *Carretera al Norte, Km 5.5, La Paz* ☎ *612/124–1988* ⊕ *visitbajasur.travel.*

EXPLORING

Nuestra Señora del Pilar. Todos Santos was the second-farthest south of Baja California's 30 mission churches, a system the Spanish instituted to convert (and subdue) the peninsula's indigenous peoples. Jesuit priests established an outpost here in 1723 as a *visita* (circuit branch) of the mission in La Paz, a day's journey away on horseback. The original church north of town was sacked and pillaged twice during its existence, before being relocated in 1825 to this site in the center of town. Additions in the past two centuries have resulted in a hodgepodge of architectural styles, but the overall effect is still pleasing, and the structure serves to this day as the community's bustling parish church. ⊠ *Calle Márquez de León, between Centenario and Legaspi* ☎ *612/145–0043.*

Teatro Cine General Manuel Márquez de León. The mouthful of a name denotes Todos Santos's 1944 movie theater, which was quite a grand movie palace back in the day for remote, small-town Mexico. A few cultural events take place here, including the annual Todos Santos Film Festival each March. ⊠ *Calle Legaspi s/n* ☎ *612/145–1083.*

WHERE TO EAT

Todos Santos's dining selection echoes the town—stylish expat with traditional Mexican—and makes a nice outing during any Los Cabos–area stay. Restaurants here do a brisk business at lunch, less so at dinner. It's well worth the trip to drive up from Los Cabos or down from La Paz for a special meal. At an hour each way, that's easier to do before dark.

$ ✕**Baja Beans.** Although Los Cabos and Baja are not coffee-growing
CAFÉ regions, the folks in the town of El Pescadero roast the finest beans from
the Sierra Norte mountains in the Mexican state of Puebla. They turn
them into the area's best gourmet coffee drinks, which may be enjoyed
at tables in the adjoining garden. **Known for:** area's best gourmet coffee
drinks; live music on Sundays; farmers' market on Sundays. $ *Average
main: $5* ⊠ *El Pescadero, Hwy. 19, Km 64* ☎ *612/130–3391* ⊕ *baja-
beans.com* ⊘ *No dinner.*

$$$ ✕**Café Santa Fe.** The setting, with tables situated in an overgrown court-
ITALIAN yard, is as appealing as the food, which includes salads and soups
made with organic vegetables and herbs, homemade pastas, and fresh
fish with light sauces. Many Cabo–area residents lunch here regularly.
Known for: scenic outdoor dining; homemade pastas; local favorite.
$ *Average main: $27* ⊠ *Calle Centenario, between Márquez de León
and Hidalgo* ☎ *612/145–0340* ⊕ *cafesantafetodossantos.com* ⊘ *Closed
Tues. and Sept. and Oct.*

$$ ✕**Caffé Todos Santos.** Omelets, bagels, granola, and whole-grain breads
ECLECTIC delight the breakfast crowd at this casual small eatery; deli sandwiches,
fresh salads, and an array of burritos, tamales, and *flautas* (fried tortillas
rolled around savory fillings) are lunch and dinner highlights. Check
for fresh seafood on the daily specials board. **Known for:** delicious deli
sandwiches; gourmet pizzas and pastas; daily seafood specials. $ *Aver-
age main: $12* ⊠ *Calle Centenario 33* ☎ *612/145–0300* ▭ *No credit
cards* ⊘ *No dinner Mon. Closed last 2 wks of Sept.*

$$ ✕**El Gusto! At Posada La Poza** Even if you don't stay at the sumptuous
ECLECTIC Posada La Poza just outside town, lunch at its equally lovely restaurant
Fodor'sChoice will be one of the highlights of your Los Cabos vacation. Owners Jürg
★ and Libusche Wiesendanger call their offerings "Swiss-Mex"—Mexican
food with European touches, and careful attention to detail. **Known
for:** Swiss-Mex cuisine; private dinners available; reservations recom-
mended. $ *Average main: $19* ⊠ *Camino a La Poza 282, La Poza*
✥ *Follow signs on Hwy. 19 and Benito Juárez to beach* ☎ *612/145–
0400* ⊕ *www.lapoza.com* ⊘ *Closed Thurs.*

$$ ✕**Los Adobes.** Locals swear by the mole poblano and chilies en nogada
MEXICAN at this pleasant outdoor restaurant. The menu is ambitious and includes
several organic, vegetarian options—rare in these parts. **Known for:**
mole poblano and chilies en nogada; vegetarian options available; adjacent desert garden. $ *Average main: $15* ⊠ *Calle Hidalgo, between
Juárez and Colégio Militar* ☎ *612/145–0203* ⊕ *www.losadobesdeto-
dossantos.com.*

$$ ✕**Michael's at the Gallery.** Everybody who dines here seems to know
ASIAN one another, but visitors are always welcome. The attraction at
Michael's—not to be confused with Miguel's, the equally recom-
mended Mexican place as you come into town—is an Asian menu
combining Chinese, Japanese, Thai, and Vietnamese cuisines. **Known
for:** Asian fusion cuisine; open just two days a week; dine behind the
Galería de Todos Santos. $ *Average main: $20* ⊠ *Huerta las Palmas,
Cañada del Diablo, Centro* ☎ *612/145–0500* ⊘ *Closed Sun.–Thurs.
No lunch.*

8

$ ✕ **Miguel's.** Deliciously prepared chiles rellenos are the attraction at
MEXICAN   Miguel's. The sign out front says so, and so does a faded *New York*
Fodor's Choice   *Times* article, which proclaims them the best in all of Baja. **Known for:**
★   friendly owner; hearty chiles rellenos with shrimp and scallops. ⑤ *Aver-age main: $8* ⊠ *Degollado at Calle Rangel, Centro* ☎ *612/134–4149* ▭ *No credit cards* ☾ *Closed Sun.*

WHERE TO STAY

The quality of lodgings in Todos Santos is surprisingly high. It's a much better value to stay here than along the Corridor or in Los Cabos, and there isn't a megaresort to be found. In fact, some of the best lodging in the region is found right here, among the lush palm trees of this former sugarcane town.

Use the coordinate (⊹ B2) at the end of each listing to locate a site on the corresponding maps.

$ ▦ **Hacienda Todos los Santos.** Within each of the three *casitas* (guest-
HOTEL   houses) here, you'll find canopied beds and antique art. **Pros:** three casitas have private terraces kitchens; great views from upstairs rooms. **Cons:** little to do here for young children. ⑤ *Rooms from: $130* ⊠ *End of Benito Juárez* ☎ *612/145–0547* ⊕ *www.tshacienda.com* ⤳ *4 suites, 3 casitas* ¶◯¶ *No meals* ⊹ *B2.*

$ ▦ **Hotel California.** This handsome structure with two stories of arched
HOTEL   terraces and rich, vibrant colors on the walls, is a testament to the artistic bent of owner Debbie Stewart. **Pros:** inn feels exotic and lush; convenient location; good value. **Cons:** some street noise; service not as smooth as other hotels in town. ⑤ *Rooms from: $105* ⊠ *Benito Juárez at Morelos* ☎ *612/145–0525, 612/145–0288* ⊕ *www.hotelcalifornia-baja.com* ⤳ *11 rooms* ¶◯¶ *No meals* ⊹ *B2.*

$ ▦ **The Hotelito.** Original art is found throughout this modern lodging
HOTEL   and has been mixed with contemporary and antique Mexican decora-
Fodor's Choice   tive pieces; the sculptural furniture is as comfortable as it is captivating.
★   **Pros:** saltwater swimming pool; mangoes fresh from the tree served at breakfast; five-minute walk to beach. **Cons:** 10-minute walk to down-town. ⑤ *Rooms from: $125* ⊠ *Rancho de la Cachora* ☎ *612/145–0099* ⊕ *www.thehotelito.com* ☾ *Closed Sept.* ⤳ *4 rooms* ¶◯¶ *Breakfast* ⊹ *A1.*

$$ ▦ **Posada La Poza.** West of town, overlooking a bird-filled lagoon that
HOTEL   gives way to the Pacific, this is the only Todos Santos property right on
Fodor's Choice   the water. **Pros:** gracious owners; very generous, delicious breakfasts;
★   gorgeous saltwater pool and hot tubs. **Cons:** no children under 12; no TV or phones; need car to stay here. ⑤ *Rooms from: $150* ⊠ *Camino a La Poza 282, La Poza* ⊹ *Follow signs on Hwy. 19 and on Benito Juárez to beach* ☎ *612/145–0400, 855/552–7692 in U.S.* ⊕ *www.lapoza.com* ⤳ *8 suites* ¶◯¶ *Breakfast* ⊹ *C3.*

$$ ▦ **Todos Santos Inn.** This converted 19th-century house, with only eight
B&B/INN   guest rooms, is unparalleled in design and comfort, owing to the loving
Fodor's Choice   care and attention of the owners. **Pros:** traditional Mexican elegance and
★   hospitality; gorgeous interior courtyard. **Cons:** street parking only; no kids under 12. ⑤ *Rooms from: $170* ⊠ *Calle Legaspi 33* ☎ *612/145–0040* ⊕ *www.todossantosinn.com* ⤳ *2 rooms, 6 suites* ¶◯¶ *Breakfast* ⊹ *C1.*

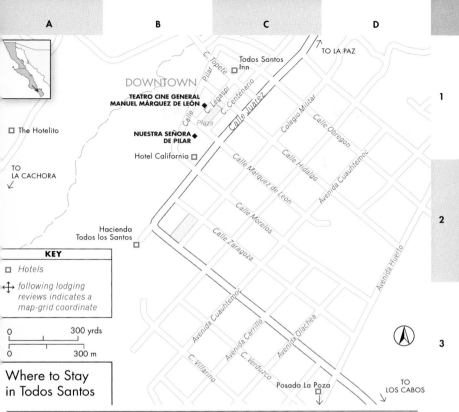

Where to Stay in Todos Santos

TO LA PAZ

Todos Santos Inn

DOWNTOWN

C. Topete
C. Pilar
Calle Legaspi
C. Centenario
Calle Juárez
Colegio Militar
Calle Obregón

TEATRO CINE GENERAL MANUEL MÁRQUEZ DE LEÓN

Plaza

Calle Hidalgo
Avenida Cuauhtémoc

NUESTRA SEÑORA DE PILAR

The Hotelito

Hotel California

Calle Márquez de León

TO
LA CACHORA

Calle Morelos

Hacienda
Todos los Santos

Calle Zaragoza

Avenida Huerta

KEY

□ Hotels

⬦ following lodging
reviews indicates a
map-grid coordinate

Avenida Cuauhtémoc
Avenida Carrillo
C. Verduzco
Avenida Olachea

0   300 yrds

0   300 m

C. Villarino

Posada La Poza

TO
LOS CABOS

1

2

3

NIGHTLIFE AND PERFORMING ARTS

As tourism grows in Todos Santos, so do its nightlife options. You'll never mistake this place for Los Cabos, however, and the town is quite fine with that state of affairs. Lingering over dinner remains a time-honored way to spend a Todos Santos evening.

FESTIVALS

Todos Santos holds three annual arts-related festivals during the high season in January and February. It's a good idea to make reservations weeks in advance if you plan to be here at those times.

Festival de Cine de Todos Santos (*Todos Santos Film Festival*). Todos Santos screens several new Latin American films during a festival in March. The 1940s-era Teatro Cine General Manuel Márquez de León serves as the main venue, with some films shown at other sites in Todos Santos, Pescadero, and La Paz. ✉ *Todos Santos*.

Festival del Arte Todos Santos (*Todos Santos Art Festival*). The city goes all out to celebrate Mexican dance, music, folklore, and culture for a week in early February each year. Local artists and several of the downtown galleries hold special events in conjunction with the festival. ✉ *Centro*.

Tropic of Cancer Concert Series. Former R.E.M. guitarist Peter Buck was the major force behind the Todos Santos Music Festival, which premiered in 2012, and is now held annually in January. The festival typically features seven nights of live music spread across two weekends, with an international lineup of performers appearing at Hotel California and the Todos Santos town square. Buck ruffled some local feathers with political comments at the 2016 festival, and did not appear in 2017. The festival was renamed as a consequence, and is now known as the Tropic of Cancer Concert Series. Proceeds benefit local children's charities. ⊠ *Centro* ⊕ *tropicofcancerconcertseries.com.*

BARS AND WINE BARS

La Bodega de Todos Santos. Twice-weekly wine tastings at this downtown wineshop make an interesting twist on a night out in Todos Santos. Stop by Monday or Wednesday evening during the October–June high season for a taste of Baja wines—a couple of vintages are featured each time—and appetizers supplied by neighboring restaurant Mi Pueblito. La Bodega also organizes the town's largest food-and-wine festival, Gastrovino, which takes place each May. ⊠ *Calle Hidalgo, between Juárez and Colegio Militar* ☎ *612/152–0181* ⊕ *www.gastrovino.mx.*

La Santeña. You'll find this upscale rendition of a Mexican cantina (with a restaurant, too) in the Hotel Casa Tota. It's a great place to stop for a quiet drink. ⊠ *Hotel Casa Tota, Calle Alvaro Obregón* ☎ *612/145–0590* ⊕ *www.hotelcasatota.com.*

Shut Up Frank's. Take your pick from the sporting events shown on seven big-screen TVs at the consummate sports bar in Todos Santos. Enjoy the scrumptious burgers here, too. ⊠ *Degollado at Rangel, across from Pemex station* ☎ *612/145–0707.*

EN ROUTE

If you're headed to La Paz on Highway 1 from San José del Cabo, a large globe-shaped monument marks 23.27° latitude north, or the Tropic of Cancer. You cross the line between Earth's temperate zone and the tropics here. Of course, Baja is Baja, and you won't detect any difference in climate no matter which side of the line you are on. Many stop for a photo posing in front of the monument, which is 2 km (1 mile) south of the turnoff to Santiago. You can decide how obligatory that seems.The Tropic of Cancer also crosses Highway 19 on the West Cape, just outside Todos Santos. There is no marker there.

SHOPPING

Although Todos Santos is gaining renown in all aspects of its tourism offerings, the name still means shopping to most Los Cabos–area visitors. Artists from the U.S. Southwest (and a few from Mexico) found a haven here some two decades ago. Their galleries and shops showcase traditional and contemporary work. There is a strong Baja emphasis in the art, and you'll find beautiful jewelry and fine crafts from all over Mexico.

ART WALKS IN TODOS SANTOS

The shops and galleries in the downtown area can be explored in an hour or two, or you can easily make a day of it. Start at **Nuestra Señora de Pilar** church in the morning, when it's cooler. Head up Legaspi a block to **Galería la Coronela**. Make a left out of the gallery and then make a right onto Topete to head over one block to Centenario—to the left is **Joyeria Brilanti**, and on the corner is **Manos Mexicanas**. Between the galleries mentioned you'll find dozens of additional shops to wander through, too.

ART GALLERIES

Benito Ortega Vargas, Sculptor. Sculptor Benito Ortega's studio and gallery showcases evocative, often sea-inspired works in wood, bronze, stone, and other materials. ⊠ *24 Centenario, at Obregon, Centro* ☎ *612/136–2760* ⊕ *www.benitoortega.mx.*

Ezra Katz Gallery. Ezra Katz is considered by many to be one of the most important and original artists ever to emerge from Baja California Sur. La Paz native Katz's evocative and inspired paintings depicting the local landscape have been on display in his latest Todos Santos gallery since 2015. ⊠ *Calle Juárez at Topete, Centro* ☎ *612/158–8294* ⊕ *ezrakatz. com* ⊗ *Closed Sun. and July–Oct.*

Galería AR. The vibrant contemporary paintings of Arturo Mendoza Elfeo are the main attraction at Galería AR. ⊠ *Centenario at Hidalgo* ☎ *612/145–0502.*

Galería de Todos Santos. Since opening in 1994, Michael and Pat Cope's *galeria* has represented a diverse group of Mexican and American painters and sculptors working in a variety of artistic mediums. The gallery's terrace opens as an Asian restaurant, Michael's at the Gallery, on Friday and Saturday evenings. ⊠ *Huerta las Palmas, Cañada del Diablo, Centro* ☎ *612/145–0500* ⊕ *galeriatodossantos-com.webs.com.*

Galería La Coronela. Galería La Coronela exhibits the work of prodigious painter Victor Vega, as well as paintings by his daughter, Sofía. ⊠ *Calle Legaspi between Hidalgo and Topete* ☎ *612/149–8294.*

Galería Logan. The namesake gallery features the work of Jill Logan, a Southern Californian who has been in Todos Santos since 1998. Jill does bold oil-on-canvas paintings and complexly layered multimedia pieces. ⊠ *Calle Juárez at Morelos* ☎ *612/145–0151* ⊕ *www.jilllogan.com.*

Gallery 365. The colors of Todos Santos provide the inspiration for the abstract paintings of artist Steve Thurston. ⊠ *Colegio Militar at Hidalgo, Centro* ☎ *612/145–1127.*

BOOKS ·

Fodor's Choice ★   **El Tecolote Bookstore.** El Tecolote Bookstore is the best bookstore in Los Cabos region. Stop here for Latin American literature, poetry, children's books, current fiction and nonfiction, and books on Baja. ⊠ *Calle Juárez at Calle Hidalgo* ☎ *612/145–0295.*

CLOTHING AND FOLK ART

Fodor's Choice ★ **Mangos.** Mangos is filled with gorgeous Guatemalan textiles, Mexican folk art, belts, purses, wood carvings, and Day of the Dead figurines, as well as paintings by esteemed Baja California Sur artist Rafael Chávez. ⊠ *Calle Centenario, between Topete and Obregón* ☎ *612/145–0315* ⊘ *Closed June–Oct.*

Manos Mexicanas. Manos Mexicanas is a treasure trove of fine Mexican crafts, jewelry, decorative objects, and work by local potter Rubén Gutiérrez. Owner Alejandra Brilanti has amassed an incredible collection of affordable pieces. You are not likely to leave empty-handed. ⊠ *Topete at Centenario* ☎ *612/145–0538.*

Nomad Chic. Eastern simplicity and the romance of exotic travel influence Nomad Chic's eclectic collection of apparel, jewelry, and accessories. ⊠ *Juárez at Hidalgo, Centro* ☎ *612/149–8962, 415/381–9087 owner Linda Hamilton in U.S.* ⊕ *www.nomadchic.mx* ⊘ *Closed Sun. and Aug. and Sept.*

JEWELRY

Fodor's Choice ★ **Joyería Brilanti.** Joyería Brilanti is a showcase for the stunning jewelry and design works of famed Taxco silversmith Ana Brilanti, in addition to a number of other contemporary jewelry artists—including Ana's son and the store's proprietor, José—whose work shares the same dramatic aesthetic. Be sure to look at the silver tea services and other functional pieces. You'll also find selected stone carvings and bronzes from local artists. ⊠ *Centenario near Topete* ☎ *612/145–0799.*

MARKETS

The Pescadero-based café Baja Beans hosts a Sunday farmers' market, with arts and crafts offerings, stands featuring locally grown produce, live music, and healthy brunch options like vegetarian frittatas.

SOUVENIRS

Got Baja? You'll find a nice selection of Baja-themed souvenirs at this small downtown shop, located next to Cafélix Coffee & Kitchen. ⊠ *Calle Juárez, between Márquez de León and Hidalgo* ☎ *612/145–0568* ⊕ *www.gotbaja.mx.*

SPORTS AND THE OUTDOORS

ECOTOURISM

Todos Santos Eco Adventures. Todos Santos Eco Adventures offers a number of land- and water-based adventures. Choose from cliff walks, rock climbing, mountain treks, or fishing trips. Friendly guides pride themselves on thorough knowledge of the area, the environment, and the culture of the region. Their weeklong Todos Santos Cooking Adventure combines Mexican lessons with local sightseeing. Whichever of the offerings you choose, you'll feel like you're traveling with a savvy friend. The Jauregui family runs the operation with great care, and it's apparent. Ask about the casitas if you need overnight accommodations. ⊠ *Guaycura 88, La Poza* ✛ *West on Calle Olachea, follow signs toward La Poza (call for detailed directions)* ☎ *612/145–0189, 619/446–6827 in U.S.* ⊕ *www.tosea.net.*

SURFING

Todos Santos offers great surfing areas for beginners to experts. The advantage here is that the crowds, including the swarming masses from the cruise ships, don't head up to these waters, which makes for a much more relaxed scene in the water and on the beach.

Los Cerritos, south of Todos Santos on Mexico 19, offers gentle waves to beginners during the summer and more challenging breaks for advanced surfers during the northwest swell from December to March. San Pedrito, also south of town, offers great surfing for experienced surfers during the winter swells, with a number of popular, low-key, surf-oriented motels along the beach. In summer, the surf is generally pretty mellow along this stretch, so locals and surfers who demand greater challenge head to the Corridor or areas along the east side of the Cape for more satisfying breaks.

Costa Azul Surf Shop. Costa Azul Surf Shop is a small shop on the north end of the beach by the cliffs at Los Cerritos. The staff is friendly, and, for such a small space, there's a good selection of board rentals, as well as T-shirts, shorts, and accessories to buy. You'll see its stickers on cars all over the Cape, and the map on its website is a great resource for information on surf spots all over Baja Sur. ⊠ *Playa Los Cerritos, Los Cerritos* ☎ *624/142–2771 San José del Cabo office* ⊕ *www.costa-azul.com.mx.*

Todos Santos Surf Shop. Swing by Todos Santos Surf Shop for board rentals, to arrange a lesson, buy gear, or get that ding in your board repaired. Other activities are also available, including day trips to Magdalena Bay during whale-watching season, and to La Paz to swim with sea lions and whale sharks. ⊠ *Calle Hidalgo, between Colégio Militar and Rangel* ☎ *612/145–1114* ⊗ *Closed Sun.*

LA PAZ

81 km (49 miles) north of Todos Santos, 178 km (107 miles) north of San José del Cabo (via Hwy. 1), 154 km (92 miles) north of Cabo San Lucas (via Hwy. 19).

Tidy, prosperous La Paz may be the capital of the state of Baja California Sur and home to about 220,000 residents, but it still feels like a small town in a time warp. This east-coast development could easily be the most traditional Mexican city in Baja Sur, the antithesis of the "gringolandia" developments to the south. Granted, there are plenty of foreigners in La Paz, particularly during snowbird season. But in the slowest part of the off-season, during the oppressive late-summer heat, you can easily see how La Paz aptly translates to "peace," and how its residents can be called Paceños (peaceful ones).

Travelers use La Paz as both a destination in itself and a stopping-off point en route to Los Cabos. There's always excellent scuba diving and sportfishing in the Sea of Cortez. La Paz is the base for divers and fishermen headed for Cerralvo, La Partida, and the Espíritu Santo islands, where parrot fish, manta rays, neons, and angels blur the clear waters by the shore, and marlin, dorado, and yellowtail leap from the sea.

LA PAZ LANGUAGE SCHOOLS

La Paz is a laid-back city with a picturesque waterfront and some fine beaches—a great spot to work on your Spanish skills at one of the language schools in the area. Being such a large tourist area, English is widely spoken; resist the temptation to hang out with other English speakers, and instead plunge in and practice your Spanish outside of class.

El Nopal Spanish Language Academy. This language school offers personalized classes and immersion programs at all levels. It arranges for students to live with local families to get the maximum possible exposure to the language and daily practice. ⊠ *Calle Legaspi 1885* ☎ *612/177–4098* ⊕ *www. elnopalspanish.com.*

Cruise ships are more and more often spotted sailing toward the bay as La Paz emerges as an attractive port. (Only small ships can berth at La Paz itself; most cruise liners dock at its port of Pichilingue, about 16 km [10 miles] north of town.)

La Paz officially became the state capital in 1974, and is its largest settlement (though the combined Los Cabos agglomeration is quickly catching up). All bureaucracy holds court here, and it's the site of the ferry port to Mazatlán and Topolobampo, the port of Los Mochis, on the mainland. There are few chain hotels or restaurants, but that's sure to change as resort developments come to fruition around the area.

La Paz region, including parts of the coastline south of the city, is slated as the future building site of several large-scale, high-end resort developments with golf courses, marinas, and vacation homes. Economic doldrums of recent years put brakes on those projects, but as Mexico's tourism finally and cautiously begins to rebound, plans have moved to the forefront again.

GETTING HERE AND AROUND

Aeropuerto General Manuel Márquez de León (LAP) is 11 km (7 miles) northwest of La Paz. Alaska Air partner Horizon Air flies daily from Los Angeles. Aereo Calafia connects La Paz with Los Cabos. Several airlines connect La Paz with Mexico City and various domestic airports in Mexico. Flying into the Aeropuerto Internacional de Los Cabos, two hours away near San José del Cabo, offers a far better selection of fares and itineraries. Ecobaja Tours operates shuttles five times daily between Los Cabos Airport and La Paz for $30 one-way. In La Paz, taxis are readily available and inexpensive. Taxis between La Paz airport and towns are inexpensive (about $15) and convenient. A ride within town costs under $5; a trip to Pichilingue costs around $15. In La Paz the main Terminal de Autobus is on the malecón at Independencia. Bus companies offer service to Todos Santos (one hour), Los Cabos (two hours).

8

THE STEINBECK CONNECTION

For an account of the Baja of years past, few works beat John Steinbeck's *The Log from the Sea of Cortez*, published in 1951. It recounts a six-week voyage he took in 1940 with marine biologist Ed Ricketts for the purpose of cataloging new aquatic species on the gulf side of Baja California. (*Phialoba steinbecki*, a previously unknown species of sea anemone discovered during the excursion, was later named for the author.)

Steinbeck lamented what he was sure would one day be the inevitable tourism growth to arrive on the peninsula. The author was mistaken on one key point however: he was certain the megaboom would come to La Paz and not to then-sleepy Cabo San Lucas.

Baja Ferries connects La Paz with Topolobampo, the port at Los Mochis, on the mainland, with daily high-speed ferries. The trip takes seven hours and costs $59 per person. Baja Ferries also connects La Paz and Mazatlán; it's a 16-hour trip and costs $67 per person. You can buy tickets for ferries at La Paz Pichilingue terminal. The ferries carry passengers with and without vehicles. If you're taking a car to the mainland, you must obtain a vehicle permit before boarding. Ferry officials will ask to see your Mexican auto-insurance papers and tourist card, which are obtained when crossing the U.S. border into Baja.

ESSENTIALS

Airlines Aereo Calafia. ☎ *612/123–2643* ⊕ *www.aereocalafia.com.mx.* **Aeropuerto Manuel Márquez de León.** ☎ *612/124–6307* ⊕ *www.aeropuertos-gap.com.mx.* **Horizon Air.** ☎ *800/252–7522* ⊕ *www.alaskaair.com.*

Bus Contacts Autotransportes Aguila. ✉ *Terminal Turística, Av. Álvaro Obregón 125, between Independencia and 5 de Mayo, Malecón* ☎ *800/824–8452, 122–7568 in Mexico* ⊕ *www.autobusesaguila.com.* **Ecobaja Tours.** ✉ *Terminal Turística, Av. Álvaro Obregón 125, between Independencia and 5 de Mayo, Malecón* ☎ *612/123–0000* ⊕ *www.ecobajatours.com.*

Currency Exchange Banamex. ✉ *Esquerro 110, Zona Comercial* ☎ *612/122–1011* ⊕ *www.banamex.com.mx.*

Emergencies Highway Patrol. ☎ *612/114–6597.* **Police.** ☎ *911.*

Ferry Lines Baja Ferries. ✉ *La Paz Pichilingue Terminal* ☎ *612/123–6397, 612/125–6324* ⊕ *www.bajaferries.com.*

Hospitals Centro de Especialidades Médicas. ✉ *Calle Delfines 110* ☎ *612/124–0400.*

La Paz

KEY

□ Hotels

⊕ following lodging reviews indicates a map-grid coordinate

Bahía de La Paz

Hotel Marina
La Concha Beach Club Resort and Condominiums

ESTERITO

Belisario
Domínguez
Fco. J. Madero
Álvaro Obregón
Revolución de 1910

Héroes del 47
Herócio Colegio Militar
Vicente Guerrero
República
Manuel T. Iglesias
Juan Ma. de Salvatierra
Aquiles Serdán
Guadalupe Victoria
José Ma. Morelos y Pavón

Canal de La Paz

Museo de la Ballena y Ciencias del Mar

Malecón Plaza
Hotel Perla
Malecón

◆ Plaza Constitución
Hotel Arte Museo Yeneka
Catedral de Nuestra Señora de la Paz
Hotel Seven Crown Malecón
el ángel azul
◆ Museo de Antropología

Miguel Hidalgo I. Costilla
Constitución
DE LA CRUZ

ZONA COMERCIAL

Paseo Álvaro Obregón
Ignacio Allende
Juárez
Manuel Pineda
Gral. Manuel Márquez de León
Miguel L. de Legaspi
Manuel Encinas
Antonio Navarro

Guillermo Prieto
Ignacio Ramírez
Ignacio Altamirano
Santos Degollado
Melchor Ocampo
Nicolás Bravo
Antonio Rosales

ZONA CENTRAL
5 de Mayo
Independencia
Reforma
16 de Septiembre
Isabel La Católica

TO AIRPORT

V. Gómez Farías
H. de la Independencia
J. Ortiz de Domínguez
Lic. Primo de Verdad

FRACC. PERLA

Serpentario de La Paz
Club El Moro

0 — 400 yards
0 — 400 meters

EXPLORING

TOP ATTRACTIONS

Malecón. Officially the Malecón Alvaro Obregón, this seaside promenade is La Paz's seawall, tourist zone, and social center all rolled into one. It runs for 5 km (3 miles) along Paseo Álvaro Obregón and has a sidewalk as well as several park areas in the directly adjacent sand. Paceños are fond of strolling the malecón at sunset when the heat of the day finally begins to subside. Teenagers slowly cruise the street in their spiffed-up cars, couples nuzzle on park benches, and grandmothers meander along while keeping an eye on the kids. (You will see people swimming here, and the water is cleaner than it used to be, but the beaches outside town are a far surer bet in that regard.) ⊠ *Paseo Alvaro Obregón.*

Malecón Plaza. A two-story white gazebo is the focus of Malecón Plaza, a small concrete square where musicians sometimes appear on weekend nights. An adjacent street, Calle 16 de Septiembre, leads inland to the city. ⊠ *Paseo Alvaro Obregón at Calle 16 de Septiembre.*

Plaza Constitución. Plaza Constitución, the true center of La Paz, is a traditional zócalo that also goes by the name Jardín Velazco. Concerts are held in the park's gazebo and locals gather here for art shows and fairs. Day-to-day life here entails shoeshines and local bingo games. ✉ *Bordered by Av. Independencia, Calles 5 de Mayo, Revolución de 1910, and Madero, Centro.*

WORTH NOTING

Catedral de Nuestra Señora de la Paz. The downtown church, Catedral de Nuestra Señora de la Paz, is a simple, unassuming stone building with a modest gilded altar but beautiful stained-glass windows.

SUNRISE, SUNSET

La Paz sits on the east coast of the Baja peninsula, but a convoluted curvature of the shoreline here positions the city to look out west over the Sea of Cortez. That means that you can enjoy beautiful sun *sets* over the water here at the end of the day.

The church was built in 1861 near the site of La Paz's first mission, which no longer exists. The two towers of the present cathedral were added a half century later. ✉ *Revolución de 1910, between 5 de Mayo and Independencia, Centro* ☎ *612/122–2596* ⊕ *diocesislapaz.com.*

FAMILY **Museo de Antropología.** La Paz's culture and heritage are well represented at the Museo de Antropología, which has re-creations of indigenous Comondu and Las Palmas villages, photos of cave paintings found in Baja, and copies of Cortés's writings on first sighting La Paz. All exhibit descriptions are labeled in both English and Spanish. If you're a true Baja aficionado and want to delve into the region's history, this museum is a must; otherwise, a quick visit is all you need. ✉ *Calle Altamirano at Calle 5 de Mayo, Centro* ☎ *612/122–0162* 🖅 *$3.*

FAMILY **Museo de la Ballena y Ciencias del Mar.** Commonly referred to by English
Fodor's Choice speakers as The Whale Museum, this popular malecón-adjacent attrac-
★ tion actually celebrates myriad forms of marine life, from dolphins and sharks to sea lions and endangered sea turtles. The enormous whale skeletons, built from bones sourced from specimens that washed up on nearby shores, are undoubtedly the most impressive items on display, however. Sperm, humpback, and other whale re-creations hang suspended from the high ceilings, with brains and other organs preserved in accompanying exhibits. Guided tours provide a wonderful introduction to the region's aquatic abundance, and are available in several languages, including English. The gift shop next door, meanwhile, offers souvenir T-shirts and other cetacean-themed memorabilia. ✉ *Malecón, Paseo Álvaro Obregón at 16 de Septiembre, Malecón* ☎ *612/129–6987* ⊕ *www.museodelaballena.org* 🖅 *$9 for adults; $7 for children and seniors* ☉ *Closed Mon.; closed Christmas, New Year's Day, and May 1.*

Serpentario de La Paz. Better that you encounter all the creatures that slip and slither here in the safety of Mexico's largest serpentarium than out in the wilds of Baja. More than 100 species are on display in indoor and outdoor exhibits, including turtles, pythons, rattlesnakes, and a rather large iguana. For less than $3, visitors may take photos with their choice of two pythons or a baby crocodile. Labeling is entirely in Spanish, but the staff offers guided tours in English with advance notice. A gift shop sells reptile-themed souvenirs. ✉ *Calle Brecha California, between Nueva Reforma and Guaycura, Centro* ☎ *612/122–5611* ⊕ *www.elserpentario.org* 🖅 *$8.*

BEACHES

Around the malecón, stick to ambling along the sand while watching local families enjoy the sunset. Just north of town the beach experience is much better; it gets even better north of Pichilingue. Save your swimming and snorkeling energies for this area. All facilities listed here exist on the weekends. Their existence on weekdays may be spottier.

Playa Balandra. A rocky point shelters a clear, warm bay at Playa Balandra, 21 km (13 miles) north of La Paz. Several small coves and pristine beaches appear and disappear with the tides, but there's always a calm area where you can wade and swim. Snorkeling is fair around Balandra's south end where there's a coral reef. You may spot clams, starfish, and anemones. Kayaking and snorkeling tours usually set out from around here. If not on a tour, bring your own gear, as rentals aren't normally available. Camping is permitted but there are no hookups. The smallish beach gets crowded on weekends, but on a weekday morning you might have the place to yourself. Sand flies can be a nuisance here between July and October. **Amenities:** camping; food concession; parking lot; toilets. **Best for:** snorkeling; swimming; walking. ⊠ *La Paz.*

Playa Caimancito. Situated just beyond La Concha Beach Club Resort, 5 km (3 miles) north of La Paz, Caimoncito is home to a scenic stretch of sand and some sun-shading palapas. Locals swim laps here, as the water is almost always calm and salty enough for easy buoyancy. There aren't any public facilities here, but if you wander over to the hotel for lunch or a drink you can use its restrooms and rent water toys. **Amenities:** parking lot. **Best for:** sunsets; swimming; walking. ⊠ *La Paz.*

Playa El Tecolote. Spend a Sunday at Playa El Tecolote, 25 km (15 miles) north of La Paz, and you'll feel like you've experienced the Mexico of old. Families set up house on the soft sand, kids race after seagulls and each other, and *abuelas* (grandmothers) daintily lift their skirts to wade in the water. Vendors rent out beach chairs, umbrellas, kayaks, and small, motorized boats; a couple of restaurants serve up simple fare such as ceviche and *almejas* (chocolate clams). These eateries are usually open throughout the week, though they sometimes close on chilly days. Facilities include public restrooms and trash cans. Camping is permitted, but there are no hookups. **Amenities:** camping; food concession; parking lot; playground; toilets. **Best for:** sunsets; swimming; walking. ⊠ *La Paz.*

FAMILY **Playa Pichilingue.** Starting in the time of Spanish invaders, Pichilingue, 16 km (10 miles) north of La Paz, was known for its preponderance of oysters bearing black pearls. In 1940 a disease killed them off, leaving the beach deserted. Today it's a pleasant place to sunbathe and watch sportfishing boats haul in their daily catches. Locals set up picnics here on weekend afternoons and linger until the blazing sun settles into the bay. Restaurants consisting of little more than a palapa over plastic tables and chairs serve oysters *diablo,* fresh clams, and plenty of cold beer. Pichilingue curves northeast along the bay to the terminals where

8

the ferries from Mazatlán and Topolobampo arrive and many of the sportfishing boats depart. If La Paz is on your cruise itinerary, you'll likely dock at Pichilingue, too. One downside to this beach: traffic buzzes by on the nearby freeway. The water here, though not particularly clear, is calm enough for swimming. **Amenities:** food concession; parking lot; toilets. **Best for:** sunset; walking. ⊠ *La Paz.*

WHERE TO EAT

$ ✕ **Bandido's Grill.** Bandido's has come a long way since opening nearly
BURGER a decade ago with three plastic tables and a grill fixed under the hood
FAMILY of an old pickup truck. The unique truck-grill is still around, but the restaurant's latest alfresco setting suggests it may be transitioning from working-class pit stop into romantic burger joint. **Known for:** popular with locals; hearty burgers and ribs; old-time rock and roll. Ⓢ *Average main: $10* ⊠ *Calle Navarro at Topete, Centro* ☎ *612/128–8338.*

$ ✕ **Caffé Gourmet.** Not far from hotels, restaurants, and important down-
CAFÉ town sights, this small café is a great place to recharge with a morning espresso, chai, or smoothie, along with great pastries. Wi-Fi is available here, so you can catch up on your email. **Known for:** great pastries; Wi-Fi available; centrally located. Ⓢ *Average main: $3* ⊠ *Esquerro at Calle 16 de Septiembre* ☎ *612/122–7710* ⊙ *Closed Sun.*

$$ ✕ **El Bismark.** The original Bismark is a bit out of the way, but it attracts
MEXICAN families who settle down for hours at long wood tables, while waitresses divide their attention between patrons and telenovelas (Latin American soap operas) on the TV above the bar. Tuck into seafood cocktails, enormous grilled lobsters, or carne asada served with beans, guacamole, and homemade tortillas. **Known for:** seafood cocktails; long dining experience; good for families. Ⓢ *Average main: $16* ⊠ *Av. Degollado at Calle Altamirano, Centro* ☎ *612/122–4854.*

$$ ✕ **Las Tres Virgenes.** Poll locals on their favorite restaurant in La Paz, and
INTERNATIONAL Las Tres Virgenes is likely to be the runaway winner. Chef and Tijuana
Fodor'sChoice native Jesús Chávez has endeared himself to Paceños over the past dozen
★ years with consistently excellent mesquite grilled fare, from seafood and enormous burgers (try the Baja 1000 with "double beef, double cheese, double everything") to slow-braised Angus short rib, Tomahawk bone-in rib eye, and Brazilian-style picaña. **Known for:** #1 favorite among locals; romantic dining; great cocktails. Ⓢ *Average main: $15* ⊠ *Calle Francisco I. Madero 1130, between Constitución and Miguel Hidalgo y Costilla, Centro* ☎ *612/123–2226.*

$$ ✕ **Mariscos Los Laureles.** A small stand that looks as if it might have been
SEAFOOD rolled along the street by a vendor is just the entryway decoration for this well-established restaurant. Whether you eat at a bench at the stand outside or dine within in the air-conditioning, if you like seafood, you will enjoy Los Laureles. **Known for:** excellent seafood; many types of fruits de mer; fresh seafood cocktails. Ⓢ *Average main: $14* ⊠ *Paseo Alvaro Obregón at Salvatierra, Centro* ☎ *612/128–8532.*

$$ ✕ **Mar y Peña.** The freshest, tastiest seafood cocktails, ceviches, and
SEAFOOD clam tacos imaginable are served in this nautical restaurant crowded with locals. If you come with friends, go for the *mariscada,* a huge

platter of shellfish and fish for four. **Known for:** huge portions; often busy; extremely fresh and tasty seafood dishes. $ *Average main: $16* ✉ *Calle 16 de Septiembre, between Isabel la Católica and Albáñez, Centro* ☎ *612/122–9949* ⊘ *Closed Christmas and New Year's Day.*

$

BAKERY

✕ **Pan d'Les.** Fortify yourself for a morning of sightseeing—the place is open only until 2:30 pm—at Pan d'Les in La Paz's central business district. Transplanted U.S. pastry chef Les Carmona hand-forms his European-style breads and pastries at his small bakery. **Known for:** daily bread specials; fresh-baked rústico sourdough; homemade ice cream sandwiches. $ *Average main: $4* ✉ *Madero, between 5 de Mayo and Constitución, Centro* ☎ *612/122–5339* ▭ *No credit cards* ⊘ *No dinner. Closed Sun.*

$$

MEXICAN

✕ **Rancho Viejo.** Everything is delicious, and prices are reasonable at this cheerful little restaurant painted in bright yellow and orange. Meats are the specialty here, but just about everything on the menu is good and choices are abundant. **Known for:** tasty tacos de arrachera; open 24 hours; abundant choices. $ *Average main: $12* ✉ *Márquez de León at Dominguez, Centro* ☎ *612/128–4647, 612/125–6633.*

$$

EUROPEAN

✕ **Restaurant Zoe.** Following a makeover and name change from the cutesy portmanteau La Pazta, this popular eatery at the Hotel Mediterrane added colorful new accents and a bit of international flair to a menu best known for its homemade pasta and pizzas. Tasty additions like carrot, ginger, and honey cream soup, grilled scallops with ginger and lime butter, and green curry with tofu are now served with lasagna, ravioli, and other traditional Italian favorites. **Known for:** homemade pastas and pizzas; creative menu additions; adjacent café is open for breakfast and lunch. $ *Average main: $13* ✉ *Hotel Mediterrane, Allende 36, Centro* ☎ *612/125–1195* ⊕ *www.hotelmed. com* ⊘ *No lunch.*

$

MEXICAN

✕ **Tacos Hermanos González.** La Paz has plenty of great taco shacks, but none are better than the small stand owned by the González brothers, who serve up hunks of fresh fish wrapped in corn tortillas and offer bowls of condiments with which to decorate your taco. The top quality draws sizable crowds. **Known for:** area's best taco shack; lots of condiments to add; draws big crowds. $ *Average main: $3* ✉ *Madero at Degollado, Centro* ☎ *612/120–5074* ▭ *No credit cards.*

WHERE TO STAY

Use the coordinate (⊕ B2) at the end of each listing to locate a site on the corresponding map.

$

RESORT

⊞ **Club El Moro.** Possibly the best bargain on the malecón, although a bit away from the city center itself, this vacation-ownership resort has very reasonable suite rentals on a nightly and weekly basis. **Pros:** handsome architecture; pool; private balconies. **Cons:** some dated decor; rooms facing pool area can be noisy. $ *Rooms from: $70* ✉ *Hwy. 11 to Pichilingue, Km 2* ☎ *612/122–4084, 866/375–2840* ⊕ *www.clubelmoro. com.mx* ⤙ *18 rooms, 20 suites* ⏉⊙ *No meals* ⊕ *A3.*

8

$ **el ángel azul.** Owner Esther Ammann converted La Paz's historic
HOTEL courthouse into a comfortable retreat in the center of the city. **Pros:**
Fodor's Choice lovely owner; attentive service; historic building. **Cons:** street parking
★ only; kids under 12 not permitted. $ *Rooms from: $80* ✉ *Av. Independencia 518, at Guillermo Prieto, Centro* ☎ *612/125–5130* ⊕ *www.
elangelazul.com* ⤳ *9 rooms, 1 suites* ⦶ *No meals* ✛ *C2.*

$ **Hotel Arte Museo Yeneka.** Thirteen budget-friendly rooms fringe a
HOTEL courtyard strewn with art and artifacts, each individually decorated
to reflect this hotel's bohemian sensibility. **Pros:** affordable room rates;
complimentary tequila shots each evening; centrally located. **Cons:**
patchy Wi-Fi; noisy ceiling fans and air-conditioning units. $ *Rooms
from: $35* ✉ *Calle Madero 1520, Centro* ☎ *612/125–4688* ⊕ *www.
hotelyeneka.com* ⤳ *13 rooms* ⦶ *Breakfast* ✛ *C2.*

$ **Hotel Marina.** Here's a hotel with a full-service marina offering fish-
RESORT ing, scuba diving, and kayaking. **Pros:** good value; amenities for fishing
vacations; tennis court. **Cons:** you may feel out of place if you're not
here on a fishing vacation. $ *Rooms from: $50* ✉ *Hwy. to Pichilingue,
Km 2.5* ☎ *612/121–6254, 866/262–7187 in U.S.* ⊕ *www.hotelmarina.
com.mx* ⤳ *84 rooms, 5 suites* ⦶ *No meals* ✛ *D1.*

$ **Hotel Perla.** The brown low-rise faces the malecón and has seen a
HOTEL flurry of activity since 1940, due largely to its nightclub, La Cabaña,
which opens on Saturday night. **Pros:** central location; friendly staff;
kitschy furnishings. **Cons:** room facing street can be noisy. $ *Rooms
from: $57* ✉ *Paseo Alvaro Obregón 1570, Malecón* ☎ *612/122–0777*
⊕ *www.hotelperlabaja.com* ⤳ *110 rooms* ⦶ *No meals* ✛ *C2.*

$ **Hotel Seven Crown Malecón.** This very reasonable, modern, minimal-
HOTEL ist hotel is perfectly situated to one side of the malecón's action. **Pros:**
central location; affordable; rooftop bar with bay views. **Cons:** very
simple rooms; some rooms facing street can be noisy. $ *Rooms from:
$52* ✉ *Paseo Alvaro Obregón 1710, Centro* ☎ *612/128–7787* ⊕ *www.
sevencrownhotels.com* ⤳ *55 rooms, 9 suites* ⦶ *No meals* ✛ *B2.*

$ **La Concha Beach Club Resort and Condominiums.** On a long beach with
RESORT calm water, this older resort (built in 1984) has a water-sports center and
FAMILY a notable restaurant. **Pros:** renovated rooms in good shape; lower-priced
rooms are good value; private beach. **Cons:** you'll need a car to stay
here. $ *Rooms from: $50* ✉ *Hwy. to Pichilingue, Km 5* ☎ *612/121–6161*
⊕ *www.laconcha.com* ⤳ *99 rooms* ⦶ *No meals* ✛ *D1.*

NIGHTLIFE AND PERFORMING ARTS

BARS AND DANCE CLUBS

The Beer Box. Craft beers are the attraction at this modestly appointed
satellite bar near the city's plaza principal, where some draught, but
many more bottled options are available from artisanal brewers
around the world. The best bets, however, are regional standouts like
Rámuri from Tijuana; Fauna and Cucapá from Mexicali; Agua Mala
from Ensenada; and Baja Brewing Company from Los Cabos. ✉ *Calle
Independencia 201, between Calle Francisco I. Madero and Belisario
Domínguez, Centro* ☎ *612/129–7299.*

Fodor's Choice
★ **La Miserable.** Don't let the name fool you: good times are typically had by all at this downtown mezcalería, thanks to its congenial late-night atmosphere and many rare and unusual examples of México's "other" national spirit. The bar's collection of smoky, agave-derived mezcals are primarily sourced from small mainland distillers, including the potent and flavorful house brand. Local artwork and vintage photos adorn the colorfully painted walls, and bar staff play a lively mix of popular hits and hard-driving rock and roll. Bottled beer is stocked for those with an aversion to strong liquors. ⊠ *Calle Belisario Dominguez 274, between 5 de Mayo and Constitución, Centro* 🕾 *612/129–7037.*

La Terraza. The best spot for both sunset- and people-watching along the malecón is La Terraza at the Hotel Perla. The place makes killer margaritas, too. ⊠ *Hotel Perla, Paseo Alvaro Obregón 1570, Malecón* 🕾 *612/122–0777* ⊕ *www.hotelperlabaja.com.*

Las Varitas. This club heats up after midnight, with live music acts playing Banda, Norteño, and other Mexican musical styles. Ladies Night is Friday 9–11, with cheap drinks and performances by male exotic dancers. ⊠ *Av. Independencia 111, at Domínguez, Centro* 🕾 *612/125–2025.*

PERFORMING ARTS

El Teatro de la Ciudad. La Paz's cultural center seats more than 1,100 and stages shows by visiting and local performers. ⊠ *Av. Navarro 700, between Ignacio Manuel Altamirano and Héroes de Independencia, Centro* 🕾 *612/125–0207, 612/125–0486.*

SHOPPING

ART AND SOUVENIRS

Antigua California. Antigua California has the nicest selection of Mexican folk art in La Paz, including wooden masks and lacquered boxes from the mainland state of Guerrero. ⊠ *Paseo Alvaro Obregón 220, Malecón* 🕾 *612/125–5230.*

Got Baja? You'll find a nice selection of Baja-themed souvenirs, including quality T-shirts, at this downtown shop that shares space with Doce Cuarenta Café & Repostería. There's also a branch in Todos Santos. ⊠ *Calle Madero 1240, between 5 de Mayo and Constitución, Centro* 🕾 *612/125–5991* ⊕ *www.gotbaja.mx.*

Ibarra's Pottery. The Ibarra family oversees the potters and painters at their namesake shop. Their geometric designs and glazing technique result in gorgeous mirrors, bowls, platters, and cups. ⊠ *Guillermo Prieto 625, between Torre Iglesias and República, Centro* 🕾 *612/122–0404.*

BOOKS

Allende Books. This bookstore stocks La Paz's best selection of English-language works, mainly about Baja and Mexico, as well as laminated nature field guides. You'll also find a terrific selection of gifts here, including handcrafted jewelry, table runners, and wall hangings. ⊠ *Independencia 518, between Serdán and Guillermo Prieto, Centro* 🕾 *612/125–9114* ⊕ *www.allendebooks.com.*

8

A diver gets up close and personal with a sea lion in the waters of the Sea of Cortez.

SPORTS AND THE OUTDOORS

BOATING AND FISHING

The considerable fleet of private boats in La Paz now has room for docking at several marinas, including Marina Palmira north of the malecón, and Marina de La Paz and Marina Cortez to the south. Most hotels can arrange trips. Fishing tournaments are typically held in July, August, and October.

Fishermen's Fleet. The Fishermen's Fleet has daylong fishing on *pangas* (skiffs), as well as multiday excursions to Magdalena Bay. ⊠ *La Paz* ☎ *612/122–1313, 408/884–3932 in U.S.* ⊕ *www.fishermensfleet.com.*

Mosquito Fleet. The Mosquito Fleet has 22-foot pangas starting at $350 for two people, and cabin cruisers from $600 for four people. ⊠ *Hwy. to Pichilingue, Km 5, between downtown and Pichilingue* ☎ *612/121–6120, 877/408–6769 in U.S.* ⊕ *www.bajamosquitofleet.com.*

KAYAKING

The calm waters off La Paz are perfect for kayaking, and you can take multiday trips along the coast to Loreto or out to the nearby islands.

Baja Expeditions. Baja Expeditions, one of the oldest outfitters working in Baja (since 1974), offers several kayak tours, including multinight trips between Loreto and La Paz. A support boat carries all the gear, including ingredients for great meals. The 10-day trip in the Sea of Cortez with camping on remote island beaches starts at $1,550 per person, based on double occupancy. ⊠ *Calle Sonora 585, between Topete and Abasolo, Manglito* ☎ *612/125–3828, 800/843–6967 in U.S.* ⊕ *www.bajaexpeditions.com.*

Fun Baja. Fun Baja offers land tours, scuba and snorkel excursions with sea lions, seasonal whale-watching trips, and camping safaris to Isla Espíritu Santo. ✉ *Marina CostaBaja, Hwy 11 to Pichilingue, Km 7.5* ☎ *612/106–7148* ⊕ *www.funbaja.com* 🐟 *2-tank scuba trips from $145.*

SCUBA DIVING AND SNORKELING

Popular diving and snorkeling spots include the coral banks off Isla Espíritu Santo, the sea-lion colony off Isla Partida, and the seamount 14 km (9 miles) farther north (best for serious divers).

Cortez Club. The Cortez Club is a full-scale water-sports center with equipment rental and scuba, snorkeling, kayaking, and sportfishing tours, as well as the complete slate of PADI instructional courses. ✉ *Hwy. to Pichilingue, Km 5, between downtown and Pichilingue* ☎ *612/121–6120, 877/408–6769 in U.S.* ⊕ *www.cortezclub.com* 🐟 *2-tank dives from $150.*

TOUR OPERATORS

KAYAKING

Nichols Expeditions. Nichols Expeditions arranges kayaking tours to Isla Espíritu Santo and between Loreto and La Paz, with camping along the way. It also offers a combination of sea kayaking in the Sea of Cortez with whale-watching in Magdalena Bay. ✉ *497 N. Main St., Moab* ☎ *800/648–8488 in U.S.* ⊕ *www.nicholexpeditions.com* 🐟 *4-day trip $695; 9-day trip $1,495.*

SCUBA DIVING

Baja Expeditions. Snorkel in sheltered coves off the coast of La Paz, or with sea lions at Los Islotes. Two- or three-tank dives at pristine sites near Isla Espíritu Santo are facilitated by a 28-foot custom dive boat. The 45-foot catamaran *El Mechudo* can carry up to eight people for weeklong snorkel and dive charters. ✉ *Calle Sonora 585, between Topete and Abasolo, Manglito* ☎ *612/125–3828, 800/843–6967 in U.S.* ⊕ *www.bajaexpeditions.com* 🐟 *Scuba diving from $140 per person.*

WHALE-WATCHING

La Paz is a good entry point for whale-watching expeditions to **Bahía Magdalena**, 266 km (165 miles) northwest of La Paz on the Pacific coast. Note, however, that such trips entail about six hours of travel from La Paz and back for two to three hours on the water. Only a few tour companies offer this as a daylong excursion, however, because of the time and distance constraints.

Many devoted whale-watchers opt to stay overnight in Puerto San Carlos, the small town by the bay. Most La Paz hotels can make arrangements for excursions, or you can head out on your own by renting a car or taking a public bus from La Paz to San Carlos, and then hire a boat captain to take you into the bay. The air and water are cold during whale season from December to April, so you'll need to bring a warm windbreaker and gloves. Captains are not allowed to "chase" whales, but that doesn't keep the whale mamas and their babies from approaching your panga so closely you can reach out and touch them.

An easier expedition is a whale-watching trip in the Sea of Cortez from La Paz, which involves boarding a boat in La Paz and motoring around until whales are spotted. They most likely won't come as close to the boats and you won't see the mothers and newborn calves at play, but it's still fabulous watching the whales breeching and spouting nearby.

Baja Expeditions. Seasonal five-day, four-night gray whale–watching excursions are offered for $2,975 per person, double occupancy. Tours are typically scheduled in February and March, and include flights, meals, an expert natural guide, and comfortable camping conditions at Laguna San Ignacio. ⊠ *Calle Sonora 585, between Topete and Abasolo, Manglito* ☎ *612/125–3828, 800/843–6967 in U.S.* ⊕ *www.bajaexpeditions.com.*

Cortez Club. The water-sports center Cortez Club runs extremely popular full-day whale-watching trips in winter. Transportation, guide, breakfast, and seafood lunch are included. ⊠ *Hwy. to Pichilingue, Km 5, between downtown and Pichilingue* ☎ *612/121–6120, 877/408–6769 in U.S.* ⊕ *www.cortezclub.com* 🖅 *$180 per person.*

BAJA CALIFORNIA BEACH TOWNS

With Ensenada and the Valle de Guadalupe Wine Region

WELCOME TO
BAJA CALIFORNIA BEACH TOWNS

TOP REASONS TO GO

★ **Scenic Driving:** Driving along the Pacific Coast, south of Tijuana, on the Carretera Transpeninsular (Highway 1) is half the fun of traveling to Baja's historic missions and remote beaches.

★ **Sampling Mexico's Wine:** The Valle de Guadalupe, near Ensenada, is a gorgeous valley blanketed with sprawling vineyards and charming inns.

★ **Whale-Watching:** Gray whales swim to Baja California every winter to mate and calve in three lagoons on the peninsula's west coast.

★ **Shopping for Handicrafts:** In Ensenada stores are filled with unique souvenirs in addition to the usual sunglasses and sombreros.

Flanked by the Pacific Ocean to the west and the Sea of Cortez to the east, Baja California (also called Baja California Norte, or simply Baja Norte) comprises the northern half of the Baja Peninsula. The majority of the narrow state is accessible by the Carretera Transpeninsular (Highway 1), but it's easy to feel as if you've gone far off the grid when a hundred miles of barren land stands between you and the nearest town or gas station. Embrace the feeling; Baja is really Mexico's Wild West, and has the stark desert landscapes, secluded coves, and striking mountains to prove it.

1 Rosarito. Just 16 km (10 miles) south of the U.S. border are Rosarito's beautiful wide beaches, fronted by a less-than-beautiful town full of touristy bars targeting college students looking for a weekend of partying.

2 Puerto Nuevo. San Diegans cross the border for the fried lobster that made ths sleepy fishing village famous.

3 Valle de Guadalupe. Explore the Ruta de Vino dotted with award-winning wineries, farm-to-table restaurants, and boutique hotels with unpretentious hosts.

4 Ensenada. A seaport town sandwiched by beaches, Ensenada is home to some of the best fish tacos and margaritas Mexico has to offer.

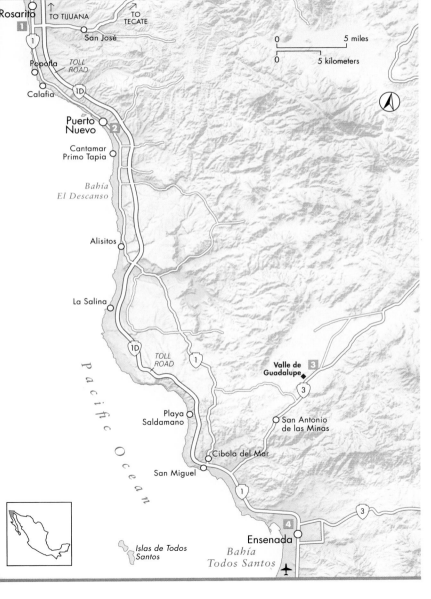

Rosarito

TO TIJUANA

TO TECATE

1

San José

Popotla

TOLL ROAD

Calafia

1D

Puerto Nuevo 2

Cantamar
Primo Tapia

Bahía El Descanso

Alisitos

La Salina

1D

TOLL ROAD

1

Valle de Guadalupe 3

3

San Antonio de las Minas

Playa Saldamano

P a c i f i c   O c e a n

Cibola del Mar

San Miguel

1

3

Ensenada 4

Islas de Todos Santos

Bahía Todos Santos

0   5 miles

0   5 kilometers

9

Updated
by Marlise
Kast-Myers

The beaches of the northern peninsula are dreamlike: fine sand, water that's refreshing but not too cold, sunshine, and some of the west coast's top waves. Part of that dream can evaporate, however, when you venture into the beach towns themselves.

More than a few of the stops along Highway 1 have been run down by years of American spring-breakers. Ensenada is the exception: a charming fisherman's enclave with a village-like feel, complete with beachside trinket stores and fish taco stands (the town's beaches, conversely, are nothing special). Along this part of the peninsula, towns are close together, and the essentials (gas, food, lodging) are never far.

PLANNING

GETTING HERE AND AROUND

The main artery of the Baja Peninsula is a road of legend: Highway 1 winds down from Tijuana to Los Cabos through deserts and coastal bluffs, past fertile estuaries and through bleak towns which eke out a few crops from the dry soil. A faster alternative to the coastal road is Highway 1D connecting Tijuana to Ensenada. Three toll booths in Tijuana, Rosarito Beach, and Ensenada charge MX$31 to pass.

If you're driving into Baja California from San Diego during peak hours, you might try heading 35 km (19 miles) east to the much less congested border crossing at Tecate. From there, Highway 3 takes you south through the Valle de Guadalupe to Ensenada.

Highway 3 continues southeast from Ensenada over the San Martír Pass, where it meets Highway 5. From here, you can head north to Mexicali or south to San Felipe, where the road ends. In northern Baja, Highway 2 hugs the border from Mexicali to Tijuana. Although the hairpin turns make for beautiful overlooks during the day, the road east of Tecate is best avoided at night.

If you're driving in from the United States, purchase Mexican insurance (required) from any of the brokers near the border. It's also possible to rent a car in Tijuana or Mexicali from any of the major chains. The only San Diego–based rental agency allowing vehicles to cross into Mexico is California Baja Rent-A-Car. Rates include insurance coverage for both sides of the border. To avoid drinking and driving, Uber offers transportation in Valle de Guadalupe. Pack plenty of water and make sure your tires are in good shape: although the major highways are well maintained, a number of smaller roads are unpaved.

There are few international flights into Tijuana, Baja California's only major airport; most travelers access the area from the border at San Diego. Aeroméxico flies to Los Cabos, to La Paz on the Baja Peninsula, and to several cities in mainland Mexico. Alaska Airlines, Spirit, US Airways, Southwest, United, Delta, and American all fly into Los Cabos.

ABOUT THE RESTAURANTS

With a modern history not much older than the Carretera Transpeninsular, most Baja California towns have appropriated their local cuisine from the cultures of mainland Mexico. In many regions, the best lunches and dinners are had at curbside taco stands, where fried fish is served atop tortillas—with shredded cabbage and salsa to add at your discretion. It's hard to find a good sit-down restaurant south of Ensenada, but the few that exist serve fantastic local seafood. There are a handful of exceptional restaurants popping up in Ensenada and Valle de Guadalupe where award-winning chefs are offering a farm-to-table experience. When restaurants are limited, opt for the local hot spot, which is always a better option than paying premium for a chef's half-baked take on "international cuisine."

ABOUT THE HOTELS

Expect private bathrooms, daily maid service, Wi-Fi, a secure parking lot, and clean quarters in all but the most basic of establishments. Many hotels offer breakfast for an extra fee, and swimming pools are prevalent. Luxury is never far in Baja Norte; almost every touristed locale has at least one "Resort & Spa" that tacks on Jacuzzis, massages, and dollar signs to the above basics (especially along the coast near Ensenada). Be aware that only camping (no hotels) is available in some of Baja Norte's smaller towns, including those on Highway 1 between Ensenada and San Quintín, and those on Highway 3 between Ensenada and San Felipe.

WHAT IT COSTS IN DOLLARS				
	$	$$	$$$	$$$$
Restaurants	under $12	$12–$20	$21–$30	over $30
Hotels	under $150	$150–$250	$251–$300	over $300

Restaurant prices are the average cost of a main course at dinner or, if dinner is not served, at lunch. Hotel prices are the lowest cost of a standard double room in high season.

Restaurant and hotel reviews have been shortened. For full information, visit Fodors.com.

WHEN TO GO

Like the American southwest, Baja California's weather is conducive to year-round travel, though "peak season" will have a different meaning for beach bums and marine-life enthusiasts. The deserts can be sweltering between May and October, and parts of the Pacific coast are chilly between November and February. Whale-watching season on the Pacific runs roughly from December to late March, and although fishing is possible all year-round, local experts consider the summer months the best time to hook a big one.

ROSARITO

29 km (18 miles) south of Tijuana.

Southern Californians use Rosarito (population 75,000) as a weekend getaway, and during school vacations, especially spring break, the crowd becomes one big party. Off-season, the area becomes a ghost town. The beach here, which stretches from the power plant at the north end of town about 8 km (5 miles) south, is long with beautiful sand and sunsets, but it's less romantic for the amateur explosives that boom every few minutes.

If staying the night, head out to the beach near the pier in front of Rosarito Beach Hotel, or hire a horse at the north or south end of Boulevard Benito Juárez for $30 per hour. ATVs and wine tours can be booked through Rosarito Beach Hotel.

GETTING HERE AND AROUND

Rosarito is off of Highway 1 about 45 minutes south of the border. Follow the exit road directly into town.

Car Rental Alamo. ⊠ *Blvd. Cuauhtemoc 1705, Zona Río* ☎ 664/686–4040 ⊕ *www.alamomexico.com.mx.* **California Baja Rent-A-Car.** ⊠ *9245 Jamacha Blvd., Spring Valley* ☎ 619/470–7368 ⊕ *www.cabaja.com.*

EXPLORING

Claudius. As Rosarito's only wine production facility, this winery brings grapes from neighboring valleys to create remarkable blends, such as their 2011 Merlot. All of the wines by owner Julio Benito Martin are organic, and are best appreciated with the winemaker himself, who has passion behind every pour. Be sure to try the Rosado de Grenache, a creamy buttery blend unique to his line. The tasting room is ideal for those who want to enjoy local wines near the border, without driving the distance to Valle de Guadalupe. To create your own blend, inquire about Julio's wine academy. ⊠ *Blvd. Sharp 3722, col Amp Benito Juarez* ☎ *661/100–0232* ⊕ *www.claudiusvino.com* 🖃 *5 wine tastings $25* ☉ *Closed Sat.*

WHERE TO EAT

$$$
STEAKHOUSE
✗ **El Nido Steakhouse.** A dark, wood-paneled restaurant with leather booths and a large central fireplace, this is one of Rosarito's oldest eateries, and the best in town for atmosphere. Diners unimpressed with newer, fancier places come here for mesquite-grilled venison, lamb, and quail from the owner's farm in the Baja wine country. **Known for:** tortillas made table-side; strong margaritas; classic bean soup. ⑤ *Average main: $30* ✉ *Benito Juárez 67* ☎ *661/612–1430* ⊕ *www.elnidorosarito.net.*

$$
MOROCCAN
Fodor'sChoice
★
✗ **Mi Casa Supper Club.** What began as an underground supper club in the home of Dennis and Bo Bendana is now the leading restaurant in Rosarito. Inspired by their international travels, the menu and decor reflect their love for Morocco and Bali. **Known for:** red velvet churros with dark chocolate; Sunday brunch and live music; seven-course tasting menu. ⑤ *Average main: $18* ✉ *Estero 54, San Antonio Del Mar* ☎ *664/609–3459* ⊕ *www.micasasupperclub.com* ☺ *Closed Mon.–Wed. No breakfast or lunch Thurs.–Sat.*

$$
ECLECTIC
✗ **Susanna's.** In addition to the fresh Southern California cuisine, many come to this restaurant to connect with the charming owner Susanna who moved to Rosarito in 2004 to open a furniture shop. Her love for fine food prevailed, thus turning her store into a restaurant that makes people feel right at home. **Known for:** fresh California cuisine; homemade breads; sweet dressings and glazes. ⑤ *Average main: $16* ✉ *Blvd. Benito Juarez 4356, Publo Plaza, Playas de Rosarito* ☎ *661/613–1187* ⊕ *www.susannasinrosarito.com* ☺ *Closed Tues.*

WHERE TO STAY

$$
HOTEL
🛏 **Rosarito Beach Hotel & Spa.** Charm and location have the slight edge over comfort at this landmark hotel built in 1925. **Pros:** close to the beach; antique charm; good Sunday brunch. **Cons:** older furnishings; overpriced; slow elevator. ⑤ *Rooms from: $190* ✉ *Blvd. Benito Juárez 31, Centro, 22710, in front of Rosarito Beach Pier* ☎ *661/612–0144, 800/343–8582* ⊕ *www.rosaritobeachhotel.com* 🛏 *495 rooms* ⑩ *No meals.*

NIGHTLIFE

Papas & Beer. Papas & Beer, one of the most popular bars in Baja Norte, draws a young, energetic spring-break crowd for drinking and dancing on the beach. The $3 beers and mechanical bull make for an entertaining combination. ✉ *Coronado 400, on beach off Blvd. Benito Juárez, 22710 Playas de Rosarito* ☎ *661/612–0444* ⊕ *www.papasandbeer.com.*

SPORTS AND THE OUTDOORS

Baja Fun Adventures. Operating out of Rosarito Beach Hotel, Baja Fun Adventures runs two-hour ATV tours for $60 and full-day wine tours to Valle de Guadalupe for $65. ✉ *Rosarito Beach Hotel, Blvd. Benito Juarez 1207* ☎ *661/527–9998* 🎫 *Tours from $60.*

9

BAJA HISTORY

It's believed that the first humans arrived in Baja some 11,000 years ago, having followed the Pacific coast down from present-day Alaska. The Yumano (northern Baja), Cochimí (central Baja), and Guaycura (southern Baja) were hunter-gatherers who slept in caves and waged frequent wars among one another. In stark contrast to the well-organized Aztec and Mayan communities of mainland Mexico, Baja's Amerindians lived this way until the arrival of the Spanish.

Led by explorer Francisco de Ulloa, the Spanish came to the peninsula in 1539, believing they had landed on an island. Ulloa, who had been commissioned by Hernán Cortés to find proof of the infamous Northwest Passage, reconnoitered the entire eastern coast of the peninsula and drafted a number of early maps, laying the groundwork for further exploration in the following century. By 1751, Jesuits had begun establishing the first Roman Catholic missions among the Amerindian tribes of Baja California, and over the next hundred years Spain used these religious outposts as a means of extending its stronghold on the territory.

But even after Mexico won its independence from Spain in 1821, Baja California remained an underdeveloped and largely uninhabitable desert. It was only with the completion of the Carretera Transpeninsular in 1973 that many towns began blossoming alongside the region's rattlesnakes and giant cardón cacti. Today, Baja California is not just a route of passage to Cabo San Lucas but a burgeoning vacation destination in its own right for fishermen, surfers, sunbathers, wine-lovers, foodies, and culture fiends from all over the world.

FAMILY **Rosarito Ocean Sports.** The ocean sports center in the heart of Rosarito rents kayaks, paddleboards, snorkeling gear, Jet Skis, and scuba diving equipment. ⊠ *Blvd. Benito Juarez, 890-7, Playas de Rosarito* ☎ *661/100–2196* ⊕ *www.rosaritooceansports.com* ⛵ *Guided kayak from $35; diving trips from $140.*

PUERTO NUEVO

19 km (12 miles) south of Rosarito.

Southern Californians regularly cross the border to indulge in the classic Puerto Nuevo meal: lobster fried in hot oil and served with refried beans, rice, homemade tortillas, salsa, and lime. At least 20 restaurants are packed into this village; nearly all offer the same menu, but the quality varies drastically; some establishments cook up live lobsters, while others swap in frozen critters. In most places prices are based on size; a medium lobster with all the fixings will cost you about $20.

Though the fried version is the Puerto Nuevo classic, some restaurants also offer steamed or grilled lobsters.

The town itself is tired and dated, with waiters standing curbside begging tourists in passing cars to stop in for the day's catch. Still, it's the best spot along the coast to try fresh lobster at an unbeatable price.

For lodging, you're better off renting a beach house in the neighboring community of Las Gaviotas or heading to a hotel north in Rosarito or south in Ensenada. Most accommodations in the town of Puerto Nuevo are in desperate need of a face-lift.

Artisans' markets and stands throughout the village sell serapes and T-shirts; the shops closest to the cliffs have the best selection.

GETTING HERE AND AROUND

Puerto Nuevo sits just beside Highway 1. When you pull off the highway and enter the town, find a parking spot (free unless otherwise marked) and hop out. There's no other transport to speak of (or needed) in this five-block hamlet.

WHERE TO EAT

$$$ ✕ **La Casa de la Langosta.** Seafood soup and grilled fish are options at
SEAFOOD the "House of Lobster," but clearly lobster is the star. It's served in
FAMILY omelets and burritos or steamed with a wine sauce. **Known for:** fresh marlin soup; large portions; lobster prepared six different ways. $ *Average main: $25* ⊠ *Av. Renteria 3, Km 44* ☎ *661/614–1072* ⊕ *www. casadelalangosta.com.*

WHERE TO STAY

$ ⛱ **Puerto Nuevo Hotel & Villas.** This Puerto Nuevo property (which even
RESORT after a remodel in 2017 could still use some TLC) is comprised of a hotel and villas and is located just beyond the archway into Puerto Nuevo's lobster village. **Pros:** nice-size rooms; convenient location; good ocean views. **Cons:** rooms a little spartan; dark rooms; loud beach music. $ *Rooms from: $145* ⊠ *Carretera Tijuana–Ensenada, Km 44.5, just past Puerto Nuevo in Ensenada direction* ☎ *661/614–1488, 877/315–1002* ⊕ *www.puertonuevohotelyvillas.com* ⇥ *178 rooms* ⏹ *No meals.*

VALLE DE GUADALUPE

80 km (50 miles) southeast of Rosarita.

The Valle de Guadalupe, 15 minutes northeast of Ensenada on Carretera 3, is filled with vineyards, wineries, and rambling hacienda-style estates. Although Mexican wines are still relatively unknown in the United States, the industry is exploding in Mexico, and the Valle de Guadalupe is responsible for some 90% of the country's production. In 2004, there were 5 wineries in production, and today there are more than 120. Along with this splurge of growth comes award-winning chefs setting up "farm-to-fork" restaurants where nearly everything on their menu is harvested right outside their door. Designers, architects, and hoteliers are getting in on the action with dreamy properties ranging from villas and ranches to haciendas and eco-lofts. Lavender fields and bougainvillea add a splash of color to hillsides framing alfresco eateries with menus that will put most culinary destinations to shame. It's the patchwork of vineyards producing impressive blends that's keeping visitor-count high.

With a region that combines the right heat, soil, and a thin morning fog, some truly world-class boutique wineries have developed in the Valle de Guadalupe, most in the past decade. Many of these are open to the public; some require appointments. Several tour companies, including Bajarama Tours (☎ 646/178-3512), leave from Ensenada on tours that include visits to wineries, a historical overview, transportation, and lunch. Better yet, visit the wineries yourself by car, as they all cluster in a relatively small area. Also worth a look is winemaker Hugo D'Acosta's school, which brings in some 30 young winemakers to use common facilities to make their own blends. The facilities are on the site of an old olive oil press (a few antique presses remain in the outlying buildings), and the grounds are augmented with artwork made from recycled wine bottles and other materials.

It seems that it's not only Mexican wine that's being discovered, but the potential of Guadalupe as a "wine destination," along with the mixed blessings that accompany such discovery. Many locals are fighting to keep it from becoming the next Napa Valley.

WHEN TO GO

The ideal time to visit Valle de Guadalupe's wine country is in April to May or October to November to avoid the scorching heat and busloads of tourists. The annual Grape Harvest Festival (Fiestas de la Vendimia) is in August. This 21-day celebration brings in thousands of wine lovers who commemorate the harvest with wine tastings, cultural blessings, live music, and elaborate feasts. Be sure to make hotel reservations well in advance.

GETTING HERE AND AROUND

If you're not on a tour, a private car (or hired taxi) is essential for touring the wine country. Main roads through the valley are paved. Once you branch off toward vineyards, you'll likely be on dirt roads. The turnoffs for the major wineries are well marked; if you're looking for a smaller destination, you may end up doing a few loops or asking a friendly bystander. The general area is not too spread out, but you'll need to drive from one winery to the other. Watch out for hidden stop signs at nearly every street crossing. You can arrange a half- or full-day tour with many of the taxi drivers in Ensenada, and some drivers in Tecate may also be willing to take you. Uber also operates out of Valle de Guadalupe under the name uberVALLE. From Tijuana, a full day of touring (including five hours of wait time) is just under $70.

ESSENTIALS

Banks are few and far between in this area, so get cash before arriving. Nearly every business accepts credit cards and U.S. dollars. There are two gas stations in town: one at the entrance to the valley near Ensenada, and the second where Highway 3 meets Highway 1.

EXPLORING

TOP ATTRACTIONS

Adobe Guadalupe. Adobe Guadalupe makes an array of fascinating old-world-style blends named after angels. Don't miss the Kerubiel, which is a blockbuster blend; the Serafiel, Gabriel, and Miguel are also excellent. Gaining notoriety is the Jardín Romántico—80% Chardonnay—and of course the powerful mezcal, appropriately named Lucifer. Owner Tru also runs a bed-and-breakfast, and the horses are available for riding tours. Tastings are offered daily 10–6 and include four reds for $12 (free to hotel guests). Be sure to visit the wine store and tapas food truck on your way out. ⊠ *Off Carretera Tecate–Ensenada, turn at sign and drive 6 km (4 miles), Guadalupe* ☎ *646/155–2094* ⊕ *www.adobeguadalupe.com.*

Baron Balché. Despite up-and-coming wineries fighting for the spotlight, this premier producer is still considered the Rolls-Royce of Valle de Guadalupe's wineries. Logos on the premium line are based on Mayan numbers, with outstanding selections like the Balché UNO, a Grenache with hints of raspberry and caramel. The Balché CERO, 100% Nebbiolo is the king of their wines, having aged four years in the barrel. Even their younger wines are exceptional, but expect to pay a hefty price to try them. Tastings for top selections will cost you about $50, but considering you are sampling $250 bottles of wine, it just might be worth it. Be sure to end your wine tour here, otherwise the rest of your tastings might pale in comparison. ⊠ *Ej. El Porvenir* ☎ *646/155–2141* ⊕ *www.baronbalche.com.*

El Cielo. Considered a giant among the region's vineyards, this winery produces 4,000 cases of wine, has its own concert venue, private villas, and the popular restaurant Latitude 32. Most stop by to sample the fine blends named after constellations in honor of the owner's love for astronomy. Behind the barrel is winemaker Jesus Rivera, responsible for much of the success of neighboring wineries where he previously consulted. For an elegant Chardonnay, try Capricornius, or for an Italian grape blend of Nebbiolo and Sangiovese, the Perseus aged 24 months in French oak barrels is also wonderful. The Orion is one of their most popular reds. Tastings and tours are available daily for $12. ⊠ *Parcela 118, Km 7.5* ☎ *646/155–2220* ⊕ *www.vinoselcielo.com.*

Fodor's Choice ★ **La Lomita.** Owned by Fernando Pérez Castro, this new-generation winery creates rich wines made with 100% local grapes. As one of the smaller wineries, their blends are sold to top restaurants and hotels in Mexico City, Riviera Maya, and Cabo. The preferred Sacro—a mix of Cabernet Sauvignon and Merlot—has hints of pomegranate, cherry, pepper, berries, and maple syrup, while the Tinto de la Hacienda has characteristics of compote and jam. The tasting room is one of the nicest in the region with wood crate ceilings, dangling vintage bulbs, and a chalkboard wall sharing tales of the grapes. Tastings are Thursday to Sunday 12–4. The cost is $10 and includes four wines, snacks, and a tour of the winery. ⊠ *Plot 13, San Marcos Village, San Antonio de las Minas* ☎ *646/156–8466* ⊕ *lomita.mx/home/index/eng.*

9

Continued on page 179

VIVA VINO

About an hour and a half south of San Diego, just inland from Ensenada, lies a region that's everything Ensenada is not. The 14-mile-long Valle de Guadalupe is charming, serene, and urbane, and—you might find this hard to believe if you're a wine buff—is a robust producer of quality vino.

There's no watered-down tequila here. Red grapes grown include Cabernet Sauvignon, Merlot, Tempranillo, and Syrah, while whites include Chardonnay, Sauvignon Blanc, and Viognier. Drive down and spend a day at the vineyards and wineries that line la Ruta del Vino, the road that stretches across the valley, or better yet, base yourself here. The inns and restaurants in the Valle de Guadalupe welcome guests with refined material comforts, which complement the region's natural desert-mountain beauty and lovely libations.

(top) Adobe Guadalupe, (bottom left) Grapes from the Guadalupe Valley, Ensenada, (bottom right) Adobe Guadalupe

WINERY-HOPPING

Some wineries along la Ruta del Vino are sizeable enterprises, while others are boutique affairs Here are a few choice picks.

THE FULL-BODIED EXPERIENCE

Serious oenophiles should visit the midsize **Monte Xanic,** which, with a new tasting, is a serious contender for Mexico's finest winery. In August, tastings are by appointment; don't miss the Gran Ricardo, a high-end Bordeaux-style blend. **L. A. Cetto** is bigger than Monte Xanic, but it offers a well-orchestrated experience with tastings. Free tours are offered daily every half-hour from 10–5. Look for celebrity winemaker Camillo Magoni's wonderful Nebbiolo. A spectacular terrazza overlooks Cetto's own bullring and a sweeping expanse of wine country.

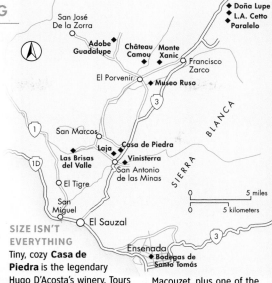

SIZE ISN'T EVERYTHING

Tiny, cozy **Casa de Piedra** is the legendary Hugo D'Acosta's winery. Tours and tastings of D'Acosta's high-end wines are by reservation only. Call ahead to visit the even smaller, but equally impressive, **Vinisterra,** where eccentric Swiss winemaker Christoph Gärtner turns out a small-production line of showstoppers called Macouzet, plus one of the only wines in the world made from mission grapes; these grapes come from vines descended from those planted by the Spanish in the 1500s for ceremonial services.

BACK TO THE BEGINNING

The imbibing of fermented fruit dates from the Stone Age (or Neolithic period; 8,500–4,000 BC), but the production of wine in the Americas is comparatively adolescent. Mexico actually has the New World's oldest wine industry, dating from 1574, when conquistadors and priests set off north from Zacatecas in search of gold; when none turned up, they decided to grow grapes instead. In 1597, they founded the Hacienda de San Lorenzo, the first winery in the Americas, in the modern-day state of Coahuila. By the late 1600s, Mexican wine production was so prolific, the Spaniards shut it down so it wouldn't compete with Spanish wine—sending Mexico's wine industry into a three-century hibernation from which it's just beginning to awaken. Now, most Mexican wine producers have moved to the Valle de Guadalupe (a cooler, more favorable climate for vineyards).

L.A. Cetto sparkling wines, Valle de Guadalupe

HOW TO EXPERIENCE WINE COUNTRY

LIVE THE VALLEY If you fancy tranquility and a perfectly starry sky, and don't mind an early bedtime, you're best off staying at one of the intimate, romantic haciendas in the middle of the valley itself, where you'll also benefit from your hosts' knowledge of the area. One of the first small wineries in Baja, **Adobe Guadalupe** is also a gracious bed-and-breakfast run by Tru Miller. A delightful and committed host—Tru might take you to neighboring wineries on horseback. **La Villa del Valle**, a luxury inn, is larger but just as nice, with spectacular countryside views and amenities like massage, a Jacuzzi, and a restaurant with its own market garden. Be sure to visit its cellar at neighboring Vena Cava Winery, made entirely of recycled boats.

DO IT BY DAY If you can't live without city buzz and nightlife, Ensenada has tons of it, and staying there is another viable option. In downtown Ensenada you can also visit **Bodegas de Santo Tomás**, one of Baja's oldest wineries. The city is less than an hour's drive to most of the wineries. It's also possible to visit the valley on a day trip from Tijuana or San Diego.

WINOS UNITE You can expect clear, sunny days in the valley for virtually the whole year, although evening temperatures dip into the 40s F (single digits Celsius) from December through March. A good time to visit is during the first two weeks of August, when the region comes alive for the **Fiestas de la Vendimia** (656/178–3088, www.provinoac.org), a harvest festival that's full of special wine tastings, dinners, and parties—both at the wineries and in Ensenada proper.

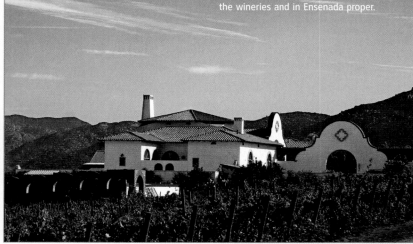

(pictured top and bottom) Adobe Guadalupe

WORTH NOTING

Casa de Piedra. The brainchild of Hugo D'Acosta, Casa de Piedra is part of an impressive portfolio that includes Paralelo, Aborigen, and La Borde Vieille, known for its Mexican and French blends. Try Casa de Piedra's flagship wine Contraste or their newer sparkling wines. The space is interesting and modern, designed by the winemaker's architect brother. Visits are by reservation only. ✉ *Carretera Tecate–Ensenada, Km 93.5, San Antonio de las Minas* ☎ *646/155–5267* ⊕ *www.vinos-casadepiedra.com* ⊘ *Closed Sun.*

L.A. Cetto. L.A. Cetto is another giant, but this is the closest thing to a California wine country experience south of the border. When tasting or buying, avoid the more affordable wines, and go straight for the premiums. They make a lovely Nebbiolo and Chardonnay, and their Don Luis Concordia is nicely balanced. Three levels of tastings (Traditional, Private Reserve, Premium) increase by $5 per level, making the Premium a good deal considering tastings are offered in a private VIP room away from the crowds. Popular with tour groups, this is one of the busiest wineries in the area. Tours take place daily 10–5 on the half hour. ✉ *Carretera Tecate–Ensenada, Km 73.5* ☎ *646/155–2179* ⊕ *www.lacetto.mx.*

Liceaga. Neighboring Casa de Piedra, this winery produces a variety of Merlot- and Cabernet-heavy blends. Try Liceaga's "L," a complex and elegant wine with hints of cherry, blackberry, cassis, plum and pepper. The tasting room is open most days 11–5, and they have live music Saturdays from July through September. ✉ *Carretera Tecate–Ensenada, Km 93, San Antonio de las Minas* ☎ *646/155–3281* ⊕ *www.vinosliceaga.com* 🍷 *4 tastings, $9.*

Mogor Badan. One of the area's few vineyards to offer organic wines, this 1950s ranch has gained notoriety for whites such as their remarkably fragrant Chasselas del Mogor. Their newer Pirineo blends a contemporary Mexican grenache with a French syrah. Wine tastings are available weekends 11–5 in their underground cave. Owner Natalia Badan hosts the local farmers' market on Wednesday and Saturday 11–1, making this *the* place to buy fresh eggs, honey, jams, breads, and salsas. After wine tasting, dine at the neighboring garden restaurant, operated by the talented Chef Drew Deckman. ✉ *Rancho El Mogor, Federal Hwy. 3 Tecate-Ensenada, Km 85.5, San Antonio de las Minas* ☎ *646/156–8156* 🍷 *3 tastings, $7.*

Monte Xanic. Tastings at Monte Xanic take place at the edge of a lovely pond and include three reds and two whites for $10. Most impressive is their consistency, right down to the cheapest table wines. During the month of August, tastings and tours are available by appointment only. Be sure to check out the impressively styled cellar. ✉ *Carretera 3, Km 70* ☎ *646/117–0027* ⊕ *www.montexanic.com.mx.*

Paralelo. Paralelo was built by the Hugo d'Acosta clan as "parallel" to Casa de Piedra. The winery makes two red blends—the excellent and balanced Arenal and the heavier, minerally Colina—as well as a Sauvignon Blanc Emblema. A reservation is necessary (ask for Gloria in the office), and construction is underway for a formal

9

tasting room. For now, tastings remain a casual and friendly affair, conducted around small tables on the deck. ⊠ *Carretera Tecate–Ensenada, Km 73.5* ☎ *646/156–5268* ⊕ *www.paralelo.com.mx* 🍽 *Tastings $5* ⊗ *Closed Sun.*

Fodor'sChoice **Vena Cava.** Even if you're not into wine, a visit to this award-winning
★ winery is well worth a visit. Winemaker Phil Gregory blended his passion for sustainable practices and wine making into the architecture of this funky wine cave made from old fishing boats. Bursting with character, these 1930s vessels once sailed the waters off the coast of Ensenada. Today they serve as the domes that cap the wine cellar, housing Vena Cava's labels considered among the best blends in Mexico. Vena Cava is one of the few wineries to produce natural wines, free of sulfites and with no added yeast. The Big Blend Tempranillo is elegant, gentle, and fruit-forward, and the 2016 Cabernet Sauvignon is remarkably smooth. This fine balance of science and art have become an obsession for the talented winemaker who uses French barrels and organic grapes from five local valleys. Tours and tastings are offered 11–5 on the hour for $16. Stay awhile and enjoy a meal at the food truck out front, serving an urban take on the cuisine from the neighboring Corazon de Tierra restaurant. ⊠ *Rancho San Marcos* ☎ *646/156–8007* ⊕ *www.venacavawine.com.*

Vinisterra. Within Vinisterra, expect to find Tempranillo and Cabernet-Merlot blends which are big and juicy. Tastings are available Saturday and Sunday 11–5. Four tastings will run you about $8. Call well in advance for reservations. ⊠ *Carretera Tecate–Ensenada, Km 94.5, San Antonio de las Minas* ☎ *646/178–3350, 646/178–3310* ⊕ *www.vinisterra.com* ⊗ *Closed weekdays.*

Wine Museum (*Museo de la Vid y el Vino*). For a better understanding of the wine-making process, the Museo de la Vid y el Vino in the heart of Valle de Guadalupe has exhibits on wine history, viticulture, and wine-inspired art. The museum showcases a vast collection of agricultural tools, more than 100 wines from the region, and a wine-tasting room where local blends are introduced daily. Don't miss the spectacular panoramic view of the valley and the outdoor amphitheater surrounded by vineyards. ⊠ *Carretera Tecate–Ensenada, Km 81.37* ☎ *646/156–8165, 646/156–8166* ⊕ *www.museodelvinobc.com* 🍽 *$4* ⊗ *Closed Mon.*

WHERE TO EAT

$$$$ ✕ **Corazon de Tierra.** A glass box restaurant surrounded by rows of veg-
ECLECTIC etables and sunflowers that are plucked and brought to the chef—and hours later to your table—is the true essence of "Heart of Earth." Adding to the rustic charm are beamed ceilings and floors recycled from an old pier, refurbished hand-stitched chairs, and burlap curtains that blow in the wind. The menu changes daily based on the harvest, but it always features six courses that are local, organic, and fresh. **Known for:** delightfully presented courses; unique desserts made with vegetables; local wine pairings. $ *Average main: $75* ⊠ *Toros Pintos s/m Km 88.3, Rancho San Marcos* ☎ *646/156–8030* ⊕ *www.corazondetierra.com* ⊗ *Closed Tues.*

$$ **✕ Deckman's En El Mogor.** Dining at Deckman's is like stepping into the
MEXICAN FUSION quintessential Pinterest photo, replete with an open-air kitchen, straw
Fodor's Choice floor, and wooden tables adorned with wildflowers. As if the chirping
★ birds, adobe structure, soft jazz, and vineyard views weren't enough,
you'll find a revolving menu built around seasonable products from
the neighboring Mogor Ranch. **Known for:** one of best restaurants in
Mexico; farm-to-table experience; artisan-ranch menu. $ *Average main:*
$18 ✉ Carretera Ensenada-Tecate, Km 85.5, San Antonio de Las Minas
☎ 646/188–3960 ⊕ www.deckmans.com ⊗ No breakfast. Closed Tues.

$$ **✕ Finca Altozano.** From the moment you see guests clinking glasses atop
MODERN wine-barrel towers, you know you're in for a memorable dining experi-
MEXICAN ence. On the edge of sprawling vineyards, this rustic setting under tin
Fodor's Choice roofs has a seasonal menu to match. $ *Average main: $18 ✉ Carret-*
★ *era Tecate–Ensenada Km 83, Ejido Francisco Zarco ☎ 646/156–8045*
⊕ www.fincaltozano.com ⊗ No breakfast.

$$$$ **✕ Laja.** Set aside three hours for this extraordinary dining experience
MEXICAN set inside a cozy little house. Celebrity chef Jair Téllez's ambitious prix-
fixe menus (there are four-course and eight-course versions) change
frequently, but may include cucumber gazpacho, yellowtail tartare,
and Swiss chard ravioli with ranch egg and beef juice, all served with
excellent regional wines. **Known for:** eight-course wine pairing; twist
on Mexican and international flavors; farm-to-table with everything
local. $ *Average main: $120 ✉ Carretera 3, Km 83 ☎ 646/155–2556*
⊕ www.lajamexico.com ⊗ Closed Sun.–Tues. and late Nov.–early Jan.
No dinner Wed. Last orders taken at 8:30 pm Thurs.–Sat.

$$$ **✕ Latitud 32.** Named for its location on the map, this upscale restau-
STEAKHOUSE rant at El Cielo Vineyards specializes in grilled cuts and Baja-Yucatán
cuisine. Chef Marco Marin brings his love for Merida to the table with
dishes baked in annatto, sour orange, and Mayan spices that pack
some heat. **Known for:** Baja-Yucatán fusion; certified Angus cuts; pan-
oramic views. $ *Average main: $30 ✉ Parcela 118, Km 7.5, at El Cielo*
☎ 646/155–2220 ⊕ www.vinoselcielo.com.

$$ **✕ Malva.** With sprawling views of vineyards, this restaurant is sur-
ECLECTIC rounded by acres of farmland where Chef Roberto Alcocer gathers
ingredients for nearly 100% of what is served, making this the most
sustainable restaurant in the region and a true farm-to-table experience. Beer, wine, vegetables, fruit, cheese, bread, meat, eggs, honey—
nearly everything he serves is from the on-site farm. **Known for:** locally
sourced food; tasting menu featuring Mexican flavors; Baja seafood
and ranch-grown foods. $ *Average main: $18 ✉ Carretera Ensenada-*
Tecate, Km 96, at Mina Penelope Vinicola, San Antonio de las Minas
☎ 646/155–3085 ⊕ www.minapenelope.com ⊗ Closed Tues.

WHERE TO STAY

Properties in Valle de Guadalupe range from ranch-style B&Bs on
orchards, to eco-lofts on boulder-strewn hillsides. A welcome drink
is fairly standard at most hotels, and some even include breakfast and
wine tasting in the room rate. Don't expect to find TVs or nightlife
in these parts, since wine tasting and early nights are top priorities.
Some hotels request that toilet paper not be flushed due to gray water

systems and clogging drains. Depending on where you're staying, remote properties are at the end of long dusty roads pitted with pot-holes. Ask the front desk for a Fast Track Pass to avoid the border wait at San Ysidro. Charging stations for electric cars are available at newer hotels and restaurants.

$$$
B&B/INN
🍽 **Adobe Guadalupe.** Brick archways, white-stucco walls, and fountains set a tone of endless pleasure and relaxation at Tru Miller's magnificent country inn surrounded by vineyards. **Pros:** on-site food truck serves great tapas; electric car charging stations; rates include wine tasting and breakfast. **Cons:** weekends usually booked six months in advance; chilly pool; no children under 12. $ *Rooms from: $275 ⊠ Off Carretera 3 through Guadalupe village, 6 km (4 miles) along same road, right turn at town of Porvenir* ☎ *646/155–2094* ⊕ *www.adobeguadalupe.com* ↪ *6 rooms* ⏐◎⏐ *Breakfast.*

$
B&B/INN
🍽 **Casa Mayoral.** This road less traveled leads to four cozy cabins in a farmy setting with clucking chickens, vegetable gardens, and ham-mocks swaying under the shade of an orange grove. **Pros:** private decks overlook the valley; friendly owners; sustainable cabins sleep up to six. **Cons:** low water pressure; bumpy road and remote; nothing fancy. $ *Rooms from: $110 ⊠ Carretera Tecate-Ensenada, Km 88.24* ☎ *664/257–2410* ⊕ *www.casamayoral.com* ↪ *4 rooms* ⏐◎⏐ *Breakfast.*

$$$$
HOTEL
🍽 **Encuentro Guadalupe** (*Endemico*). With freestanding steel box-cabins perched on a boulder-strewn hill, this property has architect Jorge Gracia to thank for its success. **Pros:** pet-friendly; unique design; rate includes Continental breakfast and wine tasting. **Cons:** no kids under 13; must sign liability waivers at check-in; room rates don't match quality of service. $ *Rooms from: $550 ⊠ Carretera Tecate-Ensenada, Km 75, San Antonio de las Minas* ☎ *646/155–2775* ⊕ *www.grupoen-cuentro.com.mx* ↪ *22 rooms* ⏐◎⏐ *Breakfast.*

$$
HOTEL
🍽 **Hacienda Guadalupe.** Privacy, comfort, and quality are the pillars of this hacienda-style property that draws a loyal clientele for the central location and reasonable rates. **Pros:** Fast Track Pass for border crossing; gorgeous waterfall pool; hospitality at its best. **Cons:** restaurant closed Tuesday and Wednesday; no TVs. $ *Rooms from: $225 ⊠ Carretera Tecate-Ensenada, Km 81.5* ☎ *646/155–2859* ⊕ *www.haciendaguada-lupe.com* ↪ *16 rooms* ⏐◎⏐ *Breakfast.*

$$$
B&B/INN
🍽 **La Villa del Valle.** Perched on a hilltop overlooking the valley, this luxury inn is part of a country retreat comprised of Vena Cava win-ery, Baja Botánica Boutique, and the restaurant Corazon de Tierra. **Pros:** attention to detail; charming; excellent breakfasts. **Cons:** no kids under 13; guests are not given keys to lock rooms. $ *Rooms from: $295 ⊠ Off Carretera 3, Km 88, between San Antonio de las Minas and Francisco Zarco* ⊕ *Exit at Rancho Sicomoro and follow signs* ☎ *646/156–8007, 818/207–7130 in U.S.* ⊕ *www.lavilladelvalle.com* ↪ *6 rooms* ⏐◎⏐ *Breakfast.*

$
B&B/INN
Fodor's Choice
★
🍽 **Terra del Valle.** Beyond the lavender fields and orange groves of this 12-acre property are ranch-style adobe suites insulated with bales of hay and equipped with surprising amenities like organic bath products, plush robes, and private terraces. **Pros:** organic breakfasts; gracious hosts; excellent value; Jacuzzi and bikes for use. **Cons:** soft mattresses; usually

booked; remote location on dirt road. $ *Rooms from: $140* ⊠ *Rancho La Concha, Camino San José de la Zorra s/n, Ejido El Porvenir* ☎ *646/117–3645* ⊕ *www.terradelvalle.com.mx* ⌇ *5 rooms* |○| *Breakfast.*

SHOPS AND SPAS

Baja Botanica (*Trista*). From the creators of Vena Cava, this lovely boutique produces its own lavender products including soaps, lotions, candles, and oils. Clothing by Mexican designer Trista features dresses, wraps, and other flowing fabrics inspired by the wildflowers of Valle de Guadalupe. ⊠ *Rancho San Marcos Toros Pintos s/n 22750 , at La Villa del Valle* ☎ *646/156–8053* ⊕ *www.bajabotanica.com.*

La Casa de Doña Lupe. Near L.A. Cetto, Dona Lupe's boutique sells berry jams, chili marmalades, olive spreads, cheeses, wines, and other local delicacies. Products can be shipped to the United States. ⊠ *Off Carretera 3, turn left and follow road past L.A. Cetto to yellow building, San Antonio de las Minas* ☎ *646/193–6291* ⊕ *www.lacasadonalupe.com.*

Viniphera Spa (*Quinta Monasterio Spa*). The creative makers of Quinta Monasterio wine combine wine tastings with spa treatments, which incorporate grapes, lavender, citrus, and olive oil directly from their property. Housed in an innovative two-story container, the small spa accommodates one to two guests and includes massages, facials, exfoliations, manicures, pedicures, and aromatherapy in the sauna created from old wine barrels. Some spa packages include lunch; appointments are by reservation only. ⊠ *Quinta Monasterio 12, San Antonio de las Minas* ✛ *Hwy. 3 to el Ejido Porvenir, turn right and follow signs* ☎ *646/668–1011* ⊕ *www.viniphera.com* ☉ *Closed Mon. and Tues.*

ENSENADA

9

65 km (40 miles) south of Puerto Nuevo.

In 1542 Juan Rodríguez Cabrillo first discovered the seaport that Sebastián Vizcaíno named Ensenada-Bahía de Todos Santos (All Saints' Bay) in 1602. Since then the town has drawn a steady stream of explorers and developers. After playing home to ranchers and gold miners, the harbor gradually grew into a major port for shipping agricultural goods, and today Baja's third-largest city (population 369,000) is one of Mexico's largest sea and fishing ports.

There are no beaches in Ensenada proper other than a man-made cove at Hotel Coral, but sandy stretches north and south of town are satisfactory for swimming, sunning, surfing, and camping. Estero Beach is long and clean, with mild waves; the Estero Beach Resort takes up much of the oceanfront, but the beach is public. Although not safe for swimming, the beaches at several of the restaurants along Highway 1 are a nice place to enjoy a cocktail with a view. Surfers populate the strands off Highway 1 north and south of Ensenada, particularly San Miguel, Tres Marías, and Salsipuedes, while scuba divers prefer Punta Banda, by La Bufadora. Lifeguards are rare, so be cautious. The tourist office in Ensenada has a map that shows safe diving and surfing beaches.

Both the waterfront and the main downtown street, Calle Primera are pleasant places to stroll. If you're driving, be sure to take the Centro exit from the highway, since it bypasses the commercial port area.

GETTING HERE AND AROUND

If you're flying into Tijuana, from Aeropuerto Alberado Rodriguez (TIJ) you can find buses that also serve Rosarito and Ensenada. Or, you can hop on a bus at Tijuana Camionera de la Línea station, just inside the border, with service to Rosarito and Ensenada along with city buses to downtown. To head south from Tijuana by car, follow the signs for Ensenada Cuota, the toll road Carretera 1D along the coast. Tollbooths accept U.S. and Mexican currency; there are three tolls of about $2.50 each between Tijuana and Ensenada. Restrooms are available near toll stations. Ensenada is an hour south of Tijuana on this road. The alternative free road—Carretera Transpeninsular Highway 1, or Ensenada Libre—is curvy and not as well maintained. (Entry to it is on a side street in a congested area of downtown Tijuana.)

Highway 1 continues south of Ensenada to Guerrero Negro, at the border between Baja California and Baja Sur, and on to Baja's southernmost resorts; there are no tolls past Ensenada. Highway 1 is fairly well maintained and signposted.

Although there are several rental car companies in Tijuana, Alamo is one of the few that includes insurance and tax in the quoted rate, rather than tacking on hidden fees at arrival. California Baja Rent-A-Car is the only agency to rent vehicles for Mexico on the San Diego side of the border. Rates start at $60 per day. Drivers must carry mandatory Third Party Liability, an expense that is not covered by U.S. insurance policies or by credit card companies.

If driving your own vehicle across the San Ysidro border, ask your hotel if they offer a Fast Track Pass, which helps eliminate the long border wait on the return. Otherwise expect to wait around two hours on an average weekend. Border wait times are available at ⊕ *bwt.cbp.gov.*

Taxis are a reliable means of getting around Ensenada, and you can flag them down on the street.

Visitor and Tour Info Ensenada Tourist Information Office. ✉ *Blvd. Costero, Zona Playitas* ⊹ *Just south of cruise ship terminal* ☎ *664/682–3367* ⊕ *www. discoverbajacalifornia.com.*

EXPLORING

TOP ATTRACTIONS

Fodor's Choice
★

La Cava de Marcelo. For many, a visit to Baja Norte must include an afternoon drive to the cheese caves of Marcelo in Ojos Negros, just 45 minutes outside of Ensenada. With Swiss-Italian roots, Owner Marcelo Castro Chacon is now the fourth generation to carry on the *queso* tradition since it first began in 1911. A visit to the farm includes a tour of the milking facilities and a tasting of seven cheeses and their signature Ramonetti red wine. Milder selections seasoned with basil, black pepper, and rosemary are more popular with locals than their sharper cheeses, aged up to two-and-a-half years, loved by foreigners. As Mexico's only cheese cave (and the first in Latin America), this beloved factory produces 450 pounds of cheese per day. Milking takes place at 5 pm daily and the small on-site shop sells the remarkable marmalade and wine that accompany your cheese tasting. Those with time and an appetite can dine under the shade of a peppertree for a lunch menu integrating Marcelo's cheeses and organic fruits and vegetables from his farm (expect flies in summer). The cactus salad and portobello mushrooms with melted cheese make the ideal starters to the regional trout served with roasted garlic. The fig mousse alone is worth a visit. ⊠ *Rancho La Campana, 48 km (30 miles) east of Ensenada, off Hwy. 3, follow signs to La Cava de Queso, Ojos Negros* ☎ *646/117–0293* ✆ *$10 tour and tasting.*

Mercado de Mariscos (*Mercado Negro*). At the northernmost point of Boulevard Costero, the main street along the waterfront, is an indoor-outdoor fish market where row after row of counters display piles of shrimp, tuna, dorado, and other fish caught off Baja's coasts. Outside, stands sell grilled or smoked fish, seafood cocktails, and fish tacos. You can pick up a few souvenirs, eat well for very little money, and take some great photographs. If your stomach is delicate, try the fish tacos at the cleaner, quieter Plaza de Mariscos in the shadow of the giant beige Plaza de Marina that blocks the view of the traditional fish market from the street. ⊠ *Ensenada.*

WORTH NOTING

Avenida Lopez Mateos (*Calle Primera*). Avenida López Mateos, commonly known as Calle Primera, is the center of Ensenada's traditional tourist zone and shopping district. Hotels, shops, restaurants, and bars line the avenue for eight blocks, from its beginning at the foot of the Chapultepec Hills to the dry channel of the Arroyo de Ensenada. The avenue also has sidewalk cafés, art galleries, and most of the town's souvenir stores where you can find pottery, glassware, silver, and other Mexican crafts. ⊠ *Av. Lopez Mateos.*

Las Bodegas de Santo Tomás. One of Baja's oldest wine producers gives tours and tastings at its downtown winery and bottling plant. Santo Tomás's best wines are the Alisio Chardonnay, the Cabernet, and the Tempranillo; avoid the overpriced Unico. The winery also operates the enormous wineshop, a brick building across the avenue. The Santo Tomás Vineyards can be found on the eastern side of Highway 1 about 50 km (31 miles) south of Ensenada, fairly near the ruins of the Misión Santo Tomás de Aquino, which was founded by Dominican priests in 1791: only a few pieces of adobe remain of the old church. ⊠ *Av. Miramar 666, Centro* ☎ *646/178–3333* ⊕ *www.santo-tomas.com* ✆ *4 tastings $6.*

Riviera del Pacífico (*Civico y Cultural de Ensenada*). Officially called the Centro Social, Cívico y Cultural de Ensenada, the Riviera is a rambling, white, hacienda-style mansion built in the 1920s. The former casino and hotel was frequented by wealthy U.S. citizens and Mexicans, particularly during Prohibition. You can tour the gardens and some of the elegant ballrooms and halls, which occasionally host art shows and civic events. ⊠ *Blvd. Lázaro Cárdenas 1421, Blvd. Costero at Av. Riviera, Centro* ☎ *646/176–4310* ⊕ *www.rivieradeensenada.com.mx* ✆ *Building and gardens free; museum entry $1.*

9

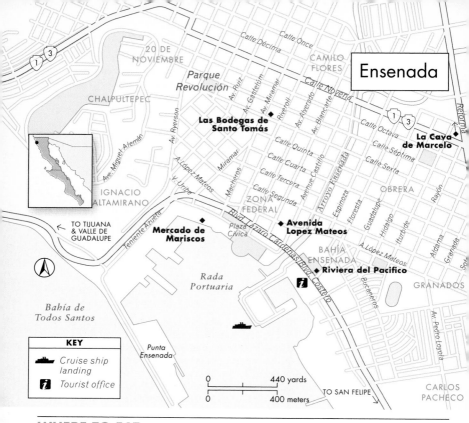

Ensenada

WHERE TO EAT

$$ ✕ **El Rey Sol.** From its chateaubriand *bouquetière* (garnished with a bou-
FRENCH quet of vegetables) to the savory chicken chipotle cooked with brandy,
port wine, and cream, this classy French restaurant has been family-
owned since 1947. It's considered one of the top restaurants in Mexico
and has won the Five Diamond Award every year since 2004. **Known
for:** French pastries; table-side Caesar salad; first-rate service. ⑤ *Aver-
age main: $20* ⊠ *Av. López Mateos 1000, Centro* ☎ *646/178–1733*
⊕ *www.elreysol.com.*

$ ✕ **La Guerrerense.** This food-cart stall off of Ensenada's bustling Calle
SEAFOOD Primera is *the* place where locals get a solid helping of the region's
Fodor's Choice seafood. Established in 1960, La Guerrerense has been featured on
★ international shows like Anthony Bourdain's *No Reservations.* **Known
for:** world's best tostadas; fresh ceviche with mango; homemade salsas.
⑤ *Average main: $10* ⊠ *Calle Primera at Alvarado* ☎ *646/206–0445*
⊕ *www.laguerrerense.com* ⊙ *Closed Tues. No dinner.*

$$ ✕ **Manzanilla.** Two of the most exciting chef-owners in Baja Norte,
ECLECTIC Benito Molina and Solange Muris, have taken a truly modern approach
to Mexican cuisine at Manzanilla, integrating the freshest catches
from the local waters—oysters, mussels, and clams, for instance—and
using ingredients like ginger, saffron, smoked tomato marmalade, and

huitlacoche (corn fungus). The ahi with ginger strawberry vinaigrette melts in your mouth and the white clam with Gorgonzola is delicious. **Known for:** fresh Baja seafood; homemade tagliatelli; grilled quail with wild mushrooms. $ *Average main: $20* ⊠ *Recinto Portuario, Teniente Azueta 139, Centro* ☎ *646/175–7073* ⊕ *www.rmanzanilla.com* ☯ *Closed Mon. and Tues.*

$$ ✕ **Ophelia.** For a garden escape along Carretera 1, check out Ophelia,
ECLECTIC opened by Rosendo Ramos. It's a favorite among the Ensenada foodie crowd. **Known for:** octopus tacos and shrimp ceviche; Zen vibe in garden patio. $ *Average main: $16* ⊠ *Carretera Tijuana-Ensenada, Km 103* ☎ *646/175–8365* ☯ *Closed Mon.*

$$ ✕ **Sano's.** This elegant restaurant, with its white linens, open trusses,
STEAKHOUSE and soft candlelight is the best steak house in Baja California. Prepared
Fodor'sChoice on mesquite wood, the steak is divine. **Known for:** best steak in Baja;
★ dishes cooked to perfection; excellent service. $ *Average main: $20* ⊠ *Carretera Tijuana-Ensenada, Km 108, just after Playitas Club del Mar, heading south to Ensenada* ☎ *646/174–4061* ⊕ *sanosrestaurant. com/main_sanos_eng.htm.*

WHERE TO STAY

$$ ⌂ **Cabañas Cuatrocuatros.** Situated among vineyards is this peaceful set-
B&B/INN tlement of 14 luxury tents with creature comforts like air-conditioning,
FAMILY a minibar, fireplace, king-size beds, and private sundecks. **Pros:** the ultimate in Baja "glamping"; mountain bikes for exploring; private beach. **Cons:** 15 minutes from town; restaurant closes at 6 pm and front desk at 8 pm; tents beginning to show some wear. $ *Rooms from: $200* ⊠ *Transpeninsular Hwy., Km 89* ☎ *646/174–6780* ⊕ *www.cabanascu-atrocuatros.com.mx* ⤳ *14 cabañas* ⦵ *No meals.*

$$ ⌂ **Estero Beach Resort.** Families love this long-standing resort on Ensena-
RESORT da's top beach, especially because of its private location and endless
FAMILY activities like horseback riding, tennis, volleyball, kayaking, and Jet Skiing. **Pros:** wonderful breakfasts; right on the beach; good for families. **Cons:** rooms by parking lot aren't great; boat launch fee; food somewhat pricey. $ *Rooms from: $180* ⊠ *Carretera Tijuana-Ensenada, intersection of Lazaro Cardenas and Lupita Novelo, Estero Beach* ✛ *10 km (6 miles) south of Ensenada* ☎ *646/176–6235, 646/176–6225* ⊕ *www.hotelesterobeach.com* ⤳ *96 rooms* ⦵ *No meals.*

$$ ⌂ **Hotel Coral & Marina.** As the most upscale accommodations in
RESORT Ensenada, this all-suites resort has indoor-outdoor pools, a spa, tennis courts, a water-sports center, and a marina with slips for 350 boats. **Pros:** midweek discounts; spacious rooms; outstanding Sunday brunch; guests receive Fast Track Pass for border crossing. **Cons:** pool can get noisy with kids; patchy Wi-Fi; slow elevator; often full on weekends. $ *Rooms from: $208* ⊠ *Carretera Tijuana-Ensenada, Km 103, Zona Playitas* ☎ *646/175–0000, 800/862–9020 in U.S.* ⊕ *www.hotelcoral. com* ⤳ *147 suites* ⦵ *No meals.*

$$ ⌂ **Las Rosas Hotel & Spa.** This intimate hotel north of Ensenada has
RESORT rooms facing the ocean and pool, and some even have fireplaces and hot tubs. **Pros:** laid-back and relaxing; great ocean views; well-appointed rooms. **Cons:** dated rooms; rocky beach; some street noise; weak Wi-Fi

9

signal in rooms. $ *Rooms from: $154 ⊠ Carretera Tijuana-Ensenada, Km 105.5, just north of Ensenada, Zona Playitas* ☎ *646/174–4310, 646/174–4360* ⊕ *www.lasrosas.com* ⤳ *48 rooms* ❍| *No meals.*

$$
RESORT   ⌂ **Punta Morro Resort.** In one of Ensenada's most beautiful settings, this 24-room hotel has charm and tranquillity to spare with spacious rooms fully remodeled in 2017. **Pros:** great views; great restaurant; Fast Track Pass for border. **Cons:** no bathtubs; uncomfortable couches in rooms; rocky beach not suitable for swimming. $ *Rooms from: $229 ⊠ Carretera Tijuana-Ensenada, Km 106, Zona Playitas* ☎ *646/178–3507* ⊕ *www.hotelpuntamorro.com* ⤳ *24 rooms* ❍| *No meals.*

NIGHTLIFE

When Valle de Guadalupe shuts down for the night, Ensenada is just getting started. The corner of Avenida Ruiz and Avenida López Mateos (Calle Primera) has the most action, with loud music and cheap beers in a cantina setting. For something a bit more refined, there are a few hip microbreweries near the coast.

Agua Mala. Don't be fooled by the name "bad water." This artisanal brewery pours a mean oatmeal stout and imperial IPA. Nearly a dozen handcrafted beers are served in the container-bar where a menu prepared by chef Drew Deckman pairs well with just about everything on tap. ⊠ *Carretera Tijuana-Ensenada Km 103* ☎ *646/174–6068* ⊕ *www.aguamala.com.mx.*

Hussong's Cantina. Hussong's Cantina has been an Ensenada landmark since 1892, and has changed little since then. Ask anyone here and they'll tell you that this is where the margarita was invented by bartender Don Carlos Orozco in October 1941; however, this is just one of several local establishments that state that claim to fame. Regardless, come by Saturday when you can get two margaritas for the price of one, or 2-for-1 beers every Tuesday and Thursday. A security guard stands by the front door to handle the often-rowdy crowd—mostly local men. The floor is covered with sawdust, and the noise is usually deafening, pierced by mariachi and ranchera musicians and the whoops and hollers of the pie-eyed. There's live music Tuesday through Sunday. ⊠ *Av. Ruíz 113, Centro* ☎ *646/178–3210* ⊕ *cantinahussongs.com/home.html* ⊗ *Closed Mon.*

Papas & Beer. The massive Papas & Beer attracts a rowdy college crowd. There are daily specials on shots and cocktails, as well as regular drinking contests. Live music takes place on weekends. For a cheap party, arrive before noon for a bucket of 10 beers and nachos for $25. ⊠ *Av. Ruíz 102, Centro* ☎ *646/178–8826* ⊕ *www.papasandbeer.com.*

Fodor'sChoice   **Wendlandt Cerveceria.** For a casual yet refined bar scene, this chic spot is
★   a favorite of Ensenada's many vintners, chefs, and brewers. Showcasing the local craft beers in the region, as well as wines from nearby Valle del Guadalupe, the friendly owners also brew their own cervezas on-site. Beer tastings in their brewery are available by reservation only. If you're hungry, Wendlandt serves elevated bar food using local ingredients. The nondescript bar is simply marked by their logo and an antique door. ⊠ *Blvd. Costero 248-1, Centro* ☎ *646/178–2938* ⊕ *www.wendlandt.com.mx.*

SHOPPING

Most of the tourist shops hold court along Avenida López Mateos (Calle Primera) beside the hotels and restaurants. There are several two-story shopping arcades, some with empty spaces for rent. Dozens of curio shops line the street, all selling similar selections of pottery, serapes, and the tackier trinkets and T-shirts.

Bazar Casa Ramirez. Bazar Casa Ramirez sells high-quality Talavera pottery and other ceramics, paintings by local artists, jewelry, wooden carvings, and papier-mâché figurines. Everything here is made in Mexico. Be sure to check out the displays upstairs. ⊠ *Av. López Mateos 498, Centro* ☎ *646/178–8209.*

Centro Artesenal de Ensenada. The Centro Artesenal de Ensenada has a smattering of galleries and shops, and it's a good place to buy quality souvenirs. ⊠ *Blvd. Costero 1094-39, Centro.*

Fausto Polanco. A former hotel from 1948, this furniture store features lovely handcrafted wood pieces, fabrics, ironwork, and home accessories. Meander the historical landmark where works of art are displayed throughout each room, reminiscent of an old Mexican hacienda. ⊠ *Av. López Mateos 1107, at Castillo, Centro* ☎ *646/174–0314* ⊕ *www.faustopolanco.com.mx.*

Los Castillo. Operated by the renowned Sanchez-Macfarland family for nearly five decades, this jewelry store has the highest quality and most unique silver pieces from famous designers from the Taxco region. ⊠ *Lopez Mateos 1084, Centro* ☎ *646/156–5274* ⊕ *www.loscastillosilver.com.*

Los Globos. Ensenada's oldest outdoor swap meet is open daily, with vendors and shoppers most abundant on weekends. ⊠ *Calle 9, 3 blocks east of Av. Reforma, Centro.*

SPORTS AND THE OUTDOORS

SPORTFISHING

The best angling takes place from April through October, with bottom fishing the best in winter. Charter vessels and party boats are available from several outfitters along the boardwalk and off the sportfishing pier. Mexican fishing licenses for the day ($10) are available from charter companies.

Sergio's Sportfishing. One of the best sportfishing companies in Ensenada, Sergio's Sportfishing has year-round private charter or open party boats. Whale-watching tours are available from December 15 to April 15. ⊠ *Sportfishing Pier, Blvd. Lázaro Cárdenas 6, Centro* ☎ *646/178–2185, 619/399–7224 in U.S.* ⊕ *www.sergiosfishing.com/whales* 🎣 *Fishing $70 per person on a group boat, including the cost of a license; whale-watching $30 per person.*

9

WATER SPORTS

Estero Beach and Punta Banda (en route to La Bufadora, south of Ensenada) are both good kayaking areas, although facilities are limited. A small selection of water-sports equipment is available at the Estero Beach Resort.

WHALE-WATCHING

Boats leave the Ensenada sportfishing pier for whale-watching trips from December through March. The gray whales migrating from the north to bays and lagoons in southern Baja pass through Todos Santos Bay, often close to shore. Binoculars and cameras with telephoto capabilities come in handy. The trips last about three hours. Vessels are available from several outfitters at the sportfishing pier. Expect to pay about $30 for a three-hour tour.

DETOUR TO LA BUFA-DORA

La Bufadora. Legend has it that La Bufadora, an impressive tidal blowhole (*la bufadora* means the buffalo snort) in the coastal cliffs at Punta Banda, was created by a whale or sea serpent trapped in an undersea cave.

The road to La Bufadora along Punta Banda—an isolated, mountainous point that juts into the sea—is lined with olive, craft, and tamale stands; the drive gives you a sampling of Baja's wilderness. If you're in need of some cooling off, turn off the highway at the sign for La Jolla Beach Camp. The camp charges a small admission fee for day use of the beachside facilities, but it's a great place to do a few "laps" of lazy freestyle or breaststroke at La Jolla Beach. At La Bufadora, expect a small fee to park, and then a half-mile walk past T-shirt hawkers and souvenir stands to the water hole itself. A public bus runs from the downtown Ensenada station to Maneadero, from which you can catch a minibus labeled Punta Banda that goes to La Bufadora. Guided tours from Ensenada to La Bufadora will run you about $15. ⊠ *Carretera 23, 31 km (19 miles) south of Ensenada, Punta Banda.*

UNDERSTANDING LOS CABOS

SPANISH VOCABULARY

SPANISH VOCABULARY

	ENGLISH	SPANISH	PRONUNCIATION
BASICS			
	Yes/no	Sí/no	see/no
	Please	Por favor	pore fah-**vore**
	May I?	¿Me permite?	may pair-**mee**-tay
	Thank you (very much)	(Muchas) gracias	(**moo**-chas) **grah**-see-as
	You're welcome	De nada	day **nah**-dah
	Excuse me	Con permiso	con pair-**mee**-so
	Pardon me	¿Perdón?	pair-**dohn**
	Could you tell me?	¿Podría decirme?	po-dree-ah deh-**seer**-meh
	I'm sorry	Lo siento	lo see-**en**-toh
	Good morning!	¡Buenos días!	**bway**-nohs **dee**-ahs
	Good afternoon!	¡Buenas tardes!	**bway**-nahs **tar**-dess
	Good evening!	¡Buenas noches!	**bway**-nahs **no**-chess
	Good-bye!	¡Adiós!/¡Hasta luego!	ah-dee-**ohss/ah**-stah **lwe**-go
	Mr./Mrs.	Señor/Señora	sen-**yor**/sen-**yohr**-ah
	Miss	Señorita	sen-yo-**ree**-tah
	Pleased to meet you	Mucho gusto	**moo**-cho **goose**-toh
	How are you?	¿Cómo está usted?	**ko**-mo es-**tah** oo-**sted**
	Very well, thank you.	Muy bien, gracias.	**moo**-ee bee-**en**, **grah**-see-as
	And you?	¿Y usted?	ee oos-**ted**
	Hello (on the telephone)	Diga	**dee**-gah
NUMBERS			
	1	un, uno	oon, **oo**-no
	2	dos	dos
	3	tres	tress
	4	cuatro	**kwah**-tro
	5	cinco	**sink**-oh
	6	seis	saice
	7	siete	see-**et**-eh
	8	ocho	**o**-cho

ENGLISH	SPANISH	PRONUNCIATION
9	nueve	new- **eh**-vey
10	diez	dee- **es**
11	once	**ohn**-seh
12	doce	**doh**-seh
13	trece	**treh**-seh
14	catorce	ka- **tohr**-seh
15	quince	**keen**-seh
16	dieciséis	dee- **es**-ee- **saice**
17	diecisiete	dee- **es**-ee-see- **et**-eh
18	dieciocho	dee- **es**-ee- **o**-cho
19	diecinueve	**dee-es**-ee-new- **ev**-eh
20	veinte	**vain**-teh
21	veinte y uno/veintiuno	**vain**-te- **oo**-noh
30	treinta	**train**-tah
32	treinta y dos	train-tay- **dohs**
40	cuarenta	kwah- **ren**-tah
43	cuarenta y tres	kwah- **ren**-tay- **tress**
50	cincuenta	seen- **kwen**-tah
54	cincuenta y cuatro	seen- **kwen**-tay **kwah**-tro
60	sesenta	sess- **en**-tah
65	sesenta y cinco	sess- **en**-tay **seen**-ko
70	setenta	set- **en**-tah
76	setenta y seis	set- **en**-tay **saice**
80	ochenta	oh- **chen**-tah
87	ochenta y siete	oh- **chen**-tay see- **yet**-eh
90	noventa	no- **ven**-tah
98	noventa y ocho	no- **ven**-tah- **o**-choh
100	cien	see- **en**
101	ciento uno	see- **en**-toh **oo**-noh
200	doscientos	doh-see- **en**-tohss
500	quinientos	keen- **yen**-tohss
700	setecientos	set-eh-see- **en**-tohss

ENGLISH	SPANISH	PRONUNCIATION
900	novecientos	no-veh-see- **en**-tohss
1,000	mil	meel
2,000	dos mil	dohs meel
1,000,000	un millón	oon meel- **yohn**

COLORS

black	negro	**neh**-groh
blue	azul	ah- **sool**
brown	café	kah- **feh**
green	verde	**ver**-deh
pink	rosa	**ro**-sah
purple	morado	mo- **rah**-doh
orange	naranja	na- **rahn**-hah
red	rojo	**roh**-hoh
white	blanco	**blahn**-koh
yellow	amarillo	ah-mah- **ree**-yoh

DAYS OF THE WEEK

Sunday	domingo	doe- **meen**-goh
Monday	lunes	**loo**-ness
Tuesday	martes	**mahr**-tess
Wednesday	miércoles	me- **air**-koh-less
Thursday	jueves	hoo- **ev**-ess
Friday	viernes	vee- **air**-ness
Saturday	sábado	**sah**-bah-doh

MONTHS

January	enero	eh- **neh**-roh
February	febrero	feh- **breh**-roh
March	marzo	**mahr**-soh
April	abril	ah- **breel**
May	mayo	**my**-oh
June	junio	**hoo**-nee-oh
July	julio	**hoo**-lee-yoh
August	agosto	ah- **ghost**-toh
September	septiembre	sep-tee- **em**-breh

ENGLISH	SPANISH	PRONUNCIATION
October	octubre	oak-**too**-breh
November	noviembre	no-vee-**em**-breh
December	diciembre	dee-see-**em**-breh

USEFUL PHRASES

ENGLISH	SPANISH	PRONUNCIATION
Do you speak English?	¿Habla usted inglés?	**ah**-blah oos-**ted** in-**glehs**
I don't speak Spanish	No hablo español	no **ah**-bloh es-pahn-**yol**
I don't understand (you)	No entiendo	no en-tee-**en**-doh
I understand (you)	Entiendo	en-tee-**en**-doh
I don't know	No sé	no seh
I am American/British	Soy americano (americana)/inglés(a)	soy ah-meh-ree-**kah**-no (ah-meh-ree-**kah**-nah)/ in-**glehs(ah)**
What's your name?	¿Cómo se llama usted?	koh-mo seh **yah**-mah oos-**ted**
My name is ...	Me llamo ...	may **yah**-moh
What time is it?	¿Qué hora es?	keh **o**-rah es
It is one, two, three ... o'clock.	Es la una./Son las dos, tres ...	es la **oo**-nah/sohnahs dohs, tress
Yes, please/No, thank you	Sí, por favor/No, gracias	**see** pohr fah-**vor** /no **grah**-see-us
How?	¿Cómo?	**koh**-mo
When?	¿Cuándo?	**kwahn**-doh
This/Next week	Esta semana/ La semana que entra	**es**-teh seh-**mah**-nah/ lah seh-**mah**-nah keh **en**-trah
This/Next month	Este mes/El próximo mes	**es**-teh mehs/el **proke**-see-mo mehs
This/Next year	Este año/El año que viene	**es**-teh **ahn**-yo/el **ahn**-yo keh vee-**yen**-ay
Yesterday/today/tomorrow	Ayer/hoy/mañana	ah-**yehr** /oy/ mahn-**yah**-nah
This morning/afternoon	Esta mañana/ tarde	**es**-tah mahn-**yah**-nah/ **tar**-deh
Tonight	Esta noche	**es**-tah **no**-cheh

ENGLISH	SPANISH	PRONUNCIATION
What?	¿Qué?	keh
What is it?	¿Qué es esto?	keh es **es**-toh
Why?	¿Por qué?	pore **keh**
Who?	¿Quién?	kee- **yen**
Where is … ?	¿Dónde está … ?	**dohn**-deh es- **tah**
the train station?	la estación del tren?	la es-tah-see-on del trehn
the subway station?	la estación del tren subterráneo?	la es-ta-see- **on** del trehn la es-ta-see- **on** soob-teh- **rrahn**-eh-oh
the bus stop?	la parada del autobus?	la pah- **rah**-dah del ow-toh- **boos**
the post office?	la oficina de correos?	la oh-fee- **see**- nah deh koh- **rreh**-os
the bank?	el banco?	el **bahn**-koh
the hotel?	el hotel?	el oh- **tel**
the store?	la tienda?	la tee- **en**-dah
the cashier?	la caja?	la **kah**-hah
the museum?	el museo?	el moo- **seh**-oh
the hospital?	el hospital?	el ohss-pee- **tal**
the elevator?	el ascensor?	el ah- **sen**-sohr
the bathroom?	el baño?	el **bahn**-yoh
Here/there	Aquí/allá	ah- **key** /ah- **yah**
Open/closed	Abierto/cerrado	ah-bee- **er**-toh/ ser- **ah**-doh
Left/right	Izquierda/derecha	iss-key- **er**-dah/ dare- **eh**-chah
Straight ahead	Derecho	dare- **eh**-choh
Is it near/far?	¿Está cerca/lejos?	es- **tah sehr**-kah/ **leh**-hoss
I'd like …	Quisiera …	kee-see-ehr-ah
a room	un cuarto/una habitación	oon **kwahr**-toh/ **oo**-nah ah-bee- tah-see- **on**
the key	la llave	lah **yah**-veh
a newspaper	un periódico	oon pehr-ee- **oh**- dee-koh

ENGLISH	SPANISH	PRONUNCIATION
a stamp	un sello de correo	oon **seh**-yo deh korr-ee-oh
I'd like to buy ...	Quisiera comprar ...	kee-see- **ehr**-ah kohm- **prahr**
cigarettes	cigarrillos	ce-ga- **ree**-yohs
matches	cerillos	ser- **ee**-ohs
a dictionary	un diccionario	oon deek-see-oh- **nah**-ree-oh
soap	jabón	hah- **bohn**
sunglasses	gafas de sol	**ga**-fahs deh sohl
suntan lotion	Loción bronceadora	loh-see- **ohn** brohn- seh-ah- **do**-rah
a map	un mapa	oon **mah**-pah
a magazine	una revista	**oon**-ah reh- **veess**-tah
paper	papel	pah- **pel**
envelopes	sobres	**so**-brehs
a postcard	una tarjeta postal	**oon**-ah tar- **het**-ah post- **ahl**
How much is it?	¿Cuánto cuesta?	**kwahn**-toh **kwes**-tah
It's expensive/ cheap	Está caro/barato	es- **tah kah**-roh/ bah- **rah**-toh
A little/a lot	Un poquito/mucho	oon poh- **kee**-toh/ **moo**-choh
More/less	Más/menos	mahss/ **men**-ohss
Enough/too much/too little	Suficiente/demasiado/ muy poco	soo-fee-see- **en**-teh/ deh-mah-see- **ah**- doh/ **moo**-ee poh-koh
Telephone	Teléfono	tel- **ef**-oh-no
Telegram	Telegrama	teh-leh- **grah**-mah
I am ill	Estoy enfermo(a)	es- **toy** en- **fehr**- moh(mah)
Please call a doctor	Por favor llame a un medico	pohr fah- **vor ya**-meh ah oon **med**-ee-koh

ON THE ROAD

Avenue	Avenida	ah-ven- **ee**-dah
Broad, tree-lined boulevard	Bulevar	boo-leh- **var**

ENGLISH	SPANISH	PRONUNCIATION
Fertile plain	Vega	**veh**-gah
Highway	Carretera	car-reh- **ter**-ah
Mountain pass	Puerto	poo- **ehr**-toh
Street	Calle	**cah**-yeh
Waterfront promenade	Rambla	**rahm**-blah
Wharf	Embarcadero	em-bar-cah- **deh**-ro

IN TOWN

Cathedral	Catedral	cah-teh- **dral**
Church	Templo/Iglesia	**tem**-plo/ ee- **glehs**- see-ah
City hall	Casa de gobierno	kah-sah deh go-bee- **ehr**-no
Door, gate	Puerta portón	poo- **ehr**-tah por- **ton**
Entrance/exit	Entrada/salida	en- **trah**-dah/ sah- **lee**- dah
Inn, rustic bar, or restaurant	Taverna	tah- **vehr**-nah
Main square	Plaza principal	plah-thah prin- see- **pahl**

DINING OUT

Can you recommend a good restaurant?	¿Puede recomendarme un buen restaurante?	**pweh**-deh rreh- koh-mehn- **dahr**- me oon bwehn rrehs-tow- **rahn**-teh?
Where is it located?	¿Dónde está situado?	**dohn**-deh ehs- **tah** see- **twah**-doh?
Do I need reservations?	¿Se necesita una reservación?	seh neh-seh- **see**-tah oo-nah rreh-sehr-bah- **syohn**?
I'd like to reserve a table ...	Quisiera reservar una mesa ...	kee- **syeh**-rah rreh- sehr- **bahr oo**-nah **meh**-sah ...
for two people.	para dos personas.	**pah**-rah dohs pehr- **soh**-nahs
for this evening.	para esta noche.	**pah**-rah **ehs**-tah **noh**-cheh
for 8 pm	para las ocho de la noche.	**pah**-rah lahs **oh**-choh deh lah **noh**-cheh

ENGLISH	SPANISH	PRONUNCIATION
A bottle of ...	Una botella de ...	**oo**-nah bo- **teh**-yah deh
A cup of ...	Una taza de ...	**oo**-nah **tah**-thah deh
A glass of ...	Un vaso de ...	oon **vah**-so deh
Ashtray	Un cenicero	oon sen-ee- **seh**-roh
Bill/check	La cuenta	lah **kwen**-tah
Bread	El pan	el pahn
Breakfast	El desayuno	el deh-sah- **yoon**-oh
Butter	La mantequilla	lah man-teh- **key**-yah
Cheers!	¡Salud!	sah- **lood**
Cocktail	Un aperitivo	oon ah-pehr-ee- **tee**-voh
Dinner	La cena	lah **seh**-nah
Dish	Un plato	oon **plah**-toh
Menu of the day	Menú del día	meh- **noo** del **dee**-ah
Enjoy!	¡Buen provecho!	bwehn pro- **veh**-cho
Fixed-price menu	Menú fijo o turistico	meh- **noo** **fee**-hoh oh too- **ree**-stee-coh
Fork	El tenedor	el ten-eh- **dor**
Is the tip included?	¿Está incluida la propina?	es- **tah** in-cloo- **ee**-dah lah pro- **pee**-nah
Knife	El cuchillo	el koo- **chee**-yo
Large portion of savory snacks	Raciónes	rah-see- **oh**-nehs
Lunch	La comida	lah koh- **mee**-dah
Menu	La carta, El menú	lah **cart**-ah, el meh- **noo**
Napkin	La servilleta	lah sehr-vee- **yet**-ah
Pepper	La pimienta	lah pee-me- **en**-tah
Please give me	Por favor déme	pore fah- **vor deh**-meh
Salt	La sal	lah sahl
Savory snacks	Tapas	**tah**-pahs
Spoon	Una cuchara	**oo**-nah koo- **chah**-rah
Sugar	El azúcar	el ah- **thu**-kar
Waiter!/Waitress!	¡Por favor Señor/ Señorita!	pohr fah- **vor** sen- **yor** /sen-yor- **ee**-tah

TRAVEL SMART
LOS CABOS

GETTING HERE AND AROUND

▌AIR TRAVEL

You can now fly nonstop to Los Cabos from Atlanta, Charlotte, Chicago, Dallas/Fort Worth, Denver, Houston, Las Vegas, Los Angeles, Mexico City, New York, Phoenix, Portland, Sacramento, Salt Lake City, San Diego, San Francisco, and Seattle. From most other destinations, you will have to make a connecting flight, either in the United States or in Mexico City. Via nonstop service, Los Cabos is about 2 hours from San Diego, about 2¼ hours from Houston, 3 hours from Dallas/Fort Worth, 2½ hours from Los Angeles, and 2½ hours from Phoenix. Flying time from New York to Mexico City, where you must switch planes to continue to Los Cabos, is 5 hours. Los Cabos is about a 2½-hour flight from Mexico City.

Airlines and Airports Airline and Airport Links.com. ⊕ www.airlineandairportlinks.com.

Airline Security Issues Transportation Security Administration. ⊕ www.tsa.gov.

AIRPORTS

Aeropuerto Internacional de San José del Cabo (SJD) is 1 km (½ mile) west of the Transpeninsular Highway (Highway 1), 13 km (8 miles) north of San José del Cabo, and 48 km (30 miles) northeast of Cabo San Lucas. The airport has restaurants, duty-free shops, and car-rental agencies. Los Cabos flights increase in winter with seasonal flights from U.S. airlines, and, despite growing numbers of visitors to the area, the airport manages to keep up nicely with the crowds.

Aeropuerto General Manuel Márquez de León serves La Paz. It's 11 km (7 miles) northwest of the Baja California Sur capital, which itself is 188 km (117 miles) northwest of Los Cabos.

Airport Information Aeropuerto General Manuel Márquez de León (*La Paz International Airport*). ✉ Carretera Transpeninsular Km 13, La Paz ☎ 612/124–6307. **Aeropuerto Internacional Los Cabos** (*Los Cabos International Airport*). ✉ Carretera Transpeninsular Km 43.5, San José del Cabo ☎ 624/146–5111 ⊕ www.aeropuertosgap.com.mx.

FLIGHTS

Calafia Airlines flies charter flights from Los Cabos for whale-watching from January through March. Aeroméxico has service to Los Cabos from San Diego, and flights to La Paz from Los Angeles, San Diego, Tijuana, and Mexico City.

Alaska Airlines flies nonstop to Los Cabos from Los Angeles, San Diego, Seattle, Portland, and San Francisco. American Airlines flies to Los Cabos from Dallas–Fort Worth, Chicago, Los Angeles, and New York (JFK). British Airways and other European carriers fly to Mexico City where connections can be made for the 2½-hour flight to Los Cabos.

United Airlines has nonstop service from Houston. Delta flies to Los Cabos from Ontario, California, and from Atlanta. They also have flights to La Paz from Los Angeles. As of 2017, Southwest offers direct flights from San Diego to Los Cabos.

Airline Contacts Aeroméxico. ☎ 800/237–6639 in U.S., 624/146–5097 in Los Cabos, 612/124–6366 in La Paz ⊕ www.aeromexico.com. **Alaska Airlines.** ☎ 800/252–7522 ⊕ www.alaskaair.com. **American Airlines.** ☎ 800/433–7300, 624/146–5303 in Los Cabos ⊕ www.aa.com. **British Airways.** ☎ 800/247–9297 in U.S. ⊕ www.britishairways.com. **Calafia Airlines.** ☎ 624/143–4302 in Los Cabos, 619/489–1439 in U.S. ⊕ www.calafiaairlines.com. **Delta Airlines.** ☎ 800/221–1212, 624/146–5005 in Los Cabos ⊕ www.delta.com. **Southwest.** ☎ 800/435–9792 ⊕ www.southwest.com. **United Airlines.** ☎ 800/241–6522, 01800/900–5000 toll-free in Mexico ⊕ www.united.com.

GROUND TRANSPORTATION

If you have purchased a vacation package from an airline or travel agency, transfers are usually included. Otherwise, only the most exclusive hotels in Los Cabos offer transfers. Fares from the airport to hotels in Los Cabos are expensive. The least expensive transport is by city bus Ruta del Desierto ($5) or by shuttle buses that stop at various hotels along the route; fares run $16 to $25 per person. Private taxi fares run from $65 to $100. Some hotels can arrange a pickup, which is much faster and costs about the same as a shuttle. Ask about hotel transfers, especially if you're staying in the East Cape, La Paz, or Todos Santos and not renting a car—cab fares to these areas are astronomical.

Sales representatives from various timeshare properties compete vociferously for clients; often you won't realize you've been suckered into a time-share presentation until you get in the van. To avoid this situation, go to the official taxi booths inside the baggage claim or just outside the final customs clearance area and pay for a ticket for a regular shuttle bus. Private taxis, often U.S. vans, are expensive and not metered, so always ask the fare before getting in. Rates change frequently, but it costs about $65 to get to San José del Cabo, $80 to a hotel along the Corridor, and $100 to Cabo San Lucas. After the fourth passenger, it's about an additional $15 per person. Usually only vans accept more than four passengers. At the end of your trip, don't wait until the last minute to book return transport. Make arrangements a few days in advance for shuttle service, and then reconfirm the morning of your departure. Or, at least a day in advance, sign up at your hotel's front desk to share a cab with other travelers, reconfirming the morning of your departure.

▌ BUS TRAVEL

In Los Cabos, the main Terminal Central Cabo San Lucas Aguila (Los Cabos Bus Terminal) is about a 10-minute drive west of Cabo San Lucas. There are also terminals in San José del Cabo and La Paz. Express buses, including Aguila and ABC, have air-conditioning and restrooms and travel frequently from the terminal to Todos Santos (one hour) and La Paz (three hours). One-way fare from Cabo San Lucas or San José del Cabo is about $10 (payable in pesos or dollars) to Todos Santos. From either terminal to La Paz will cost around $20. From the Corridor, expect to pay about $25 for a taxi to the bus station.

The area's city bus, Ruta del Desierto, has nine stops along the highway between the airport in San José del Cabo and Terminal Aguila in Cabo San Lucas. Although affordable ($5), the trip from the airport to Cabo San Lucas takes over an hour and only departs from Terminal 1 (international flights arrive in Terminal 2). Plus, drop-off points are on Carretera Transpeninsular, meaning you'll still have to get from the highway to your hotel. If you have time and a sense of adventure, this is your cheapest way into the city.

In La Paz the main Terminal de Autobus is in front of the *malecón*, the seaside promenade.

Bus Information ABC. ☏ 664/104–7400 ⊕ www.abc.com.mx. **Ruta del Desierto.** ☏ 624/146–5320 ⊕ www.rutadeldesierto. travel. **Terminal Central Cabo San Lucas Aguila** (*Transportes Águila*). ✉ Av. Hidalgo , Block Ejidal, Cabo San Lucas ☏ 01800/026–8931 toll-free in Mexico ⊕ www.autobusesaguila.com. **Terminal Central La Paz Aguila.** ✉ Alvaro Obregon 125, entre 5 de Mayo e Independencia, La Paz ☏ 01800/026–8931 toll-free in Mexico ⊕ www.autobusesaguila. com. **Terminal Central San José del Cabo Aguila.** ✉ Calle Valerio González 1, Colonia Primero de Mayo, Centro ☏ 800/026–8931 ⊕ www.autobusesaguila.com.

▌CAR TRAVEL

Rental cars come in handy when exploring Baja. Countless paved and dirt roads branch off Highway 1 beckoning adventurers toward the mountains, ocean, and sea. Baja Sur's highways and city streets are under constant improvement, and Highway 1 is usually in good condition except during heavy rains. Four-wheel drive comes in handy for hard-core backcountry explorations, but isn't necessary most of the time. Just be aware that some car-rental companies void their insurance policies if you run into trouble off paved roads. If you are even slightly inclined to impromptu adventures, it's best to find out what your company's policy is before you leave the pavement.

GASOLINE

Pemex (the government petroleum monopoly) franchises all gas stations in Mexico. Stations are to be found in both towns as well as on the outskirts of San José del Cabo and Cabo San Lucas and in the Corridor, and there are also several along Highway 1. Gas is measured in liters. Prices run higher than in the United States. Premium unleaded gas (*magna premio*) and regular unleaded gas (*magna sin*) are available nationwide, but it's still a good idea to fill up whenever you can. Fuel quality is generally lower than that in the United States and Europe. Vehicles with fuel-injected engines are likely to have problems after driving extended distances.

Gas-station attendants pump the gas for you and may also wash your windshield and check your oil and tire air pressure. A tip of MX$10 or MX$20 (about 50¢ or $1) is customary depending on the number of services rendered, beyond pumping gas.

ROAD CONDITIONS

Mexico Highway 1, also known as the Carretera Transpeninsular, runs the entire 1,700 km (1,054 miles) from Tijuana to Cabo San Lucas. Do not drive the highway at high speeds or at night—it is not lighted and is very narrow much of the way. For a faster option, the toll road begins just after the airport with exit points in San José del Cabo ($2) and Cabo San Lucas ($3). From there, you can jump on Highway 19 to Todos Santos.

Highway 19 runs between Cabo San Lucas and Todos Santos and was widened in 2014 to two lanes in each direction, joining Highway 1 below La Paz. The four-lane road between San José del Cabo and Cabo San Lucas is usually in good condition. Roadwork along the highway is common and may cause delays or require detours.

In rural areas, roads tend to be iffy and in unpredictable conditions. Use caution, especially during the rainy season, when rock slides and potholes are a problem, and be alert for animals—cattle, goats, horses, coyotes, and dogs in particular—even on highways. If you have a long distance to cover, start early, fill up on gas, and remember to keep your tank full as gas stations are not as abundant here as they are in the United States or Europe. Allow extra time for unforeseen obstacles.

Signage is not always adequate in Mexico, and the best advice is to travel with a companion and a good map. Take your time. Always lock your car, and never leave valuable in plain sight (the trunk will suffice for daytime outings, but be smart about stashing expensive items in there in full view of curious onlookers).

The Mexican Tourism Ministry distributes free road maps from its tourism offices outside the country. Guía Roji and Pemex publish current city, regional, and national road maps, which are available in bookstores and big supermarket chains for under $10; but stock up on every map your rental-car company has, as gas stations generally do not carry maps. Most car-rental agencies have GPS units available for around $15 per day with regional maps preprogrammed.

ROADSIDE EMERGENCIES

The Mexican Tourism Ministry operates a fleet of more than 350 pickup trucks, known as the Angeles Verdes, or Green Angels. Bilingual drivers provide mechanical help, first aid, radio-telephone communication, basic supplies and small parts, towing, tourist information, and protection. Services are free; spare parts, fuel, and lubricants are provided at cost. Tips are always appreciated ($15–$20 for big jobs, $5–$10 for minor repairs). The Green Angels patrol sections of the major highways daily 8–8 (later on holiday weekends). If you break down, call Green Angels, or if you don't have a cell phone, **pull off the road as far as possible,** lift the hood of your car, hail a passing vehicle, and ask the driver to **notify the patrol.** Most bus and truck drivers will be quite helpful. If you witness an accident, do not stop to help—it could be a ploy to rob you or could get you interminably involved with the police. Instead, notify the nearest official.

Contacts Federal Highway Patrol. 🕾 624/125–3584. **Green Angels, La Paz.** 🕾 01800/987–8224 toll-free in Mexico, 078 from any Baja phone.

SAFETY ON THE ROAD

The mythical *banditos* are not a big concern in Baja. Still, **do your best to avoid driving at night,** especially in rural areas. Cows and burros grazing alongside the road can pose as real a danger as the ones actually in the road—you never know when they'll decide to wander into traffic.

Though it isn't common in Los Cabos, police may pull you over for supposedly breaking the law, or for being a good prospect for a scam. If it happens to you, remember to be polite. Tell the officer that you would like to talk to the police captain when you get to the station. The officer will usually let you go. If you're stopped for speeding, the officer should hold your license until you pay the fine at the local police station, but he will always prefer taking a *mordida* (small bribe) to wasting his time at the police station. Corruption is a fact of life in Mexico, and the $20–$40 it costs to get your license back is supplementary income for the officer who pulled you over with no intention of taking you to police headquarters.

RENTAL CARS

When you reserve a car, ask about cancellation penalties, taxes, drop-off charges (if you're planning to pick up the car in one city and leave it in another), and surcharges (for being under or over a certain age, for additional drivers, or for driving across state or country borders or beyond a specific distance from your point of rental). All these things can add substantially to your costs. Request car seats and extras such as GPS when you book.

Rates are sometimes—but not always—better if you book in advance or reserve through a rental agency's website. There are other reasons to book ahead, though: for popular destinations, during busy times of the year, or to ensure that you get certain types of cars (vans, SUVs, exotic sports cars). We've also found that car-rental prices are much better when reservations are made ahead of travel, from the United States. Prices can be as much as 50% more when renting a car upon arrival in Los Cabos. Shockingly low rates through third-party sites usually result in hidden fees when you actually pay for the car on-site. Cactus Car include insurance, taxes, and unlimited mileage in the quoted rate and have a solid fleet of compact cars, SUVs, and vans. Los Cabos–based Cactus Car has some of the best prices in the area and includes 30% discounts on local attractions when booking through their website. If you plan on renting a car in the United States and driving it across the border, the only agency that allows (and encourages) this is California Baja Rent-A-Car. Keep in mind that your pickup point is San Diego County.

▐ TIP➡ Make sure that a confirmed reservation guarantees you a car. Agencies sometimes overbook, particularly for busy weekends and holiday periods.

Taxi fares are especially steep in Los Cabos, and a rental car can come in handy if you'd like to dine at the Corridor hotels, travel frequently between the two towns, stay at a hotel along the Cabo Corridor, spend more than a few days in Los Cabos, or plan to see some of the sights outside Los Cabos proper, such as La Paz, Todos Santos, or even farther afield. If you don't want to rent a car, your hotel concierge or tour operator can arrange for a car with a driver or limousine service.

Convertibles and jeeps are popular rentals, but beware of sunburn and windburn and remember there's nowhere to stash your belongings out of sight. Specify whether you want air-conditioning and manual or automatic transmission. If you rent from a major U.S.-based company, you can find a compact car for about $60 per day ($420 per week), including automatic transmission, unlimited mileage, and 16% tax; however, having the protection of complete coverage insurance will add another $25 per day, depending on the company, so you should figure the cost of insurance into your budget. You will pay considerably more (probably double) for a larger or higher-end car. Most vendors negotiate considerably if tourism is slow; ask about special rates if you're renting by the week.

To increase the likelihood of getting the car you want and to get considerably better car-rental prices, make arrangements before you leave for your trip. You can sometimes find cheaper rates online. No matter how you book, rates are generally much lower when you reserve a car in advance outside Mexico.

In Mexico your own driver's license is acceptable. In most cases, the minimum rental age is 25, although some companies will lower it to 22 for an extra daily charge. A valid driver's license, major credit card, and Mexican car insurance are required.

Contacts Cactus Car. ✉ *Carretera Transpeninsular, Km 45, at Aeropuerto Internacional de Los Cabos, San José del Cabo* ☎ *624/146–1839, 866/225–9220 in U.S.* ⊕ *www.cactuscar. com.* **California Baja Rent-A-Car.** ✉ *9245 Jamacha Blvd., Spring Valley* ☎ *619/470–7368* ⊕ *www.cabaja.com.*

CAR-RENTAL INSURANCE

In 2013, the Mexican government passed a law stating that drivers must carry mandatory Third Party Liability, an expense that is not covered by U.S. insurance policies or by credit card companies. To be safe, agree to at least the minimum rental insurance. It's best to be completely covered when driving in Mexico.

If you own a car, your personal auto insurance may cover a rental to a degree, though not all policies protect you abroad; always read your policy's fine print.

Even if you have auto insurance back home, you should buy the collision- or loss-damage waiver (CDW or LDW) from the car-rental company, which eliminates your liability for damage to the car. Some credit cards offer CDW coverage, but it's only supplemental to your own insurance and rarely covers SUVs, minivans, luxury models, and the like. If your coverage is secondary, you may still be liable for loss-of-use costs from the car-rental company. But no credit-card insurance is valid unless you use that card for *all* transactions, from reserving to paying the final bill. In general, U.S. and Canadian auto insurance policies are not recognized in Mexico, and the few that are only cover specific coverage like damage and theft. Rather than fear what *might* happen, it is best to purchase a Mexican liability insurance package from your rental car company so that you know you're covered.

■TIP➔ **American Express offers primary CDW coverage on all rentals reserved and paid for with the card. This means that the American Express company—not your** own car insurance—pays in case of an accident. This does not cover Third Party Liability, nor does it mean your car-insurance company won't raise your rates once it discovers you had an accident—but it provides a welcome amount of security for travelers.

▌ TAXI TRAVEL

Taxis are plentiful throughout Baja Sur, even in the smallest towns. Government-certified taxis have a license with a photo of the driver and a taxi number prominently displayed. Fares are exorbitant in Los Cabos, and the taxi union is very powerful. Some visitors have taken to boycotting taxis completely, using rental cars and buses instead, the latter of which can be the most time-consuming. The fare between Cabo San Lucas and San José del Cabo runs about $50–$60—more at night. Cabs from Corridor hotels to either town run at least $30 each way. Expect to pay at least $65 from the airport to hotels in San José, and closer to $100 to Cabo.

In La Paz, taxis are readily available and inexpensive. A ride within town costs under $5; a trip to Pichilingue costs between $10 and $15. Illegal taxis aren't a problem in this region.

ESSENTIALS

▌COMMUNICATIONS

PHONES

Los Cabos is on U.S. Mountain Time. The region has good telephone service and wide cell-phone reception. Phone numbers in Mexico change frequently; a recording may offer the new number, so it's useful to learn numbers 1 through 9 in Spanish. Beware of pay phones and hotel room phones with signs saying "Call Home" and other enticements. Some of these phone companies charge astronomical rates. Some all-inclusive resorts include free calls to the United States and Canada, which will be clearly stated in your amenities upon check-in.

The country code for Mexico is 52. When calling a Mexico number from abroad, dial the country code and then the area code and local number. At this writing, the area code for all of Los Cabos is 624. All local numbers have seven digits.

CALLING WITHIN MEXICO

For local or long-distance calls, one option is to contact your cell phone provider and add the Mexico plan to your account for the days you are traveling, usually a flat rate of $5 per day. From your computer or a smartphone you can download Skype onto your device and purchase $10 to $20 of talk time, which will actually go quite far. Alternatively, if the person you are calling has Skype, it will be free for both parties. If you are tech-savvy, purchase a local SIM card for an "unlocked" cell phone and use a prepaid phone card to deduct minutes from your talk time. TelCel is a reliable Mexican company that offers this service. When all else fails, you can always use the phone in your hotel room.

Contact TelCel. ☎ *264, *111 ⊕ www.telcel.com.

CALLING OUTSIDE MEXICO

To make a call to the United States or Canada, dial 001 before the area code and number. For operator assistance in making an international call, dial 090.

AT&T, Verizon, and Sprint access codes make calling long-distance relatively convenient, but you may find the local access number blocked in many hotel rooms. First ask the hotel operator to connect you; if they balk, ask for an international operator, or dial the international operator yourself. One way to improve your odds of getting connected to your long-distance carrier is to travel with more than one company's calling card (a hotel may block Sprint, for example, but not MCI). If all else fails, call from a pay phone.

Access Codes AT&T Direct. ☎ 800/331–0500 ⊕ www.att.com. **Sprint International Access.** ☎ 866/866–7509 ⊕ www.sprint.com. **Verizon.** ☎ 800/922–0204 ⊕ www.verizonwireless.com.

DIRECTORY AND OPERATOR ASSISTANCE

Directory assistance in Mexico is 040 nationwide. For international assistance, dial 020 first for an international operator and most likely you'll get one who speaks English; indicate in which city, state, and country you require directory assistance and you will be connected with directory assistance there.

MOBILE PHONES

If you have a multiband phone (some countries use different frequencies from what's used in the United States) and your service provider uses the world-standard GSM network (as do T-Mobile, AT&T, and Verizon), you can probably use your phone abroad. Roaming fees can be steep, however: 99¢ a minute is considered reasonable. And overseas you normally pay the toll charges for incoming calls. It's almost always cheaper to send a text message than to make a call, since text messages have a very low set fee (often less than 5¢). Verizon offers very reasonable Mexican calling plans that can be added to your existing plan.

If you just want to make local calls, consider buying a new SIM card (note that your provider may have to unlock your phone for you to use a different SIM card) and a prepaid service plan in the destination. You'll then have a local number and can make local calls at local rates. If your trip is extensive, you could also simply buy a new cell phone in your destination, as the initial cost will be offset over time.

■TIP➡ If you travel internationally frequently, save one of your old mobile phones or buy a cheap one on the Internet; ask your cell phone company to unlock it for you, and take it with you as a travel phone, buying a new SIM card with pay-as-you-go service in each destination.

There are now companies that rent cell phones (with or without SIM cards) for the duration of your trip. You get the phone, charger, and carrying case in the mail and return them in the mailer.

Contacts Cellular Abroad. ☎ 800/287–5072 ⊕ www.cellularabroad.com. **Mobal.** ☎ 888/888–9162 ⊕ www.mobalrental.com. **Planet Fone.** ☎ 888/988–4777 ⊕ www. planetfone.com.

TOLL-FREE NUMBERS
Toll-free numbers in Mexico start with an 800 prefix. To reach them, you need to dial 01 before the number. *In this guide, Mexico-only toll-free numbers appear as follows: 01800/123–4567 (numbers have seven digits).* Most of the 800 numbers *in this book* work in the United States only and are listed simply: 800/123–4567; you cannot access a U.S. 800 number from Mexico. Some U.S. toll-free numbers ring directly at Mexican properties. Don't be deterred if someone answers the phone in Spanish. Simply ask for someone who speaks English. Toll-free numbers that work in other countries are labeled accordingly.

▮ CUSTOMS AND DUTIES

Upon entering Mexico, you'll be given a baggage declaration form and asked to itemize what you're bringing into the country. You are allowed to bring in 3 liters of spirits or wine for personal use; 400 cigarettes, 25 cigars, 10 packs of cigarettes; a reasonable amount of perfume for personal use; one video camera and one regular camera; and gift items not to exceed a total of $500. If driving across the U.S. border, gift items shouldn't exceed $300, although foreigners aren't usually hassled about this.
■TIP➡ Although the much-publicized border violence doesn't usually affect travelers, it is real. To be safe, don't linger long at the border.

You aren't allowed to bring firearms, ammunition, meat, vegetables, plants, fruit, or flowers into the country. You can bring in one of each of the following items without paying taxes: a cell phone, a musical instrument, a laptop computer, and portable copier or printer. Compact discs are limited to 30 total and DVDs to 10.

Mexico also allows you to bring up to three pets as long as you have a pet health certificate signed by a registered veterinarian in the United States and issued not more than 72 hours before the animal enters Mexico, and a pet vaccination certificate showing that the animal has been treated (as applicable) for rabies, hepatitis, distemper, and leptospirosis.

For more information or information on bringing other animals or more than one type of animal, contact the Mexican consulate, which has branches in many major American cities as well as border towns. To find the consulate nearest you, check the Ministry of Foreign Affairs website (go to the "Servicios Consulares" option).

Information in Mexico Mexican Embassy. ☎ 202/728–1600 ⊕ www.embassyofmexico. org. **Ministry of Foreign Affairs.** ☎ 55/3686–5100 ⊕ www.sre.gob.mx.

U.S. Information U.S. Customs and Border Protection. ☎ 877/227–5511 in U.S., 202/325–8000 outside the U.S. ⊕ www.cbp.gov.

▌ ELECTRICITY

For U.S. and Canadian travelers, electrical converters are not necessary because Mexico operates on the 60-cycle, 120-volt system. If you're coming from Europe, you'll need a converter to go from 240V to 120V.

▌ EMERGENCIES

In 2017, Mexico switched to 911 as the emergency number for police and the fire department. The number can be used throughout the state, and there are English-speaking operators. Another option is air medical services—find a provider through the Association of Air Medical Services (AAMS); several of the U.S.-headquartered operations have bases around Mexico so they can reach you more quickly.

Emergency Services AAMS. ☎ 703/836–8732 ⊕ www.aams.org. **Highway Patrol.** ☎ 624/143–0135 in Los Cabos, 612/122–0429 in La Paz. **Police.** ☎ 624/142–0361 in San José del Cabo, 624/143–3977 in Cabo San Lucas, 612/122–0477 in La Paz.

Foreign Consulates Consular Agent in Cabo San Lucas. ⊠ Hwy. 1, Km 27.5, Shoppes at Palmilla, The Corridor ☎ 624/143–3566.

Hospitals and Clinics AmeriMed. ⊠ Av. Cárdenas at Paseo Marina, in front of Seven Crown Resort, Cabo San Lucas ☎ 624/105–8500 ⊕ www.amerimed.com.mx. **Centro de Especialidades Médicas.** ⊠ Calle Delfines 110, La Paz ☎ 612/124–0400.

▌ HEALTH

FOOD AND DRINK

In Mexico the biggest health risk is *turista* (traveler's diarrhea) caused by consuming contaminated fruit, vegetables, or water. To minimize risks, avoid questionable-looking street stands and bad-smelling food even in the toniest establishments; and if you're not sure of a restaurant's standards, pass up ceviche (raw fish cured in lemon juice). The Mexican Department of Health warns that marinating in lemon juice does not constitute the "cooking" that would make the shellfish safe to eat. Also avoid raw vegetables that haven't been, or can't be, peeled (e.g., lettuce and tomatoes).

In general, Los Cabos does not pose as great a health risk as other parts of Mexico. Nevertheless, watch what you eat, and drink only bottled water or water that has been boiled for a few minutes. Water in most major hotels is safe for brushing your teeth, but to avoid any risk, use bottled water. Hotels with water-purification systems will post signs to that effect in the rooms.

When ordering cold drinks at establishments that don't seem to get many tourists, skip the ice (order it *sin hielo*). You can usually identify ice made commercially from purified water by its uniform shape.

Stay away from uncooked food and unpasteurized milk and milk products. Mexicans excel at grilling meats and seafood, but be smart about where you eat—ask locals to recommend their favorite restaurants or taco stands, and if you have the slightest hesitation about cleanliness or freshness, skip it. Fruit and *licuados* (smoothies) stands are wonderful for refreshing treats, but again, ask around, be fanatical about freshness, and watch to see how the vendor handles the food. Mexico is a food-lover's adventure land, and many travelers wouldn't dream of passing up the chance to try something new and delicious.

Mild cases of turista may respond to Imodium (known generically as loperamide), Lomotil, or Pepto-Bismol, all of which you can buy over the counter. Keep in mind that these drugs can complicate more serious illnesses. You'll need to replace fluids, so drink plenty of purified water.

Chamomile tea (*té de manzanilla*) and peppermint tea (*té de menta/hierbabuena*) can be good for calming upset stomachs, and they're readily available in restaurants throughout Mexico.

It's smart to travel with a few packets of drink mix such as EmergenC when you travel to Mexico. You can also make a salt-sugar solution (½ teaspoon salt and 4 tablespoons sugar per quart of water) to rehydrate. Drinking baking soda dissolved in water can neutralize the effects of an acidic meal and help with heavy indigestion or an upset stomach. It might also help prevent a painful hangover if taken after excessive drinking.

If your fever and diarrhea last longer than a day or two, see a doctor—you may have picked up a parasite or disease that requires prescription medication.

DIVERS' ALERT

■TIP➔ Do not fly within 24 hours of scuba diving.

SHOTS AND MEDICATIONS

According to the U.S. National Centers for Disease Control and Prevention (CDC), there's a limited risk of Zika in Mexico, which can cause serious birth defects. Women who are pregnant are advised to avoid travel to Mexico.

Health Information National Centers for Disease Control & Prevention (*CDC*). ☎ *800/232–4636 international travelers' health line* ⊕ *www.cdc.gov/travel.* **World Health Organization** (*WHO*). ☎ *22/791–2111, 202/974–3000 in U.S.* ⊕ *www.who.int.*

MEDICAL INSURANCE AND ASSISTANCE

Consider buying trip insurance with medical-only coverage. Neither Medicare nor some private insurers cover medical expenses anywhere outside the United States. Medical-only policies typically reimburse you for medical care (excluding that related to preexisting conditions) and hospitalization abroad, and provide for evacuation. You still have to pay the bills and await reimbursement from the insurer, though.

Another option is to sign up with a medical-evacuation assistance company.

Membership gets you doctor referrals, emergency evacuation or repatriation, 24-hour hotlines for medical consultation, and other assistance. International SOS Assistance Emergency and AirMed International provide evacuation services and medical referrals. MedjetAssist offers medical evacuation.

Medical Assistance Companies AirMed International. ☎ *800/356–2161, 205/443–4840 in Mexico* ⊕ *www.airmed.com.* **International SOS Assistance Emergency.** ☎ *800/523–8662* ⊕ *www.internationalsos. com.* **MedjetAssist.** ☎ *800/527–7478* ⊕ *www.medjetassist.com.*

Medical-Only Insurers International Medical Group (*IMG*). ☎ *800/628–4664* ⊕ *www.imglobal.com.* **Wallach & Company.** ☎ *800/237–6615, 540/687–3166* ⊕ *www. wallach.com.*

▮ HOLIDAYS

Banks and government offices close during Holy Week (the week leading to Easter Sunday) and on Cinco de Mayo, Día de la Raza, and Independence Day. Government offices usually have reduced hours and staff from Christmas through New Year's Day. Some banks and offices close for religious holidays.

Official holidays include New Year's Day (January 1); Constitution Day (February 5); Benito Juárez's Birthday (March 21); Good Friday (Friday before Easter Sunday); Easter Sunday (the first Sunday after the first full moon following spring equinox); Labor Day (May 1); Cinco de Mayo (May 5); Independence Day (September 16); Día de la Raza (Day of the Race; October 12); Dia de los Muertos (Day of the Dead; November 2); Anniversary of the Mexican Revolution (November 20); Christmas (December 25).

▌ HOURS OF OPERATION

Banks are usually open weekdays 8:30–3 (although sometimes banks in Cabo and San José stay open until 5). Government offices are usually open to the public weekdays 8–3, and are closed on national holidays, along with banks and most private offices. Stores are generally open weekdays and Saturday from 9 or 10 to 7 or 8. In tourist areas, some shops don't close until 10 and are open Sunday. Most galleries are closed on Sunday. Some shops close for a two-hour lunch break, usually 2–4. Shops extend their hours when cruise ships are in town.

▌ MAIL

Airmail letters from Baja Sur can take up to two weeks and often much longer to reach their destination. The *oficina de correos* (post office) in San José del Cabo is open 8–7 on weekdays (with a possible closure for lunch) and 9–1 Saturday. Offices in Cabo San Lucas and La Paz are open 9–1 and 3–6 weekdays; La Paz and San Lucas offices are also open 9–noon on Saturday.

Post Offices **Cabo San Lucas Oficina de Correo.** ⊠ *Lázaro Cárdenas 22* ☎ *624/143-0048.* **San José del Cabo Oficina de Correo.** ⊠ *Mijares and Margarita Maya de Juárez* ☎ *624/142-0911.*

SHIPPING PACKAGES

FedEx does not serve Los Cabos area, other than FedEx freight. DHL has express service for letters and packages from Los Cabos to the United States and Canada; most deliveries take three to four days (overnight service is not available). To the United States, letters take three days and boxes and packages take four days. Cabo San Lucas, San José del Cabo, and La Paz have a DHL drop-off location.

Major Services **DHL Worldwide Express.** ⊠ *Blvd. Mauricio Castro 1738, San José del Cabo* ☎ *624/142-2148* ⊕ *www.dhl.com* ⊠ *Plaza Los Arcos 8 and 9, Leona Vicario, corner of Revolución 1810, Cabo San Lucas* ☎ *624/143-3885* ⊕ *www.dhl.com.*

▌ MONEY

Mexico has a reputation for being inexpensive, but Los Cabos is one of the most expensive places to visit in the country. Prices rise from 10% to 18% annually and are comparable to those in Southern California.

Prices in this book are quoted most often in U.S. dollars, which are readily accepted in Los Cabos (although you should always have pesos on you if you venture anywhere beyond the walls of a resort). *For information on taxes, see Taxes.*

ATMS AND BANKS

ATMs (*cajas automáticas*) are commonplace in Los Cabos and La Paz. If you're going to a less-developed area, though, go equipped with cash. Cirrus and Plus cards are the most commonly accepted. The ATMs at Banamex, one of the oldest nationwide banks, tend to be the most reliable. Bancomer is another bank with many ATM locations.

Many Mexican ATMs cannot accept PINs with more than four digits. If yours is longer, change your PIN to four digits before you leave home. If you've entered your PIN is correctly yet your transaction still can't be completed, chances are that the computer lines are busy, the machine has run out of money, or it's being serviced. Don't give up. Expect to pay a $5 withdrawal fee with each ATM transaction.

CREDIT CARDS

When shopping, you can often get better prices if you pay with cash, particularly in small shops. But you'll receive wholesale exchange rates when you make purchases with credit cards. These exchange rates are usually better than those that banks give you for changing money. The decision to pay cash or to use a credit card depends on whether the establishment finds bargaining acceptable, and whether you want the safety net of your card's purchase protection. To avoid fraud or errors, it's wise to make sure that pesos are clearly marked on all credit-card receipts. Keep in mind that foreign transaction fees tack on an additional 3% for every purchase made abroad. If you travel often, consider getting a credit card with no foreign transaction fees and flexible travel rewards.

Before you leave for Mexico, contact your credit-card company to let them know you'll be using your card abroad, and get lost-card phone numbers that work in Mexico; the standard toll-free numbers often don't work abroad. Carry these numbers separately from your wallet so you'll have them if you need to call to report lost or stolen cards. American Express, MasterCard, and Visa note the international number for card-replacement calls on the back of their cards.

CURRENCY AND EXCHANGE

The currency in Los Cabos is the Mexican peso (MXP), though prices are often given in U.S. dollars. Mexican currency comes in denominations of 20-, 50-, 100-, 200-, and 500-peso bills. Coins come in denominations of 1, 2, 5, 10, and 20 pesos and 20 and 50 centavos (20-centavo coins are only rarely seen). Many of the coins are very similar, so check carefully; bills, however, are different colors and easily distinguished.

At this writing, US$1 was equivalent to approximately MXP 18.14.

▮ PASSPORTS AND VISAS

A passport, or other WHTI (Western Hemisphere Travel Initiative) compliant document, is required of all visitors to Mexico, including U.S. citizens who may remember the days when only driver's licenses were needed to cross the border. Upon entering Mexico all visitors must get a tourist card (FMM card). If you're arriving by plane from the United States or Canada, the standard tourist card will be given to you on the plane. They're also available through travel agents and Mexican consulates and at the border if you're entering by land.

▮TIP→ You're given a portion of the tourist card form upon entering Mexico. Keep track of this documentation throughout your trip: you will need it when you depart. You'll be asked to hand it, your ticket, and your passport to airline representatives at the gate when boarding for departure.

If you lose your tourist card, plan to spend some time (and about $60) sorting it out with Mexican officials at the airport on departure.

A tourist card costs about $23. The fee is generally tacked onto the price of your airline ticket. If you enter by land or boat you'll have to pay the fee separately. You're exempt from the fee if you enter by sea and stay less than 72 hours, or by land and do not stray past the 26- to 30-km (16- to 18-mile) checkpoint into the country's interior.

Tourist cards and visas are valid from 15 to 180 days, at the discretion of the immigration officer at your point of entry (90 days for Australians). Americans, Canadians, New Zealanders, and the British may request up to 180 days for a tourist card or visa extension. The extension fee is about $20, and the process can be time-consuming. There's no guarantee that you'll get the extension you're requesting. If you're planning an extended stay, plead with the immigration official for the maximum allowed days at the time of entry. It will save you time and money later.

▮TIP→ Mexico has some of the strictest policies about children entering the country. Minors traveling with one parent need notarized permission from the absent parent.

If you're a single parent traveling with children up to age 18, you must have a notarized letter from the other parent stating that the child has his or her permission to leave his or her home country. The child must be carrying the original letter—not a facsimile or scanned copy—as well as proof of the parent-child relationship (usually a birth certificate or court document), and an original custody decree, if applicable. If the other parent is deceased or the child has only one legal parent, a notarized statement saying so must be obtained as proof. In addition, you must fill out a tourist card for each child over the age of 10 traveling with you.

Info Mexican Embassy. ☎ 202/728–1600 ⊕ www.embassyofmexico.org.

U.S. Passport Information U.S. Department of State. ☎ 877/487–2778, 888/407–4747 ⊕ www.state.gov.

▮ RESTROOMS

Expect to find clean flushing toilets, toilet tissue, soap, and running water in Los Cabos. The exception may be small roadside stands or restaurants in rural areas. If there's a bucket and a large container of water sitting outside the facilities, fill the bucket and use it to flush. Some public places, such as bus stations, charge a few pesos for use of the facility, but toilet paper is included in the fee. Still, it's always a good idea to carry some tissue. Throw your toilet paper and any other materials into the provided waste bins rather than the toilet. Mexican plumbing simply isn't equipped to deal with the volume of paper Americans are accustomed to putting in toilets.

▮ SAFETY

Due to criminal activity and violence in 2017, the U.S. State Department warned U.S. citizens about the risk of traveling to Los Cabos and La Paz. Stay up to date with travel warnings on the U.S. State Department website. Carjacking, pickpocketing, mugging, and being asked for bribes are still threats.

General Information and Warnings Transportation Security Administration (*TSA*). ☎ 866/289–9673 ⊕ www.tsa.gov. **U.S. Department of State.** ☎ 202/501–4444 in Mexico, 888/407–4747 in U.S. ⊕ www.travel.state.gov.

▮ TAXES

Mexico charges a departure and airport tax of about $50 which is almost universally included in the price of your ticket, but check to be certain.

A 3% tax on accommodations is charged in Los Cabos, with proceeds used for tourism promotion.

All of Mexico has a federal tax, or Value-Added Tax of 16%, called I.V.A. (*impuesto de valor agregado*), which is occasionally (and illegally) waived for cash purchases. Other taxes and charges apply for phone calls made from your hotel room.

▮ TIME

Baja California Sur is on Mountain Standard Time, Baja California is on Pacific Standard Time. And the unofficial standard for behavior is "Mexican time"—meaning stop rushing, enjoy yourself, and practice being *tranquilo*.

▮ TIPPING

When tipping in Baja, remember that the minimum wage is equivalent to a mere $4 an hour, and that the vast majority of workers in the tourist industry of Mexico live barely above the poverty line. However, there are Mexicans who think in dollars and know, for example, that in the United States porters are tipped about $2 a bag; many of them expect the peso equivalent from foreigners but are sometimes happy to accept MX$10 (about 50¢) a bag from Mexicans. They will complain either verbally or with a facial expression if they feel they deserve more—you and your conscience must decide. Following are some guidelines. Naturally, larger tips are always welcome.

For porters and bellboys at airports and at moderate and inexpensive hotels, $2 (about MX$13) per bag should be sufficient. At expensive hotels, porters expect at least $4 per bag. Leave at least $3 per night for maids at all hotels. The norm for waiters is 15% to 20% of the bill, depending on service (make sure a 15% service charge hasn't already been added to the bill, although this practice is more common in resorts). Tipping taxi drivers is necessary only if the driver helps with your bags; $1 to $2 should be enough, depending on the extent of the assistance. Tip tour guides and drivers at least $5 per half day or 10% of the tour fee, minimum. Gas-station attendants receive 50¢ to $1, more if they check the oil, tires, etc. Parking attendants—including those at restaurants with valet parking—should be tipped $1 to $3.

▮ TRAVEL INSURANCE

Comprehensive travel insurance is valuable if you're booking a very expensive or complicated trip (particularly to an isolated region) or if you're booking far in advance. Comprehensive policies typically cover trip-cancellation and interruption, letting you cancel or cut your trip short because of a personal emergency, illness, or, in some cases, acts of terrorism in your destination. Such policies also cover evacuation and medical care. (For trips abroad you should at least have medical-only coverage). Some also cover you for trip delays because of bad weather or mechanical problems as well as for lost or delayed baggage. If you plan on engaging in extreme activities like surfing, bungee jumping, scuba diving, or zip-lining, consider buying an extended plan that covers such sports.

Another type of coverage to look for is financial default—that is, when your trip is disrupted because a tour operator, airline, or cruise line goes out of business. Generally you must buy this when you book your trip or shortly thereafter, and it's only available to you if your operator isn't on a list of excluded companies.

Always read the fine print of your policy to make sure that you are covered for the risks that are of most concern to you. Compare several policies to make sure you're getting the best price and range of coverage available.

Insurance Comparison Sites Insure My Trip. com. ☏ 800/487–4722 ⊕ www.insuremy-trip.com. **Square Mouth.** ☏ 800/240–0369 ⊕ www.squaremouth.com.

Comprehensive Travel Insurers Allianz. ☏ 800/284–8300 ⊕ www.allianztrav-elinsurance.com. **CSA Travel Protection.** ☏ 877/243–4135 ⊕ www.csatravelprotection. com. **Travel Guard.** ☏ 800/826–4919 ⊕ www. travelguard.com. **Travel Insured International.** ☏ 800/243–3174 ⊕ www.travelinsured. com. **Travelex Insurance.** ☏ 800/228–9792 ⊕ www.travelex-insurance.com.

▮ VISITOR INFORMATION

Avoid tour stands on the streets; they are usually associated with time-share operations. The *Gringo Gazette* newspaper and the *Baja Traveler Guide* are good resources for the Cabo scene, as is *Los Cabos Magazine*. These publications are free and easy to find in hotels and restaurants throughout the region. Discover Baja, a membership club for Baja travelers, has links and info at its website. For information about eco-tourism and environmental issues, visit ⊕ *www.planeta.com.*

The Baja California Sur State Tourist Office is in La Paz about a 10-minute drive north of the malecón, the seaside promenade. It serves as both the state and city tourism office. There's also an information stand on the malecón across from Los Arcos hotel. The booth is a more convenient spot, and it can give you info on La Paz, Scammon's Lagoon, Santa Rosalia, and other smaller towns. Both offices and the booth are open weekdays 9–5.

Contacts Baja California Sur State Tourist Office. ✉ Mariano Abasolo s/n, La Paz ☏ 612/124–0100 ⊕ www.visitbajasur. travel. **Discover Baja.** ☏ 800/727–2252 in San Diego ⊕ www.discoverbaja.com. **Gringo Gazette.** ⊕ www.gringogazette.

com. **Los Cabos Tourism Board.** ⊠ *Plaza Providencia, Hwy 1, Km 43, next to Costco, Cabo San Lucas* ☎ *624/143–5531 in Mexico, 01800/746–2226 toll-free in U.S.* ⊕ *www. visitloscabos.travel.* **Mexican Government Tourist Board.** ☎ *800/446–3942 in U.S. and Canada* ⊕ *www.visitmexico.com.* **Planeta. com.** ⊕ *www.planeta.com.* **TodosSantos-Baja.com.** ⊕ *www.todossantos-baja.com.*

INDEX

PHOTO CREDITS

Front cover: SIME / eStock Photo [Description: Land's End, Cabo San Lucas, Los Cabos, Mexico]. 1, carlos sanchez pereyra/Shutterstock. 2-3, Chad Ehlers/Alamy. 4, Grigory Fedyukovich/iStockphoto. 5 (top), quitthistown / Stockimo / Alamy. 5 (bottom), niknikon/iStockphoto. 6 (top left), Douglas Peebles Photography / Alamy. 6 (top right), toddtaulman/iStockphoto. 6 (bottom right), Los Cabos Tourism Board. 6 (bottom left), ferrantraite/iStockphoto. 7 (top), Garrettandrewchong | Dreamstime. com. 7 (bottom), Hoatzinexp | Dreamstime.com. 8 (top left), Chileno Bay Resort/Los Cabos Tourism Board. 8 (top right), Michael Braun/iStockphoto. 8 (bottom right), Michael Seidl/Puerto Los Cabos. 8 (bottom left), Leswrona | Dreamstime.com. 9 (top), Las Ventanas al Paraiso/Los Cabos Tourism Board. 9 (bottom), francisco estrada PHOTOMEXICO37. 11, Kato Inowe/Shutterstock. **Chapter 1: Experience Los Cabos:** 14-15, Victor Elías/age fotostock. **Chapter 2: Beaches:** 31, Heeb Christian/age fotostock. 32, Brian Florky/Shutterstock. 37, National Geographic Creative / Alamy, 38 (top), Jim Russi/age fotostock. 38 (center), Kato Inowe/Shutterstock. 38 (bottom), RCPPHOTO/Shutterstock. 39, Henry William Fu/Shutterstock. 40, Kato Inowe/Shutterstock. 43, Mark A. Johnson / Alamy. 46-47, Heeb Christian/ age fotostock. **Chapter 3: Sports and Outdoor Activities:** 49 and 50, Bruce Herman/Mexico Tourism Board. 54-55, Ralph Hopkins/age fotostock. 57, Robert Chiasson/age fotostock. 60, tonobalaguerf/Shutterstock. 61, Larry Dunmire. 62 (top), Sam Woolford/iStockphoto. 62 (bottom), Larry Dunmire. 65, Michele Westmorland/age fotostock. 67, Reinhard Dirscherl/age fotostock. 69, Adalberto Ríos Szalay/age fotostock. 70 (top), gary718/Shutterstock. 70 (bottom), Michael S. Nolan/age fotostock. 71, Ryan Harvey/Flickr. **Chapter 4: Where to Eat:** 73, Hemis / Alamy. 74, Matthieu Fiol. **Chapter 5: Where to Stay:** 91, Las Ventanas al Paraiso. 92, Chileno Bay Resort. 102, Esperanza, An Auberge Resort. 104, One&Only Palmilla. **Chapter 6: Shops and Spas:** 109, Terrance Klassen/age fotostock. 110, Tony Hertz/Alamy. 120, John Mitchell/Alamy. 121, María Lourdes Alonso/age fotostock. 122, María Lourdes Alonso/age fotostock. 123(top), Ken Ross. 123 (bottom left), Ken Ross. 123 (bottom 2nd from left), Ken Ross. 123 (bottom 3rd from left), Ken Ross. 123 (right), Jane Onstott. 124 (top left), patti haskins/Flickr. 124 (bottom left), fontplaydotcom/ Flickr. 124 (top right), Wonderlane/Flickr. 124 (center right), Jose Zelaya Gallery/ArtedelPueblo.com. 124 (bottom right), Jane Onstott. **Chapter 7: Nightlife:** 129, Gerasimovvv | Dreamstime.com. 130, Elena Koulik/Shutterstock. **Chapter 8: Los Cabos Side Trips:** 139, Efrain Padro / Alamy. 142, Sherwin McGehee/iStockphoto. 149, San Rostro/ age fotostock. 162, Michael S. Nolan/age fotostock. **Chapter 9: Baja California Beach Towns:** 165, Photo Network / Alamy. 168, Peter Coombs / Alamy. 176 (top and bottom right), Adobe Guadalupe. 176 (bottom left), Tomas Castelazo/Wikipedia.org. 177, María Lourdes Alonso. 178 (top and bottom), Adobe Guadalupe. **Back cover, from left to right:** Gary718 | Dreamstime.com; Leonardospencer | Dreamstime.com; Dgirard12 | Dreamstime.com. **Spine:** Khewey | Dreamstime.com. **About Our Writers:** Photos of our writers are courtesy of the following: Marlise Kast-Myers, courtesy of Benjamin Myers; Chris Sands, courtesy of Camilla Fuchs.

NOTES

NOTES

ABOUT OUR WRITERS

San Diego–based writer Marlise Kast–Myers has contributed to over 50 publications, including *San Diego Union Tribune, Surfer, San Diego Magazine,* and *Forbes.* Her passion for traveling has taken her to 80 countries and residency in Switzerland, Dominican Republic, Spain, and Costa Rica. Following the release of her memoir *Tabloid Prodigy* (Running Press, 2007) Marlise coauthored Fodor's Guides to Cancun, San Diego, Los Cabos, Panama, Vietnam, Costa Rica, Peru, Puerto Rico, Corsica, and Sardinia. In promotion of her work, she has appeared on CNN, NPR, FOX News, CNBC, "O'Reilly Factor," and "Entertainment Tonight." Marlise served as a photojournalist for *Surf Guide to Costa Rica* (Airborn Media, 2009) and wrote *Day Hikes & Overnights on the Pacific Crest Trail* (Countryman Press, 2014). For more info, visit ⊕ *www.marlisekast.com.*

In addition to his work for Fodor's, Chris Sands is co-founder of CaboVivo, editor at Baja.com, and a contributor to *Forbes* and 10Best at *USA Today,* as well as other travel websites and publications. He is a full-time resident of Cabo San Lucas.